D1503478

The "Barberian" Presidency

American University Studies

Series X
Political Science

Vol. 14

PETER LANG
New York • Bern • Frankfurt am Main • Paris

William David Pederson

The "Barberian" Presidency

Theoretical and Empirical Readings

PETER LANG
New York • Bern • Frankfurt am Main • Paris

Library of Congress Cataloging-in-Publication Data

The "Barberian" presidency : theoretical and empirical
readings / [edited by] William David Pederson.

    p. cm. — (American University studies. Series X,
Political science ; vol. 14)
      Bibliography: p.
      Includes articles by James David Barber.
      1. Presidents—United States—Case studies.
2. Presidents—United States—Psychology.
I. Pederson, William D. II. Barber, James David.
III. Series: American university studies. Series X,
Political science ; v. 14.
JK511.B38   1989   353.03'1'0926—dc19   88-39146
ISBN 0-8204-0693-7   CIP
ISSN 0740-0470

CIP-Titelaufnahme der Deutschen Bibliothek

Pederson, William David:
The "Barberian" presidency : theoretical and
empirical readings / William David Pederson. —
New York; Bern; Frankfurt am Main; Paris:
Lang, 1989.
  (American University Studies: Ser. 10,
  Political Science; Vol. 14)
  ISBN 0-8204-0693-7

NE: American University Studies / 10

© Peter Lang Publishing, Inc., New York 1989

Printed by Weihert-Druck GmbH, Darmstadt, West Germany

FOR MY PARENTS
Jon Moritz Pederson and Rose Marie Ryan Pederson

Contents

PART III. Comparative Tests and Case Studies: The
Empirical Presidency

PART III. Comparative Tests and Case Studies: The
Empirical Presidency

7 Amnesty and Presidential Behavior: A "Barberian" Test 113
   William David Pederson
8 The President and the White House Staff 129
   William David Pederson and Stephen Neal Williams
9 Putting Gippergate into Perspective 149
   William David Pederson
10 The Behavior of Lawyer-Presidents: A "Barberian" Link 153
   Thomas Meredith Green and William David Pederson
11 Presidential Reaction to Security: A Longitudinal Study 169
   Dwight L. Tays
12 Truman's Seizure of the Steel Mills as an Exercise of Active-Positive Combat 189
   Frank Schwartz
13 On Presidential Character 219
   Jeffrey Tulis
14 "Presidential Senator" Ted Kennedy and a Character Test 253
   William David Pederson
   An Annotated Bibliography 263
   William David Pederson

Contributors

JAMES DAVID BARBER (b. 1930, Charleston, West Virginia). A political scientist who received his Ph.D. from Yale University in 1960. He is the author of *The Lawmakers* (1965); *Presidential Character* (1972); and the *Pulse of Politics* (1980). Department of Political Science, Duke University, Durham, North Carolina, 27706.

THOMAS MEREDITH GREEN (b. 1958, Murfreesboro, Tennessee). A farmer who received his B.A. from Westminister College (Fulton, Missouri) in 1981. He is the co-author of "The Behavior of Lawyer-Presidents," *Presidential Studies Quarterly* (1985). Sikeston, Missouri, 63801.

MICHAEL BOYD NELSON (b. 1944, Minneapolis, Minnesota). A political scientist who received his Ph.D. from Johns Hopkins University in 1978. He is the author of *Culture of Bureaucracy* (1979); *Presidents, Politics, and Policy* (1984); and *Presidency and the Political System* (1984). Department of Political Science, Vanderbilt University, Box 9, Station B, Nashville, Tennessee, 37235.

WILLIAM DAVID PEDERSON (b. 1946, Eugene, Oregon). A political scientist who received his Ph.D. from the University of Oregon in 1979. He is the author of "Inmate Movements and Prison Uprisings," *Social Science Quarterly* (1978); "Pardons in Russia and the Soviet Union," in *Modern Encyclopedia of Russian and Soviet History* (1982); and *The Rating Game in American Politics* (1987). Department of History and Political Science, Louisiana State University, Shreveport, 71115-2399.

FRANK SCHWARTZ is a political scientist who received his law degree from Villanova University. He is the author of "Truman's Seizure of the Steel Mills as an Exercise of Active-Positive Combat," *Harry S. Truman* (1986). He teaches in the Department of Political Science, Beaver College, Glenside, Pennsylvania, 19038.

DWIGHT L. TAYS (b. 1950, Florence, Alabama). A political scientist who received his Ph.D. from the University of Mississippi in 1982. He is the author of "Presidential Reaction to Security," *Presidential Studies Quarterly* (1980). Department of History and Political Science, David Lipscomb College, Nashville, Tennessee, 37204-3951.

JEFFREY TULIS is a political scientist who received his Ph.D. from the

Contributors

ersity of Chicago in 1982. He is the co-editor of *The Presidency in the
stitutional Order* (1981). Department of Politics, Princeton University,
iceton, New Jersey, 08544.

HEN NEAL WILLIAMS (b. 1957, Beaumont, Texas). A lawyer who
ceived his B.A. from Lamar University in 1980, and law degree from
exas Tech University in 1985. He is the co-author of "The President and
he White House Staff," *Dimensions of the Modern Presidency* (1981).
Hullett, Roth and Williams, 700 North Street, Suite 101, Beaumont, Texas,
77701.

Preface

This collection of readings on James David Barber's theory of presidential behavior is designed to present briefly the theory, critiques, and empirical tests of the "Barberian" presidency. It brings together the scattered critiques and case studies of Barber's approach to predicting performance in the White House, one of the most controversial theories in modern political science. A brief annotated bibliography is also included for those who desire to do additional reading and research.

Although the material is designed for undergraduate and graduate courses on the American presidency, interested citizens may learn from Barber's effort to distinguish the psychologically healthiest politicians from the most dangerous ones. Students of the presidency will find material relevant to psychological theories of the presidency.

The editor is grateful to Thomas Hovet, Jr. and James C. Davies for their early assistance on this subject. Thanks are particularly due to James R. Klonoski for his course on the American presidency, and to the National Endowment for the Humanities for making it possible to attend a summer seminar at New York University with Louis W. Koenig in 1981. Appreciation is also extended to Eugene McCarthy's Workshop on the American Presidency which was offered at the 1979 International Society of Political Psychology Meeting in Washington, D.C. The assistance of R. Gordon Hoxie and the Center for the Study of the Presidency over the past decade has been most helpful.

I am grateful to Martha N. Bordelon for her secretarial services on the manuscript, and to Sally D. Montgomery for her administrative assistance. I also wish to express my appreciation to Dr. Mary Ann McBride, Dean of the College of Liberal Arts at Louisiana State University in Shreveport, for her editorial assistance. Final responsibility for the end result rests with the contributors and the editor.

William D. Pederson
December 12, 1987

Introduction:

Dimensions of the "Barberian" Presidency

William D. Pederson

After two decades it is time to evaluate James David Barber's psychological approach to the presidency. While critics have tended to ignore the case studies and empirical studies of Barber's theory, his early prediction of Richard Nixon's downfall has been followed by another even earlier and impressive assessment of Ronald Reagan's personality which suggested the possibility of a "Gippergate" episode.[1] The chapters in this book are meant to balance those critics finding fault with Barber and those supporters embracing his stunning predictions. The book suggests the need for an "empirical presidency" to help resolve conflicts between either personality or policy theories as the most important factors in the selection of presidential candidates.

Barber's Theory

Barber argues that presidential candidates should be judged more on the basis of their personalities than on their policy preferences or promises. He argues that most people can predict a political personality through a careful examination of a candidate's "style" (rhetorical skills, maintaining personal relations, and doing homework). In addition, one needs to consider whether a candidate's outlook on life ("worldview") is optimistic or pessimistic. The most important factor is personality ("character"). Most presidents tend to be either: (1) compulsive power seekers (active-negatives); (2) lazy good guys searching for affection (passive-positives); or (3) withdrawn, abstract, and passive figures seeking to confirm their civic virtues (passive-negatives). However, some presidents are flexible progressives who self-actualize through the arena of politics (active-positives). Though often impatient, they search for practical results to public policy problems. Barber thinks that active-positive personalities make the healthiest presidents.[2]

Chapter 1 presents Barber's theory, and Chapter 2 elaborates on the external variables in his approach. The "Barberian" theory of the presidency is based on his early quantitative study of state legislators (Chapter 5). Barber's courage to classify current candidates is reflected in his analysis of the 1972 presidential election, which was published in the *Saturday Review* in September of that year. It is reprinted here (Chapter 4) for it contains a "Barberian" sketch of Senator George McGovern. Because so many presidential candidates are legislators, particularly senators, it is useful to see how Barber approaches these candidates.

Critiques of Barber's Approach

Scholars have been quick to point out possible faults in Barber's model,[3] and readers are referred to the bibliography for several qualitative and quantitative studies which find shortcomings in the "Barberian" presidency, as well as to the first part of Chapter 13, where several troublesome aspects of Barber's approach to presidential personality are presented.

Michael Nelson's essay (Chapter 6) is presented in this volume as a balanced critique of Barber's work on the American presidency. Nelson's criticism that Barber fails to provide a checklist of criteria to type candidates remains a crucial concern. For example, presidential scholar Bruce Buchanan has recently presented four "guidelines" for assessing the real personalities of political candidates: (1) how they typically react to roadblocks or frustrations; (2) how they react to excess glory;

(3) how they work or burn out; and (4) how they handle the truth or evade it.[4]

Even those scholars who are sympathetic to Barber's psychological approach to the American presidency have great difficulty in classifying particular presidents and candidates. The rating of American presidents will remain a subjective exercise until researchers refine the crude clues to character posited in Barber's theory. Perhaps the classic case of this subjectivity is reflected in the historian who worked for Lyndon Johnson. Even at close range, the scholar failed to see the president as a potentially dangerous personality. On the other hand, the same scholar continues to believe personality is more important than policy and promises.[5] Besides suggesting one may be blinded by one's political heroes, better measures of character would be helpful.

The Empirical Presidency

Despite the barage of initial criticism of Barber's theory, it remains one of the best known theoretical approaches to the study of the American presidency. Most introductory American government textbooks use the theory, even though most American presidency textbooks are quick to cite its limitations. The bulk of the studies in this volume have tried to test the theory at an appropriate level. Readers can determine for themselves the success of this effort. At the very least, there is solid ground for keeping an open mind to Barber's approach.

Chapters 7 to 10 present an empirical check of Barber's theory and an expansion of his classification scheme to include pre-twentieth century presidents. The results tend to support Barber's theory, and suggest that about one-fourth of American presidents have been the healthiest types of personalities (active-positives), while another fourth have been the "most dangerous types" (active-negatives). The majority of presidents have exhibited passive personality characteristics.

Most important, the approach taken in these chapters offers a basis for comparative judgments about presidents. It also suggests one of the reasons Barber's theory remains controversial. Some presidents rank higher and lower on the base dimensions of activity and flexibility. Presidential personalities exhibiting extremes of these dimensions within each of the four classifications might easily be inaccurately classified—even by careful critics.

Although Chapters 11 and 12 use different methodologies, both writers find utility in Barber's approach. The findings are consistent with his theory and the results presented in Chapters 7 to 10.

Chapters 13 and 14 raise the issue of how soon the "character" of a politician may be determined, as well as the difficulty of applying Barber's classification scheme to complex personalities. Jeffrey Tulis concludes from his research that Abraham Lincoln was an active-negative politician, while the findings in Chapters 7 to 10 suggest that Lincoln was an active-positive, capable of psychological growth. Readers need to evaluate carefully the evidence presented in these chapters. The six "indexes" presented in Chapter 14 offer a possible means to measure presidential character empirically.

Barber's theory is a controversial one which has nevertheless enlivened scholarly and public debate about presidential character. The studies included in this volume suggest that the evidence marshalled in support of the "Barberian" approach to the presidency will be increasingly sophisticated. In the final analysis, despite the criticism, the emphasis on personality as central to successful leadership is an ancient concept within the Western political tradition, tested by centuries of experience in all varieties of organizations. Because the Barberian presidency is consistent with the democratic ideal, it will endure.

References

[1] James David Barber, "Worrying About Reagan," *New York Times*, September 8, 1980, p. 19.

[2] For a brief but enlightening sketch of Barber's theory, see James David Barber, "If You Were Hiring a President," *Boston Globe*, March 22, 1987.

This article serves as an excellent one-page introduction to the "Barberian" theory of the presidency.

3 Alexander L. George's, "Assessing Presidential Character," *World Politics*, Vol. 26, No. 2 (January, 1974), 234-282 provides a lengthy analysis of Barber's theory; for an elaborate quantitative study which would impose an overly rigid standard of consistency on Barber's work, see James H. Qualls, "Barber's Typological Analysis of Political Leaders," *American Political Science Review*, Vol. 71, No. 1 (September, 1977), 182-211.

4 Bruce Buchanan, "Open All Candidates Before Election," *New York Times*, October 2, 1987.

5 John P. Roche, "Focus on Candidates, Not Issues," *Houston Chronicle*, April 26, 1980.

PART I.

Theory. A Psychological Approach to the American Presidency

1

Analyzing Presidents: From Passive-Positive Taft to Active-Negative Nixon

James David Barber

The President is a lonely figure in a crowd of helpers: he must share the work; he cannot share the responsibility. He may try, as Harding did, to escape this tension by surrounding himself with advisors he can give in to; but if he does, he will find no way out when their counsel is divided. He may, as Wilson did, seek escape by turning inward, with a private declaration of independence; but if he does, he will risk mistake and failure in ventures where cooperation is imperative.

Now as before, the endless speculation about who has a President's confidence—and who is losing it or gaining it as issues shift—reflects a general recognition that the way a President defines and relates to his close circle of confidants influences policy significantly. Detailed studies of such relationships as Wilson with House, Franklin Roosevelt with Howe and Hopkins, and Eisenhower with Sherman Adams, tend to confirm this view.

How, then, might we go about predicting a President's strengths and weaknesses in his personal relations? I think a close examination of his style—the political habits he brings to the office—and his *character*—his basic orientation toward his own life—can reveal a good deal.

Through his style, a President relates himself to three main elements: the national audience (through rhetoric); his advisors, enemies, and subordinates (through personal relations): and the details of policy-making (through what I shall call decision management). In other words, Presidents have to make speeches, conduct negotiations, and solve problems. Each President distributes his energies differently among these tasks, and each shapes his style in a distinctive way. No President is born again on Inauguration Day. Like most people past middle age, a President tries to use his experience; he draws from what has worked for him before in coping with new work.

Where in a man's past are the best clues to his Presidential style? Strangely, they may not come from the way he has acted in immediately pre-Presidential roles. One thinks of Truman as Vice President, Kennedy as Senator, Hoover as Secretary of Commerce. As President, a man emerges as sole king of the mountain—suddenly on top all by himself, no longer one of the many climbing the ladder. His reactions are highly individualized; elements of his old Eriksonian identity crisis jump out of the past. He tends to hark back to that time when he had an analogous emergence—to his first independent political success, usually in early adulthood, when he developed a personal style that worked well for him.

Character has deeper and much less visible roots than style. But two gross dimensions outline the main types. First, divide the Presidents into the more active and the less active. Then cut across that with a division between those who seemed generally happy and optimistic and those who gave an impression of sadness and irritation. These crude clues tend to symptomize character packages. The "active-positive" type tends to show confidence, flexibility, and a focus on producing results through rational mastery. The "active-negative" tends to emphasize ambitious striving, aggressiveness, and a focus on the struggle for power against a hostile environment. "Passive-positive" types come through as receptive, compliant, other-directed persons whose superficial hopefulness masks much inner doubt. The "passive-negative" character tends to withdraw from conflict and uncertainty, to think in terms of vague principles of duty and regular procedure.

William Howard Taft: Passive-Positive

What lends drama to Presidential performances is the interplay of character and style. Consider William Howard Taft. In character, Taft was from the beginning a genial, agreeable, friendly, compliant person, much in need of affection from wife, family, and friends. He fits the passive-positive category most closely, with his slow-moving pace and his optimistic grin. Taft endured several illnesses and a severe accident during childhood. His family was remarkable for its close, affectionate relationships. I think he was spoiled. His father expected his children to do well in school, and Will did. By his Yale days he was a big, handsome campus favorite, with many friends but no really intimate ones. By his twenties he was a fat man. Always sensitive to criticism and anxious for approval, he repeatedly entered new offices with a feeling of personal inadequacy to the tasks before him. He was a humane friend of the men and women around him. His mother often said that "the love of approval was Will's besetting fault." As Secretary of War under Theodore Roosevelt, he won the President's approval by complying willingly with every assignment and by repeatedly expressing his devotion to him.

Taft's political style developed in his career as a lawyer and judge. By a series of family connections and historical accidents (Taft said he always had his plate turned right side up when offices were being handed out), he found his way into the judiciary and adopted the style of the legalist, the law-worshipper. He found the bench comfortable and secure, stable and safe, honorable and respected. He developed a decision-management style based firmly in a narrow, literal, conservative concept of a judge's relationship to the law. Principles were applied to cases to give verdicts, period.

The conflict between Taft's character and style was largely latent until after he became President in 1909. In the White House he had to choose between loyalty and law. His biographer, Henry F. Pringle, wrote that:

Indeed, one of the astonishing things about Taft's four years in the White
House was the almost total lack of men, related or otherwise, upon
whom he could lean. He had no Cabot Lodge. He had no Colonel House.
For the most part he faced his troubles alone.

Again there is the pattern of his earlier years; many friends, no
intimates. And from his character came also his worshipful,
submissive orientation toward Theodore Roosevelt, which he
continued to express in letters and conversation as President. "I
can never forget," he wrote to Roosevelt from the White House,
"that the power that I now exercise was a voluntary transfer
from you to me, and that I am under obligation to you to see to
it that your judgment in selecting me as your successor and in
bringing about the succession shall be vindicated according to
the standards which you and I in conversation have always
formulated."

Taft saw himself as a follower of TR—but not as an imitator of
the TR style. "There is no use trying to be William Howard Taft
with Roosevelt's ways," he wrote. Taft had learned, as a lawyer
and judge, to manage decisions by the application of legal
principles: "Our President has no initiative in respect to legislation given to him by law except that of mere recommendation,
and no legal or formal method of entering into argument and
discussion of the proposed legislation while pending in
Congress." Taft said in a post-Presidential lecture in which he
disagreed explicitly with Roosevelt's view that the "executive
power was limited only by specific restrictions and prohibitions
appearing in the Constitution." This was more than a matter of
intellectual principle. Taft's judicial stance worked—as long as
he was in judicial roles—to protect him from the fires of
controversy. But in the White House, he abhorred the heat of
the kitchen. As his Presidential aide wrote, "I have never known
a man to dislike discord as much as the President. He wants
every man's approval, and a row of any kind is repugnant to
him."

President Taft had once told an aide that "if I only knew what
the President [i.e., Roosevelt—for a long time Taft referred to

TR this way] wanted . . . I would do it, but you know he has held himself so aloof that I am absolutely in the dark. I am deeply wounded." But Taft's character-rooted affectionate loyalty to Roosevelt inevitably came into conflict with Taft's legalistic style. The initial issue was the Ballinger-Pinchot controversy over conservation policy. The details are not important here. What is significant to this discussion is that Taft attempted to solve a broad but intensely political conflict within his Administration through a strict application of the law. As he wrote of the controversy at the time: "I get very impatient at criticism by men who do not know what the law is, who have not looked it up, and yet ascribe all sorts of motives to those who live within it."

Slowly he began to see the Roosevelt Presidency as less than perfection, flawed by irregular procedures. He tried to find a way out which would not offend TR. But as criticisms from TR's followers mounted, negative references to Roosevelt crept into Taft's correspondence. The two managed to maintain a surface amiability in their meeting when Roosevelt returned from Africa, but as Roosevelt began making speeches, Taft found more and more cause for Constitutional alarm. When Roosevelt attacked property rights and then the Supreme Court, Taft became edgy and nervous. He lost his temper on the golf links. He began criticizing Roosevelt in less and less private circles. The man who had written in 1909 that "my coming into office was exactly as if Roosevelt had succeeded himself," wrote in 1912 of "facing as I do a crisis with Mr. Roosevelt."

The crisis came a piece at a time. In 1911, Taft still hoped to avoid a fight, though he saw Roosevelt as "so lacking in legal knowledge that his reasoning is just as deficient as Lodge's." Roosevelt continued to criticize. Taft stuck by his legal guns. However, he confided to his chief aide, Archie Butt: "It is hard, very hard, Archie, to see a devoted friendship going to pieces like a rope of sand."

By the end of 1911, it was clear that TR would not support Taft for re-election. As Pringle says of Taft's mood:

He was heartsick and unhappy. "If I am defeated," he wrote, "I hope that somebody, sometime, will recognize the agony of spirit that I have undergone." Yet Taft remained in the contest. He fought to the limit of his too-tranquil nature because he envisioned the issue as more than a personal one. The "whole fate of constitutional government," he said, was at stake.

Roosevelt attacked "legalistic justice" as "a dead thing" and called on the people to "never forget that the judge is as much a servant of the people as any other official." At first Taft refrained from answering what he privately called TR's "lies and unblushing misrepresentations," but in April of 1912, confessing that "this wrenches my soul" and "I do not want to fight Theodore Roosevelt," he defended himself in public:

> Neither in thought nor word nor action have I been disloyal to the friendship I owe Theodore Roosevelt. . . . I propose to examine the charges he makes against me, and to ask you whether in making them he is giving me a square deal.

Taft's nerves were shattered by the ordeal of attacking TR, that man "who so lightly regards constitutional principles, and especially the independence of the judiciary, one who is so naturally impatient of legal restraints, and of due legal procedure, and who has so misunderstood what liberty regulated by law is. . . ." Exhausted, depressed and shaken, Taft was found by a reporter with his head in his hands. He looked up to say, "Roosevelt was my closest friend," and began to weep.

In 1912 the Republican party split apart and the Democrats captured the government.

The break between Taft and Roosevelt had numerous levels and dimensions; one of those was clearly the conflict within Taft between his legalistic style and his submissive character. Taft's decision-management approach—the application of principles to cases—served him well, both before and after he was President. It failed him as President. If he had had a different character, he might have pushed Roosevelt aside as soon as he won the Presidency, as Woodrow Wilson did the New Jersey bosses when he won his governorship. As it was, Taft nearly tore himself apart—and did help tear his party apart—by hanging onto his leader long after Roosevelt had, in Taft's eyes, broken the law.

Harry S. Truman: Active-Positive

Harry S. Truman belongs among the active-positive Presidents. His activity is evident; beginning with a brisk walk early in the morning, he went at the job with all his might. And despite occasional discouragement, he relished his experience. His first memory was of his laughter while chasing a frog across the backyard; his grandmother said, "It's very strange that a two-year-old has such a sense of humor." When Democratic spirits hit the bottom in the 1948 campaign, Truman said, "Everybody around here seems to be nervous but me." And he played the piano.

Although he was in his sixties throughout his long stay in the White House, he put in 16 to 18 hours a day at Presidenting, but "was fresher at the end than I was at the beginning," according to Charles Ross. Truman often got angry but rarely depressed. Once he compared the criticism he got with the "vicious slanders" against Washington, Lincoln, and Andrew Johnson. Truman expressed his bouyancy under attack in these words (quoted in William Hillman's *Mr. President*):

> So I don't let these things bother me for the simple reason that I know that I am trying to do the right thing and eventually the facts will come out. I'll probably be holding a conference with Saint Peter when that happens. I never give much weight or attention to the brickbats that are thrown my way. The people that cause me trouble are the good men who have to take these brickbats for me.

And then there is that ultimate, almost implausible indication of persistent optimism: he is said to have enjoyed being Vice President. The White House staff called him "Billie Spunk."

Truman had a strong father (nicknamed "Peanuts" for his short stature) and an affectionate mother. The family had more than its share of difficulties, especially financial ones. They moved several times in Harry's early years. His severe vision problem kept him out of school until he was eight, and at nine he nearly died of diphtheria. But he appears to have come through it with an unusually strong store of self-confidence, ready to endure what had to be, ready to reach out when opportunities presented themselves. He drew on a home in which the rules said: Do the right thing, Love one another, and By their fruits shall ye know them. When he telephoned his mother to ask if she had listened to his inauguration as Vice President on the radio, she answered: "Yes. I heard it all. Now you behave yourself up there, Harry. You behave yourself!"

Truman's drive for decisions, his emphasis on results, his faith in rational persuasion, his confidence in his own values, his humor about himself, and his ability to grow into responsibility all fit the active-positive character. The character shows itself as an orientation, a broad direction of energy and affect, a tendency to experience self and others in a certain way. Truman attacked life; he was not withdrawn. He emphasized his independence; he was not compliant. He laughed at himself; he was not compulsive (though he showed some tendencies in that direction). His character thus provided a foundation for the transcendence of his defenses, for devoting his attention to the realities beyond himself.

Style is what he built on those foundations. Truman's style developed in two main spurts. "So far as its effect on Harry Truman was concerned," his biographer writes, "World War I released the genie from the bottle." He had worked in a bank, farmed, taken a flier on an oil-drilling enterprise, joined the Masons, and fallen in love with Bess Wallace. The family was having financial difficulties again. His father died in 1914, when Harry was 30. At the outbreak of the war, he joined the National Guard and was elected lieutenant by his friends. Sent away from home to Oklahoma, he became regimental canteen officer, with Eddie Jacobson as his assistant. The other Ft. Sill canteens had heavy losses, but the Truman-Jacobson enterprise returned 666 per cent on the initial investment in six months. In charge for the first time, Truman had shown that he could succeed through careful management. Later in France, he was put in charge of a rowdy flock of Irish pranksters loosely organized as a field-artillery battery. One former officer who could not control the men had been thrown out of the Army; another had broken down under the strain. Upon assuming command, Truman recalled later, "I was the most thoroughly scared individual in that camp. Never on the front or anywhere else have I been so nervous." Alfred Steinberg, in *The Man from Missouri*, gives this account of how Truman handled himself:

> "Men," he told the sergeants and corporals, "I know you've been making trouble for your previous commanders. From now on, you're going to be responsible for maintaining discipline in your squads and sections. And if there are any of you who can't, speak up right now and I'll bust you back right now."

Truman did his own reconnaissance at the front, to get his information first-hand. When his troops broke and ran under fire in "The Battle of Who Run":

> "I got up and called them everything I knew," said Truman. The curses that poured out contained some of the vilest four-letter words heard on the Western Front. Said Father Curtis Tiernan, the regiment's Catholic chaplain, who was on the scene, "It took the skin off the ears of those boys." The effect was amazing. Padre Tiernan recalled with pleasure. "It turned those boys right around."

"Captain Harry" came out of the war with the respect and admiration of his men. He had learned that his angry voice could turn the tide and that he could decide what to do if he got the facts himself and paid attention to the details. Most important, his style developed around intense loyalty in personal relations: everything depended on the stick-togetherness of imperfect allies.

After the war, Truman and Jacobson opened their famous haberdashery, serving mostly old Army buddies. An Army friend who happened to be a Missouri Pendergast got him into politics—not against his will. He ran for county judge and won; his performance in that office reconfirmed his faith in hard personal compaigning and in careful, honest business practice. During the campaign he was charged with voting for a member of the other party and he answered with this speech:

> You have heard it said that I voted for John Miles for county marshal. I'll have to plead guilty to that charge, along with 5,000 ex-soldiers. I was closer to John Miles than a brother. I have seen him in places that made hell look like a playground. I have seen him stick to his guns when Frenchmen were falling back. I have seen him hold the American line when only John Miles and his three batteries were between the Germans and a successful counterattack. He was of the right stuff, and a man who wouldn't vote for his comrade under circumstances such as these would be untrue to his country. I know that every soldier understands it. I have no apology to make for it.

These experiences reinforced and confirmed an emphasis Truman had grown up with. "If Mamma Truman was for you," he said, "she was for you, and as long as she lived I always knew there was one person who was in my corner." Throughout his political life Truman reiterated this for-me-or-against-me theme:

> "We don't play halfway politics in Missouri. When we start out with a man, if he is any good at all, we always stay with him to the end. Sometimes people quit me but I never quit people when I start to back them up."

> [To Admiral Leahy:] "Of course, I will make the decisions, and after a decision is made, I will expect you to be loyal."

> [Margaret Truman, on her father's philosophy:] " . . . 'the friends thou hast and their adoption tried, grapple them to thy soul with hoops of steel'. . . ."

> [From Truman's own memoirs:] "Vinson was gifted with a sense of personal and political loyalty seldom found among the top men in Washington. Too often loyalties are breached in Washington in the rivalries for political advantage."

> [Truman on Tom Pendergast:] "I never deserted him when he needed friends. Many for whom he'd done much more than he ever did for me ran out on him when the going was rough. I didn't do that—and I am President of the United States in my own right!"

[Truman to Harry Vaughn:] "Harry, they're just trying to use you to embarrass me. You go up there, and tell 'em to go to hell. We came in here together and, God damn it, we're going out together!"

[Of Eisenhower's refusal to stand up for Marshall:] "You don't kick the man who made you."

What did this emphasis on loyalty mean for the Truman Presidency? The story of Truman's wrangles with aides high and low is well known. Conflicts, misunderstandings, scandals, and dismissals piled up: Byrnes, Wallace, Ickes, Louis Johnson, J. Howard McGrath, Morgenthau, MacArthur, Baruch, Clifford vs. Steelman, and the ragtag crew of cronies and influenceables typified by Harry Vaughan. The landscape of the Truman administration was littered with political corpses. Both Presidential candidates in 1952 promised to clean up what Eisenhower called "the mess in Washington."

I think Patrick Anderson, in *The President's Men*, is right when he sees the key to Truman's loyalty troubles "in the man himself, not in those who so poorly served him." Anderson continues:

Truman once said that his entire political career was based upon his World War I experience, upon the friends he made and the lessons he learned. It was as an army captain under fire in France that Harry Truman first learned that he was as brave and as capable as the next man. He learned, too, the rule that says an officer must always stand by his men. Perhaps he learned that rule too well; in later years he seemed to confuse standing by Harry Vaughan when he was under fire from Drew Pearson with standing by the men of the 35th Division when they were under fire from the Germans at Meuse-Argonne and Verdun.

After the war, he was a failure as a businessman; his success came in politics. It must have galled Truman that he owed his political success to the corruption-ridden Pendergast machine. But he kept quiet, he kept his hands clean, he learned to mind his own business. That may be another lesson he learned too well. The most simple, most harsh explanation of Truman's tolerance is just this: You can take the politician out of the county courthouse, but you can't take the county courthouse out of the politician.

But it is not that simple. Another reason Truman stood by Vaughan and the others was no doubt simple political tactics: If you fire a man, you in effect admit wrongdoing; if you keep him, you can continue to

deny it. More than by politics, however, Truman seems to have been
motivated by stubborn loyalty to his friends. It was a sadly misguided
loyalty, for Presidents owe a loyalty to the nation that transcends any
allegiance to erring friends. Roosevelt understood this instinctively;
Truman would not recognize it. Truman's dilemma was complicated by
the fact that his nature was more sentimental than that of any of the other
recent Presidents. It is often helpful for a President to be a ruthless
son-of-a-bitch, particularly in his personal relationships; this, for better
or worse, Truman was not.

There appears to have been a lapse in communication in each of
Truman's "breaks" with such high-level personages as Wallace,
Byrnes, Baruch, and MacArthur. Truman believed that he had
made clear to the other fellow just how he must change his
behavior; each of the others believed that Truman had endorsed
him in the course he was pursuing. Truman seems to have been
slowly, and then radically, disillusioned with men in whom he
had placed his trust. He was not able to realize that the loyalties
around a President are not black and white—as they are in battle
or in a Missouri political campaign—but rather shade off from
Vaughan-like sycophancy at one end of the spectrum to Mac-
Arthur-like independence at the other. For Truman, loyalties
were hard and brittle; when they broke they broke. Before he
became President, he had, after all, been the chief of loyal
subordinates only twice: in the Army and as a "judge" in
Missouri. It was natural for him to revert back to those times
when he was again in charge.

In terms of character and style analysis, Truman shows one
form of danger inherent in the political adaptation of the active-
positive type. To oversimplify what is really much more complicated: the character who has overcome his own hang-ups,
who has leaped over the barriers between himself and the real
world, whose bent is toward rational mastery of the environment, is likely to forget, from time to time, that other persons,
publics, and institutions maintain themselves in rather messier
ways. In another context I have said this type may want a
political institution "to deliberate like Plato's Academy and then
take action like Caesar's army," neglecting the necessities of

emotional inspiration and peaceful procedure. The type is also vulnerable to betrayal when he assumes that others who seem to share his purposes will see those purposes precisely as he does and govern their actions accordingly. He is especially prone to this mistake with respect to the active-negative types who is, on the surface, like him in many ways.

Truman's style exaggerated these characteristic vulnerabilities. What he had learned of himself when he was under 20 was shaped and channeled by what he learned of life when he was over 30. Character fed style, style digested character. Amid many Presidential successes, most of his failures can be traced to a particular way in which style reinforced character trends.

Dwight D. Eisenhower: Passive-Negative

Eisenhower as President is best approximated in the passive-negative category, in which tendencies to withdraw predominate. On a great many occasions in the biographies, Eisenhower is found asserting himself by denying himself; that is, by taking a strong stand against the suggestion that he take a strong stand.

No, he would not get down in the gutter with Joseph McCarthy; no, he would not stop the Cohn and Schine highjinks. Franklin Roosevelt had usurped Congressional powers, he thought, and he would not do that: "I want to say with all the emphasis at my command that this Administration had absolutely *no* personal choice for a new Majority Leader. *We* are not going to get into *their* business." When "those damn monkeys on the Hill" acted up, he would stay out of it. Press conferences were another Rooseveltian mistake: "I keep telling you fellows I don't like to do this sort of thing." Was he under attack in the press? "Listen," Eisenhower said, "anyone who has time to listen to commentators or read columnists obviously doesn't have enough work to do." Should he engage in personal summitry on the international front? "This idea of the President of the United States going personally abroad to negotiate—it's just damn stupid."

With a new Cabinet, wouldn't it make sense to oversee them

rather carefully? "I guess you know about as much about the job as I do," he told George Humphrey. His friend Arthur Larson wrote that Eisenhower found patronage "nauseating" and "partisan political effect was not only at the bottom of the list—indeed it did not exist as a motive at all." In 1958 the President said, "Frankly, I don't care too much about the Congressional elections." Eisenhower disliked speechmaking (he had once been struck by lightning while delivering a lecture). Urged to address some meeting, he would typically say, "Well, all right, but not over 20 minutes." Sherman Adams writes that Eisenhower "focused his mind completely on the big and important aspects of the questions we discussed, shutting out with a strongly self-disciplined firmness the smaller and petty side issues when they crept into the conversation." In other words, he did not so much select problems upon which to concentrate as he selected an *aspect* of all problems—the aspect of principle.

When someone aggravated Eisenhower, he would "write his name on a piece of paper, put it in my lower desk drawer, and shut the drawer." When it came time to end his four-pack-a-day cigarette habit, "I found that the easiest way was just to put it out of your mind."

Eisenhower's tendency to move away from involvements, to avoid personal commitments, was supported by belief: "My personal convictions, no matter how strong, cannot be the final answer," he said. The definition of democracy he liked best was "simply the opportunity for self-discipline." As a military man he had detested and avoided politics at least since his first command, when a Congressman had pressed him for a favor. His beliefs were carved into epigrams:

He that conquereth his own soul is greater than he who taketh a city.

Forget yourself and personal fortunes.

Belligerence is the hallmark of insecurity.

Never lose your temper, except intentionally.

It is the tone, the flavor, the aura of self-denial and refusal that counts in these comments. Eisenhower is not attacking or rejecting others; he is simply turning away from them, leaving them alone, refusing to interfere.

His character is further illuminated by his complaints, which cluster around the theme of being bothered. His temper flared whenever he felt that he was either being imposed upon or interfered with on matters he wanted others to handle. He "heatedly gave the Cabinet to understand that he was sick and tired of being bothered about patronage." "When does anybody get any time to think around here?" he complained to Adams. Robert Donovan said of Eisenhower: "Nothing gets him out of sorts faster than for a subordinate to come in and start to hem and haw about a decision. He wants the decision and not the thinking out loud." Eisenhower felt that his 1955 heart attack was triggered when he was repeatedly interrupted on the golf links by unnecessary phone calls from the State Department. In 1948, when he finally managed to stop the boomlet for his nomination, he said he felt "as if I'd had an abscessed tooth pulled." He told a persistent reporter as the 1948 speculations continued: "Look, son, I cannot conceive of any circumstance that could drag out of me permission to consider me for any political post from dogcatcher to Grand High Supreme King of the Universe."

Why, then, did Eisenhower bother to become President? Why did he answer those phone calls on the golf links? Because he thought he ought to. He was a sucker for duty and always had been. Sentiments which would sound false for most political leaders ring true for Eisenhower:

My only satisfaction in life is to hope that my effort means something to the other fellow. What can I do to repay society for the wonderful opportunities it has given me?

. . . a decision that I have never recanted or regretted [was the decision] to perform every duty given me in the Army to the best of my ability and to do the best I could to make a creditable record, no matter what the nature of the duty.

. . . in trying to explain to you a situation that has been tossed in my teeth more than once (my lack of extended troop duty in recent years),

all I accomplished was to pass up something I *wanted* to do, in favor of
something I thought I *ought* to do.

He did not feel a duty to save the world or to become a great
hero, but simply to contribute what he could, in the best way he
was able. From the family Bible readings, from the sportsman-
ship of a boy who wanted nothing more than to be a first-rate
athlete, from the West Point creed, Eisenhower felt, amid
questions about many other things, that duty was a certainty.

In all these respects, and also in his personal comradeliness,
Eisenhower fits the passive-negative (or "reluctant") type. The
orientation is toward performing duty with modesty; the political
adaptation is characterized by protective retreats to principle,
ritual, and personal virtue. The political strength of this character is its legitimacy. It inspires trust in the incorruptibility and
the good intentions of the man. Its political weakness is its
inability to produce, though it may contribute by preventing.
Typically, the passive-negative character presides over drift and
confusion, partially concealed by the apparent orderliness of the
formalities. Samuel Lubell caught the crux of this character
when he saw in Eisenhower "one man's struggle between a
passion for active duty and a dream of quiet retirement."

Eisenhower's political style, particularly his style in personal
relations, channeled these character forces in an interesting
way. At West Point he was a minor hellraiser (eventually ranking
125th in a class of 164 in "conduct") and a dedicated athlete until
an injury, incurred because he would not tell a sadistic riding
instructor that he had a weak knee, removed him from competition. He missed combat in World War I and kicked around for
a good many years in staff jobs and football coaching; he served
seven years on the staff of that flamboyant self-dramatist,
Douglas MacArthur, for whom Eisenhower learned to make a
newly-developing kind of military administration work.

The old structure of military command—the hierarchy—was
giving way to a system less like a pyramid, more like a floating
crap game, a system of interdependent functional specialties—
teams—that had to be brought together around new technolog-

ical and strategic concepts. Eisenhower mastered the skills this system increasingly demanded, particularly the ability to coordinate, to gather together the right threads into the right knot. It was *this* style, the style of the modern administrative team-coordinator, that stuck with Eisenhower on into his White House years. The danger of his "military mind" was not that he would be a martinet, a MacArthur; here Harry Truman misestimated him. It was Eisenhower's command habit of central coordination that shaped his behavior. The President, he said,

> must know the general purpose of everything that is going on, the general problem that is there, whether or not it is being solved or the solution is going ahead according to principles in which he believes and which he has promulgated; and, finally, he must say "yes" or "no."

The well-known staff system Eisenhower put into the Presidency was designed to leave him free to coordinate at the highest level. The trouble was that the level got higher and higher, more and more removed from the political battlefield, until, in his second term, Eisenhower had to break through a good many layers and circles to get at the controls of policy.

In the Army, Eisenhower's brand of coordination went forward in a context of command; the colonels were dependent on the generals. An order announced (after however much coordination) was an order to be executed. Not so in politics, where promulgation is just the beginning. In an Army at war, coordination takes place behind the advancing flag: the overriding purposes are not in question. Not so in the political "order" where the national purpose is continually questioned and redefined.

When Eisenhower had to deal with military matters as President, such as Lebanon and the Suez crisis, he could act with celerity and precision. He took his greatest pride in the fact that there had been eight years of peace during his administration. But at the same time his character and style fit together to contribute—along with many external factors—to a long list of less happy incidents and trends (Dixon-Yates, Dullesian brinksmanship, the Faubus and U-2 bumbles, the McCarthy contagion). He didn't mean it this way, but when Eisenhower said that "our system demands the Supreme Being," he was probably right.

Lyndon B. Johnson: Active-Negative

For this generation of President-watchers, it would be tedious to document President Lyndon B. Johnson's difficulties in personal relations. The bully-ragging, the humiliations visited upon the men around him, are nearly as familiar as his rages against the Kennedy clan. By mid-1966 it was hard to find an independent voice among his intimate advisors. What had happened to a political style whose cornerstone was the expert manipulation of personal relations?

Johnson experienced his first independent political success as a student at Southwest Texas State Teachers College. Lyndon's mother pushed the boy to get an education; when he was four years old she persuaded the local schoolteacher to let him attend classes. In 1924, he graduated from high school at 15, the youngest of the six-member senior class as well as its president. That year he had lost an important debating contest ("I was so disappointed I went right into the bathroom and was sick"). The year before the family had moved back to a farm in Johnson City and stayed "just long enough for Daddy to go broke," Lyndon's sister recalled.

After high school, Lyndon told all his friends he was through with school forever, despite his mother's urgings to go on. That summer he tried a clerical job for a few weeks but got discouraged and came home. Then Lyndon and two friends left home for California in an old car. A year and a half later, thin, broke, and hungry, he came back and found a job on a road gang for a dollar a day. There was some beer and girls and fights; once his mother looked at his bloodied face and said, "To think that my eldest-born should turn out like this." By February, 1927, Lyndon had had enough; "I'm sick of working with just my hands, and I'm ready to try working with my brain. If you and

Daddy can get me into a college, I'll go as soon as I can." On borrowed money, he set off for San Marcos.

Johnson's intense ambition—and his style in personal relations, rhetoric, and decision management—took shape in his college years. The academic side of life did not trouble him much at unaccredited Southwest Texas Teachers; he attacked his courses "with an intensity he had never before revealed." But his main energies went into operating, getting on top of the institution. President Evans got him a job collecting trash, but Lyndon soon cajoled his way into a position as assistant to the President's secretary, with a desk in the outer office. In *Sam Johnson's Boy*, Alfred Steinberg continues the story:

> According to Nichols [the secretary], what next unfolded was flabergasting. Lyndon jumped up to talk to everyone who came to the office to see Evans, and before days passed, he was asking the purpose of the visit and offering solutions to problems. The notion soon spread that it was necessary to get Lyndon's approval first in order to see Dr. Evans. At the same time, faculty members came to the conclusion that it was essential for them to be friendly to Lyndon, for they believed he could influence the president on their behalf. This erroneous idea developed because the school lacked a telephone system tying President Evans' office with those of department heads, and when the president wanted to send a message to a department head or a professor, he asked his part-time aide, rather than Nichols, to run over with a note. Lyndon's tone and attitude somehow gave the impression he was far more than a messenger.

Soon this student assistant was slapping the president on the back, accompanying him to the state capitol, answering mail, and writing reports to state agencies. "Lyndon," President Evans said, "I declare you hadn't been in my office a month before I could hardly tell who was president of the school—you or me."

Johnson was off and running. Black-balled by the dominant fraternity, he helped start a rival one, the White Stars, who won campus elections in part by fancy parliamentary tactics. Johnson sold more Real Silk socks than his customers had use for. He became a star debater, significantly in a system where he and his partner had to prepare both sides of each question because the assignment of negative or affirmative turned on the flip of a coin just before the debate. Johnson's strength was in finding the opponents' key weakness, and then exploiting it to the hilt. Later he began to win office: president of the press club, senior legislator of his class, student council member, secretary of the Schoolmakers Club, editor of the newspaper. His editorials were full of positive thinking. They came out for courtesy, "honesty of soul," and the Fourth of July, along with some more personal sentiments:

> Personality is power; the man with a striking personality can accomplish greater deeds in life than a man of equal abilities but less personality.

> The great men of the world are those who have never faltered. They had the glowing vision of a noble work to inspire them to press forward, but they also had the inflexible will, the resolute determination, the perfectly attuned spiritual forces for the execution of the work planned.

> The successful man has a well-trained will. He has under absolute control his passions and desires, his habits and his deeds.

> There are no tyrannies like those that human passions and weaknesses exercise. No master is so cruelly exacting as an indulged appetite. To govern self is a greater feat than to control armies and forces.

> Ambition is an uncomfortable companion many times. He creates discontent with present surroundings and achievements; he is never satisfied but always pressing forward to better things in the future. Restless, energetic, purposeful, it is ambition that makes of a creature a real man.

In 1928, Johnson left college with a two-year teaching certificate. He returned a year later after having served, at the age of 20, as principal of an elementary school in Cotulla, Texas. As principal (over five teachers and a janitor). Lyndon was in his first chief executive position. His friendly biographers report he was "a firm administrator, a strict disciplinarian, and a good teacher." He insisted that Mexican children speak only English, and he required his teachers to keep constant supervision of the students. Laziness or misbehavior "was likely to bring some form of punishment. A hard worker himself, Johnson expected others to work with equal energy and determination. He was persistent, sometimes high-tempered, energetic, aggressive, and creative.'' His march into the classroom each morning was the signal for the students to sing out:

How do you do, Mr. Johnson,
How do you do?
How do you do, Mr. Johnson,
How are you?
We'll do it if we can,
We'll stand by you to a man.
How do you do, Mr. Johnson,
How are you?

Mr. Johnson spanked at least one boy who ridiculed his walk. His energy was incredible. He introduced school assemblies, inter-school public-speaking contests, spelldowns, baseball games, track meets, parental car pools for transporting children, coached debating and basketball at the high school, organized a literary society, courted a girl who taught 35 miles away, and took courses at the Cotulla extension center.

Enough. Johnson's style—the whirlwinded energy, the operator-dominator personal relations, the idealistic rhetoric, the use of information as an instrument—all of it was there when he emerged from road-gang bum to big wheel in the world of San Marcos and Cotulla. Obviously personal relations was at the core of his style. It displayed itself in two interesting variations: Johnson on the make, and Johnson in charge. In the first he was the operator who repeated, as secretary to a conservative Congressman and as Senate party leader, the story of his San Marcos takeover, showing a remarkable ability to expand his roles—and his influence—through energetic social manipulation. Johnson in charge used domination successfully, forcing subordinates into conformity.

I think Johnson's character infused this stylistic pattern with a compulsive quality, so that he was virtually unable to alter it when it proved unproductive. Clearly Johnson belongs among the active-negative characters. His fantastic pace of action in the Presidency was obvious. He was also characteristically discouraged much of the time. On the wall of his Senate office he hung this quotation from Edmund Burke:

> Those who would carry on great public schemes must be proof against the worst fatiguing delays, the most mortifying disappointments, the most shocking insults, and worst of all, the presumptuous judgment of the ignorant upon their designs.

He was, he said, "the loneliest man in the world," "the most denounced man in the world," for whom "nothing really seems to go right from early in the morning until late at night," who was "not sure whether I can lead this country and keep it together, with my background." Even at the height of his success—at the close of the remarkable first session of the 89th Congress— Johnson, convalescing from a gallstone operation, complained:

> What do they want—what *really* do they want? I am giving them boom times and more good legislation than anybody else did, and what do they do—attack and sneer! Could FDR do better? Could anybody do better? What *do* they want?

Johnson's remarkable effectivness *in situations where the social environment provided direction* is not to be doubted. As Senate Democratic Leader he reached the high point of success in consensus-building by catching issues at the right stage of development, mapping the terrain of Senatorial opinion, and manipulating members' perceptions and expectations to get bills passed. The raw materials were given: Johnson did not take a stand, he worked with the range of stands he found among other members, pushing here, pulling there, until he had a workable configuration of votes. "I have always thought of myself as one who has been moderate in approaching problems," he said. But "moderation"—like Eisenhower's middle-of-the-road—is a relational concept definable only in terms of the positions others take. In the legislative setting, Johnson *had* to work that way. In the Presidency, Johnson had around him, not a circle of Senatorial barons, each with his own independence and authority, but a circle of subordinates. There his beseeching for knowledge of "what they *really* want," his feeling that "no President ever had a problem of doing what is right; the big problem is knowing what is right," and especially his plea to his advisors that "all you fellows must be prudent about what you encourage me to go for," indicated the disorientation of an expert middle-man elevated above the ordinary political marketplace.

Put crudely: Johnson's style failed him, so he fell back on character. There he found no clear-cut ideology, no particular direction other than the compulsion to secure and enhance his personal power. As his real troubles mounted, he compounded them by so dominating his advisors that he was eventually left even more alone, even more vulnerable to the exaggerations of his inner dramas, until he took to wondering aloud: "Why don't people like me?" "Why do you want to destroy me?" "I can't trust anybody!" "What are you trying to do to me? Everybody is trying to cut me down, destroy me!"

Richard Nixon: Active-Negative

The description accompanying Richard Nixon's figure at the Fisherman's Wharf Wax Museum in San Francisco calls the President "industrious and persistent," "ambitious and dedicated from childhood." Like Woodrow Wilson, Herbert Hoover, and Lyndon B. Johnson, Nixon in the early months of his presidency seemed happy in his work.

He began cautiously. Recognizing the national mood as calling for peace and quiet, empowered by a narrow, minority victory in the election, and confronting a Congress and a bureaucracy dominated by Democrats, he opted for an undramatic beginning. He devoted much of his attention in these early days to gathering around him the men who would help him shape a program, and in arranging them in relation to his own style of operation.

The recruitment process had its difficulties—Nixon received refusals from his first choices for Secretaries of State, Defense, and Treasury and Attorney General; his friend Finch had decided not to accept the Vice Presidential nomination; Warren

Burger was at least fifth on his list of candidates for Chief Justice. But it was probably Nixon's own preference which brought together in the Cabinet a collection of competent, quiet, relatively obscure men whose "extra dimensions" he had to describe to the unknowing national audience, and in the White House a crew of younger lieutenant-colonel types leavened with two brillant Harvardians. He intended to disperse power in his administration. In 1968 he had said: "Publicity would not center at the White House alone. Every key official would have the opportunity to be a big man in his field." If so, their reputations would be made, largely, within and through the Nixon Administration.

Nixon's Presidential style was not entirely clear as of September, 1969; he had not yet been through the fires of large-scale political crisis. But a few features emerged that seemed likely to persist. In several ways, Nixon appeared to have adopted a judgelike stance:

- He takes up one case at a time and tries to dispose of it before moving on to the next case.
- He relies on formal, official channels for information and advice. In his ABM decision, for example, "Although he instructed his aides to seek out all sides of the argument, the President appears to have had little direct contact with opponents or advocates of the missile system outside his own circle." Senators and scientists opposed to the ABM sought out Kissinger, who prepared a "devil's advocate" paper.
- At official meetings, Nixon is the presider, the listener who keeps his own counsel while other members of the group present their cases and options and briefs, like lawyers in a court. He asks questions; he himself rarely tosses out suggestions for critical comment.
- Evidence in hand, he retires to his chambers (usually a small room off the Lincoln bedroom), where he may spend hours in complete solitude reaching his decision.
- He emerges and pronounces the verdict.

By September, this system had already produced some Presidential stumbles. Decisions or near-decisions taken in this fashion had to be reversed or abruptly modified as they set off political alarms. There was the $30,000 job for Nixon's brother Edward; Franklin Long and the National Science Foundation directorship; Willie Mae Rogers's appointment as consumer consultant; the Knowles appointment; the nomination and then withdrawal of Peter Bove to be Governor of the Virgin Islands; the shelving and then unshelving of the "hunger" question; the backing and filling regarding desegregation guidelines; and the various changes in the Job Corps. In these cases "decisions" came unglued in the face of indignant and surprised reactions from the press, interest groups, and Congress. The resignation of Clifford Alexander and the appointment of Senator Strom Thurmond's protégé as chief White House political troubleshooter seemed to indicate inadequate consultation, as did certain exaggerations by Secretary Laird on defense and Attorney General Mitchell on "preventive detection." On the ABM, Nixon emerged, despite his victory, with about half the Senate confirmed in opposition. These bobbles may be seen, some years hence, as nothing more than the inevitable trials of shaking down a new crew. Through them all, Nixon's popularity with the public rose.

It is the isolation, the lonely seclusion adopted consciously as a way of deciding, that stands out in Nixon's personal-relations style. That style was defined, in its main configurations, at the time of his first independent political success in 1948.

Following a childhood marred by accident, severe illness, the deaths of two brothers, and much family financial insecurity. Richard Nixon made his way to the Law School of Duke University, where he succeeded as a student but failed in his fervent desire to land a position in New York or Washington upon his graduation in 1937. Instead, his mother arranged a place for him in a smaller Whittier firm, where he spent the late 1930's in a practice featuring a good deal of divorce and criminal law, holding town attorney office, and serving as a trustee of Whittier College. He and "a group of local plungers" gambled $10,000 to start a frozen-orange-juice company which went broke after a year and a half. In 1938, he proposed to Pat Ryan the night they met; they were married in May of 1940 and took an apartment over a garage.

After Pearl Harbor he worked briefly in the OPA tire-rationing office in Washington before entering the Navy as a lieutenant junior grade—at which, Nixon remembered in 1968, his "gentle, Quaker mother . . . quietly wept." He met William P. Rogers in the Navy. He served as a supply officer in the South Pacific, where he ran a kind of commissary, called "Nixon's Hamburger Stand." When he returned from the war, he struck acquaintances as unusually contemplative, "dreaming about some new world order," possibly feeling guilty about his "sin" of serving in the armed forces." Then there was an unexpected outburst: at a homecoming luncheon for some 30 family and friends, an elderly cousin gave an arm-chair analysis of the war. Suddenly Richard leaned across the table and cursed the old man out. Talk stopped. His folks were amazed. Nixon thought no one there would ever forget this uncharacteristic outburst.

He was returning to be, in his own words, "Nothing . . . a small-time lawyer just out of the Navy." Then, as he was winding up his service in Baltimore, he received a call from a Whittier banker asking if he would run for Congress against Jerry Voorhis. He accepted almost immediately. The year was 1945; Nixon was 32. He flew back to California and appeared in his uniform before the Republican group; he brought along a collection of pictures he had had taken; in his lieutenant commander's uniform, for use in the campaign. He impressed the group with his calm, crisp answers. They took him as their candidate in what seemed like a hopeless campaign against the popular Voorhis. In his letter of acceptance he said he planned to stress "a group of speeches." Voorhis's "conservative reputation must be blasted," he said. His campaign became an aggressive rhetorical performance in which he won with little help from anyone else.

Nixon's success at this period was independent of his family; it was his first clearly political commitment in a personal sense;

it was then, he wrote later, that "the meaning of crisis [took] on sharply expanded dimensions"—a fine paraphrase of Alexander George's concept of the expansion of one's "field of power." Perhaps most important is the independence dimension: he had tried several times to make it into the big time in a big city away from home and now he had achieved that.

The shape of Nixon's style, confirmed in his subsequent success with the Hiss case, was clear in its general outline at this point. Close inter-personal relations were simply not very important to his success. He was, and remained, a loner. His style was centered in speaking and in hard work getting ready to speak. Later he attributed his victory over Voorhis to three factors: "intensive campaigning; doing my homework; and participating in debates with my better-known opponent." From then on, Nixon was primarily a man on his own—a hard-working, careful student of one issue or case at a time, continually preparing for a public presentation, highly sensitive to his rhetorical style and the reactions of audiences to him. Throughout his career, including his stint with Eisenhower, Nixon was never a full-fledged member of a cooperative team or an administrator used to overseeing the work of such a team. He stood apart, made his own judgments, relied on his own decisions.

All this should have made it evident that Nixon in the Presidency would (a) develop a rhetorical stance carefully attuned to his reading of the temper of the times (and of the public's reaction to him); (b) work very hard at building a detailed case to back up each of his positions, and (c) maintain a stance of interpersonal independence and individual final authority with respect to his Cabinet and his White House staff.

It is the way this style interacts with Nixon's character which is of interest here. Despite his current air of happy calm, similar in many ways to the early Presidential experience of others of his type, Nixon belongs, I think, among the active-negative President. On the activity side there is little doubt. Nixon has always been a striver, an energetic doer who attacks his tasks vigorously and aggressively. He has often driven himself to grey-faced exhaustion. But even the less demanding 1968-69 Nixon schedules leave him on the side of activists, in contrast, to, say, Taft, Harding, Coolidge, and Eisenhower.

As for his affect toward his experience, I would put more stock in the way he has typically felt about what he was doing over a lifetime than I would put in his current euphoria. Over more than 20 political years, Nixon has seen himself repeatedly as being just on the verge of quitting. Furthermore, on many occasions he has experienced profound depression and disappointment, even when he was succeeding. As a new Congressman, he said he had "the same lost feeling I had when I went into military service." With the Hiss case victory, "I should have felt elated. . . . However, I experienced a sense of letdown which is difficult to describe or even to understand." Running for the Senate in 1950 he was a "sad but earnest underdog." The Nixon Fund episode in 1952 left him "gloomy and angry;" after the Checkers speech, he said, "I loused it up, and I am sorry. . . . It was a flop," and then he cried. He was "dissatisfied" and "disappointed" in his Vice Presidency; in "semi-shock" at Eisenhower's heart attack; he found the President's 1956 hesitations about him "an emotional ordeal;" he was "grim and nervous" in 1960, and he exploded bitterly and publicly after his 1962 defeat.

There have been a few piano-thumping exceptions, but the general tone of Nixon in politics—even when he has not been in a crisis—has been the doing of the unpleasant but necessary. It is this lifelong sense that the burdens outweigh the pleasures which must be set up against the prospect of a new Nixon continuing to find the White House a fun place. In the introduction, to *Six Crises*, Nixon writes, "I find it especially difficult to answer the question, does a man 'enjoy' crises?" He goes on to say that he had not found his "fun," but that "surely there is more to life than the search for enjoyment in the popular sense." Crisis engages all a man's talents; he loses himself in a larger cause. Nixon contrasts enjoyment with "life's mountaintop experiences"—what he calls the "exquisite agony" of crisis. When Nixon begins to feel pleasantly relaxed, or playfully enjoying, I think, some danger sign goes up, some inner commandment says no, and he feels called back into the quest for worlds to conquer.

There are many more aspects of Nixon's character that fit the active-negative type: the unclear and discontinuous self-image; the continual self-examination and effort to construct a "Richard Nixon;" the fatalism and pessimism; the substitution of technique for value; the energies devoted to controlling aggressive feelings; the distrust of political allies; and, most of all, the perpetual sensitivity to the power dimensions of situations. I think that if Nixon is ever threatened simultaneously with public disdain and loss of power, he may move into a crisis syndrome. In that case, the important resonances will be direct ones between character and the political environment; style would play a secondary part. But in the ordinary conduct of the Presidency (and there are long stretches of that), Nixon's personal-relations style may interact with his character to produce a different kind of danger, a kind the President and his friends could, I think, steer away from.

The danger is that Nixon will commit himself irrevocably to some disastrous course of action, as, indeed, his predecessor did. This is precisely the possibility against which Nixon could defend himself by a stylistic adjustment in his relations with his White House friends. Yet it is made more likely than it need be by the way he appears to be designing his decision-making process in the critical early period of definition.

It may seem that the danger of the Nixon Presidency lies not in exaggeration but in timidity, that his administration will turn out to be more Coolidgean than Johnsonian. Yet unless there has been a fundamental change in his personality (as Theodore White and others think there has been), Nixon has within him a very strong drive for personal power—especially—*independent* power—which pushes him away from reliance on anyone else and pulls him toward stubborn insistence on showing everyone that he can win out on his own. Throughout his life he has experienced sharp alternations between periods of quiet and periods of crisis. These discontinuities in his experience have contributed to the uncertainties nearly all observers have felt in interpreting the "real" Nixon. On the one hand, he is a shrewd, calm, careful, proper, almost fussily conventional man of moderation, a mildly self-deprecating common-sense burgher. On the other hand, he has been a fighter, a rip-snorting indignant, a dramatic contender for his own moral vision. To say that the first theme traces to his mother and the second to his father is but the beginning of an explanation of a pattern in which alternation has substituted for resolution. The temptation for one of his character type is to follow a period of self-sacrificing service with a declaration of independence, a move which is necessary exactly because it breaks through the web of dependencies he feels gathering around him.

Add to this character a style in which intimacy and consultation have never been easy and in which isolated soul-searching is habitual. Add to that an explicit theory and system of decision-making in which the President listens inquiringly to his committees of officials (who have been encouraged in their own independence), then retires to make his personal choice, then emerges to announce that choice. The temptation to surprise them all and, when the issue is defined as critically important, to adhere to it adamantly is exacerbated by the mechanisms of decision. Add also hostile reporters given unusual access, an increasingly independent Senate, a generationally-polarized nation, and a set of substantive problems nearly impossible to "solve" and the stage is set for tragic drama.

Another President once dismissed Nixon as a "chronic campaigner." In a campaign, day by day, the product is a speech or other public appearance. The big decisions are what to say. In the Presidency, rhetoric is immensely important, but preliminary: the product is a movement by the government. To bring that about Nixon needs to succeed not only with the national audience (where the danger of impromptu, "sincere" commitment is already great) and with the audience of himself alone (where the danger of self-deception is evident), but also with that middle range of professional President-watchers in Washington. Managing their anticipated reactions requires not only the development of "options," but widening circles of consultation around a tentative President decision—in other words, consultation *after* the President has reached a course of action satisfactory to him. It is at that point that the President's friends can help him most. For it is not true in the Presidency that, as Nixon wrote of 1960: "In the final analysis I knew that what was most important was that I must be myself."

2

Three Old Sagas in American Politics

James David Barber

Every four years a gong goes off, and a new Presidential campaign surges into the national consciousness: new candidates, new issues, a new season of surprises. But underlying the syncopations of change there is a steady, recurrent rhythm from election to election, a pulse of politics that brings up the same basic themes in order, over and over again. If the rhythm holds for the future, the dominant theme of the next election is already being formed in this one and will in turn set the theme for the one after that. Understanding how this cycle works is the key to bucking it, to breaking out of a pattern of drift and reaction in that most critical of all political choices, the choice of a President.

From the turn of the century to the present day, three themes have dominated successive campaign years: politics as conflict, politics as conscience, and politics as conciliation. That sequence runs its course over a 12-year period and then starts over again.

The stress on conflict is the clearest case: the campaign is a battle for power. Like a real war, the political war is a rousing call to arms. Candidates mobilize their forces for showdowns and shoot-outs, blasting each other with rhetorical volleys. It is a risky adventure; its driving force is surprise, as the fortunes of combat deliver setbacks and breakthroughs contrary to the going expectation, and the contenders struggle to recover and exploit the sudden changes. It is the myth of the fighting candidate. It is John Wayne galloping over the horizon at the head of the cavalry troop, just as the Indians are about to descend on the settlement. It is Harry S. Truman battling through to victory against overwhelming odds.

Over the next four years, reaction sets in. Uplift is called for. Political conflict seems more and more like mere "politics," in the low sense of stab and grab, a clash of merely selfish interests. Attention focuses on the dangers of blind ambition, corruption, even tyranny, the degeneration of politics into a gut-level contest for preference and place, culminating in rule by the most aggressive of the feral few, the politics of the jungle. It is time to remember that America is God's country, founded for a high purpose. The call goes out for a revival of social conscience, the restoration of the Constitutional covenant, the cleansing of the temple of democracy. Matters of principle dominate; missionary zeal emerges. In our relatively unideological politics, relatively simple moral verities are invoked and applied to the search for a President who, in his very person, stands for strong character and visceral American values. We think of Jimmy Stewart in *Mr. Smith Goes to Washington*, a victory of innocence over cynicism. We think of the Jimmy Carter of 1976, an unsullied outsider who meant to restore a measure of decency to the White House.

But despite all the President's virtue, the troubles do not go away. The sermons grow tiresome, righteousness turns into self-righteousness, and fiery philosophers threaten to burn down the national barn. Moral uplift strains the fabric of our sense of ourselves as one people, not polarized as the Good Guys versus the Bad Guys. We worry about the drift from disagreement to disruption, from civil conflict to civil war, threatening the union so laboriously patched together over all those years of mutual adjustment and forbearance. The public yearns for solace, for domestic tranquillity, for the politics of conciliation. The watchword is "Blessed are the peacemakers"; the byword is "the politics of joy"—and tolerance, comfort, good will, patient forgiveness, even laughter, and especially confidence.

Having been so "serious" last time, we are ready to touch base with our humanity, to get past our galling guilts and anxieties to some island of ease, some peaceable kingdom where the lamb can lie down with the lion. It is time to smile away the blues. We want a President we can like. We'll take the Wizard of Oz. We'll settle for Warren G. Harding.

Give that four years to settle in, and the time for a fight will come around again. We itch for adventure once more. It seems a long time since the last straight political fight, the last real test of courage, the last blood-and-guts political contest. An illustrative example: the 1960 election was a straight fight between two young warriors, Kennedy and Nixon. In 1964 we saw a circus of morals: Goldwater, with his conservative conscience, versus "Preacher Lyndon" Johnson, the civil rights crusader. In 1968, every candidate of consequence came on as a peacemaker, particularly "Bring Us Together" Nixon and the happy harmonizer Hubert Humphrey. By the time the primaries opened in 1972, the nation was geared up for another political fight. The dominant theme of each election led into the dominant theme of the next one, in a dynamic historical pattern.

This pattern is a deliberate oversimplification, an approximation. It is not offered as yet another tin key to the Iron Law of history. The cycle does not necessarily pinpoint the winning candidate, though it shows the rough shape of the odds. It falls short of characterizing the electorate in general, though I think it catches the thinking of those who are interested but not obsessed. On reflection, it is not all that mysterious that these three themes repeatedly grip the public imagination.

Part of the explanation may be that they resonate with the most deeply rooted and primitive human memories. No one knows how tale-telling got its start, long before life was reduced to writing. The conflict theme may trace all the way back to preliterate hunting stories recounted by survivors returning to the fireside to report the frantic search and kill and escape—the origin of the "Embroidered Exploit," one writer thinks. The conscience theme may echo the primordial "Warning Example": a mother straining to "persuade her child from the fire" tells how another child, another time, ignored the commandment and suffered for it. The conciliation theme may draw on the appeal of ancient acts of union: the young woman or man driven by the incest taboo to seek a mate among foreigners comes back with a tale of courtship and consummation, giving birth to an endless series of sweet stories of love.

Reflections of these old sagas might be discerned in the psychological paradigm that dominates our age's thinking; the ego, instrument for coping with the struggles of the external world; the superego, warning against harmful violations; the id, longing after the thrill and ease of sexual satifaction. They are reflected again in the never-ending popularity of the war story, the morality play, the romantic comedy.

But there are also specifically American reasons for these emphases. The American war story, from which the theme of politics as conflict derives its very language, reflects our peculiar experience. Here, as elsewhere, war has had its powerful appeal—cutting through the ambiguities and complexities and frustrations of life with a simple, exciting, rejuvenating release of aggression. But war often came to other nations by the shock of invasion. In isolated America, the warmakers repeatedly confronted the special problem of arousing the martial spirit against distant enemies who had not yet attacked us. That arousal required propaganda—the substitution of drama for experience as a stimulus to action. Thus our history vibrates with *talk* about war, advertising its anticipated glories in rip-roaring tales of heroism. The war story echoes through the culture; no wonder political storytellers pick up on its thrilling, threatening theme.

The politics of conscience bites deep in the American experience. From the Old Testament on, the tense drama of the making and breaking of the covenant between God and His people electrified Western civilization. The American civilization was founded by godly people determined to build a New Zion in the wilderness, a newly chosen people set apart by the Almighty Himself from the heathen Europeans to the East and the heathen Indians to the West. The Puritan God was no bemused observer of human folly, content to sit back and watch what His original act of creation had set in train. God was *in* history, the Calvinist God directing every flight of birds over Plymouth, every blast of lightning, the rise of every crop and plague, and the exact course of human events. America was a mission. The Declaration of Independence announces our "firm reliance on the protection of Divine Providence."

Thus, America stepped into the family of nations claiming a kind of ordination. Lincoln confirmed it: we were a nation "under God." From then to now, our conscience has never been satisfied by government as a mere practical arrangement to secure our survival and see to the feeding of our animal appetites. If it was never perfectly clear who God favored for President, it seemed self-evident that the question must be asked.

The politics of conciliation has its own essential suspense: will Romeo and Juliet succeed in getting together, despite the Montagues and Capulets? But again, the specifically American experience underscores the theme. We became a nation of nationalities, of strangers with conflicting heritages, scattered across a continent. Had we not found the path to union, there would have been no United States. Holding the vast and varied enterprise together became urgent American work, its necessity never more deeply burnt into the national consciousness than when union failed in the 1860s.

Just as we are about to smash up the political saloon, someone has to have the sense to yell, "Don't shoot the piano player!" That calls for laughing off our oh-so-serious differences, for positive thinking, for the continual rediscovery of what we have in common. At least since Ben Franklin, Americans have stood apart from the world's stern aristocracies, dour dictatorships, and aching slumlands as a nation of incorrigible hopers and boosters. If we did not invent Santa Claus, we made him our own. Our politics is something we *play*, a great game, and a President is supposed to play that game with a smile on his face. The superficially light and vulgar story of forgive and forget amuses the ironists, but it is, in fact, the rock-bottom myth of our political existence.

These modern myths of politics are brought to our doorsteps and living rooms by journalists. They are no more mere messenger boys than Homer was. Today, with the political parties virtually disbanded and even their symbolic configurations fading from view, political journalism itself supplies the key judgments that shape the key decisions. If improvement in the way we choose our Presidents is vital, journalists will have to see what they can do, with their hasty and dramatic craft, to get the story straight.

Over the years, inventive candidates and journalists translated the battle story into a tale of calculation and maneuver that is set apart from the story of governing the country. Critics of the fighting story call for "issues, not personalities," for a rational debate on the candidates' programs and party platforms. But as President after President has discovered, particularly in recent years, the gap between what he wants to do in January of an election year and what he can do the following January is enormous.

Pressed for specifics during the campaign, the candidate and his aides and advisers expend their intellectual energies composing tedious position papers. These papers are not frequently cited after Inauguration Day. The fundamental reason is not that the candidates lie, though some do, but that such detailed blueprints for government action are drawn up abstractly, disconnected from an as yet unknown context of forces and changes, in Washington, and of necessity shaped for an immediate purpose: to win the election. It is like asking a doctor to prescribe for a patient he has yet to meet.

The party platforms try to beat those uncertainties by including a little of everything. At best, they become registries of access—who could marshal enough clout to nail in a plank—and at worst, mere laundry lists of more or less plausible hopes. To center campaign debate on specific candidate plans is to shift the conversation away from evidence and toward opinions which cannot readily be tested, however sincerely they are advanced.

The story of conflict reduces itself to a competition among assertions. Reporters closeted with the candidates on the campaign trail badger them for statements of intention, hoping for some bit of quotable idiocy, usually making do with some hypothetical clash between what A says and what B says. Their reports from the field become grist for the editorial mill; the columnists and commentators take over, producing analysis after analysis in which their own confident opinions on issues are contrasted with the uncertain and ineloquent proposals candidates make. In practice, the battle between candidate and journalist supersedes the battle among the candidates themselves. Because an issue's focus must, by definition, highlight the hypothetical and abstract—a story told in the subjunctive language of what one would do *if* certain conditions prevailed—the way is opened for endless speculation, and theory rules the roost.

Journalism's strength is not theory but fact. And to reason toward a choice, the public's first need is to get a grip on the contemporary reality. As for candidates, each offers a picture of the facts as he sees them, a picture very likely to shape whatever he would try to do as President. A battle among *those* visions—visions of what is actually happening—could prove much more enlightening and enlivening than war stories out of Iowa or New Hampshire. In 1932, for example, Hoover claimed the economy was picking up, Roosevelt the opposite. Their visions of reality clashed. The facts of life were there to report—and bore directly on the task of assessing the candidates. Hoover favored local, voluntary relief. Whatever the philosophical validity of his viewpoint, it rested on a fact question: what local and private resources were available to relieve how many of the unemployed? In 1980, amidst all the challenges and promises, it would be interesting to know which candidates have already mastered the facts of the energy crisis, and which are making do with merely plausible assertions.

Testing potential Presidents on the facts of the national condition would test their capacity for realistic perception and judgment, their grasp of the actual shape of the situation at home and abroad. That would be an important test of a genuine Presidential ability. For, time and again in recent decades, we have seen a President cut himself off from the real world, isolate himself in the White House with his cozy crew of flattering advisers, and drift into illusion and tragedy. It happened to as cool a rationalist as John F. Kennedy, when he fell for the Bay of Pigs invasion mirage, though he quickly recovered his bearings.

We need a President highly curious about what is happening in the world—and ready to respond to the evidence of change. The time to assess a President's world view is before, not after, he raises his hand on Inauguration Day and swears to preserve, protect, and defend the Constitution. During the campaign, his fantasies should he be held to the fire of fact. Whatever he may hope to do, can he bear to see the truth? Does he know what he is talking about? A President-to-be should never again be allowed to pass through the gate of an election without first paying the admission of realism.

The moralists in politics go wrong when they wrench the story of morals away from its pragmatic American plot. Claiming that their political preferences are derived from eternal principles, they wind up investing debatable policies with the force of holy writ. Goldwaterism follows: sweeping away the conditional uncertainties of the historical present as simply irrelevant, demanding not calculation but application of received truth. That stance stops argument dead in its tracks. If it is God who prescribes the League of Nations or militant anticommunism or free enterprise, the devil must be running the opposition—and you turn your back on the devil, you do not argue with him. History is seen as fundamentally beside the point. Therefore, such superficially startling leaps as Wilson's shift from peace to war and such low-level contradictions as Goldwater's desire to cut federal spending while financing much stronger military forces are not so surprising. The political fundamentalist looks up the answer in his book of Natural Laws or Divine Revelations and pronounces: Q.E.D., like Euclid with his triangles. Nor is it surprising that moralizing candidates so often wind up practicing the wily arts of public relations and psychological manipulation. Since the derivation from principle to policy is perfectly clear, the obstacles to implementation must be emotional—problems of the will, not the mind. People need selling, not convincing.

That leads a Dwight Eisenhower to the commercial-making studio where, however reluctantly, he mouths little inspiration platitudes for his ad men.

The modern skeptical story of conscience fumbles after character in the Campaign Stress Test—the totally unrealistic supposition that he who is good at running for President will be good at running the Presidency. Especially since the race became a marathon, campaigning—with its endless exhaustions, brief encounters, and pleadings for money and attention—tests qualities of physical endurance and superficial plausibility, but not much else.

The moment of truth is the gaffe, which starts a running story predictably racing along from the supposed slip to the apology and absolution. Carter's "ethnic purity" mistake and Ford's "Polish blunder" were the great gaffes of 1976, neither of which bore the slightest relationship to the man's public policies, much less his character. But the story takes off and lives, sometimes for weeks of front-page attention and editorial fulmination, before it finds its rightful place in oblivion. The gaffe is our era's prime example of symbolic politics run wild. Its early retirement would make space for the story we eventually turn to for enlightenment on the question of Presidential virtue.

That is the life story, the biography. As the early magazine moralists discovered, that was their most appealing product. It sold far better than all the shrill denunciations and atmospheric pontifications put together.

People could connect with it. Everyone lives a life history. Everyone is interested in how to do that and, through the human connection, how lives very different from their own take shape and plunge on. The poetic sage of Odysseus, the history of Moses, the parable of the life of Christ, Caesar's story, the tragedies of King Oedipus and Prince Hamlet, on down to the lives of Napoleon and Lincoln and Victoria and Churchill, to our age's fascination with the biographies of every sort of hero and villain from Gandhi to Hitler—the story of a person grips the imagination as nothing else can. The stories of "ordinary" people (each, in fact, extraordinary) told by the likes of Robert

Coles or Studs Terkel light up the contemporary scene with a
clarity unmatched by any public-opinion poll.

For people sense that all our theoretical constructs and
elaborate fantasies take their human meaning from their incar-
nation in the flesh and blood of persons. The theory no one lives
by remains a theory only. Biography brings theory down to
earth, history to focus, fantasy to reality. It is the narrative of
existence, of being-in-becoming. No wonder people indifferent
to mere speculation take to biography as if the life they read
might be their own.

Political observers of the "realist" school are forever under-
rating the problem of conciliation in American democracy. The
appeal that celebrates the common hope for harmony is dismissed as mere rhetoric masking darker purposes. Every candidate is suspected of being consumed with personal ambition and
of possessing an infinite capacity for meaningless blather. Conflict is real; concord is an illusion. Thus the tough-minded
wordsmith, who need never bear the responsibility of action,
sets out to unmask the fakers and correct the naive. In fact, of
course, it is not possible for the government to move forward
except by developing alliances among politicians—the politics of
conciliation.

The story of that search periodically dominates the national
narrative. Too often, the hunger for the relief of tension and
anxiety has led us to accept the terms of a peace too fragile to
last, a truce in place of a social contract. Politics can be
transformed into romance, with the candidates posturing off into
fiction, the electorate making itself into a mere audience of
appreciators. Magic tricks of policy appeal, as does the wistful
hope that all will be well if people will just be nice to one
another. Political discussion collapses into cheerleading. The
celebrity candidate gets across the sense that he as President,
backed by the people at large, will somehow make everything all
right.

That of course is nonsense, but it points the way to a more
productive path for the story of politics as conciliation. That
story could tell of the gathering of forces and persons who might

well wind up leading the nation, not just to victory at the polls but in the years thereafter. Journalists would press Presidential candidates to articulate the areas of agreement they share with actual and potential congressmen and senators, governors and Cabinet members, advisers and interest-group leaders—with the range of politicians preparing to join in running the country. Stories on the interesting characters running for "lesser" offices, highlighting their connections with the Presidential candidates, would enrich the drama.

Even during the primary season, now so preoccupied with conflict, emerging candidates would be asked not just what they would do with power, but with whom they might do it and what the basis for their concord could be. At and after the national convention, now a television extravaganza of doubtful instructional benefit, reporters could press the candidate for President not to name his Cabinet, but to elaborate where he and leaders of Cabinet stature agree on the issues. That challenge would test a genuine Presidential skill, because, in fact, the government works by an endless round of negotiation.

Such might be the turn of events as the 1980 election approaches: a season of conciliation after the moralism of 1976. By the summer of 1979, President Carter's preacherly rhetoric was wearing thin with the attentive public. The very themes that had served him so well in his amazing rise to the Presidency—the stress on honesty and decency and compassion—now sounded shrill and unconvincing. Escalating inflation, energy shortfalls, and a new round of supposedly authoritative recession predictions had the public nervous, ready for a healing time. Carter's popularity fizzled down to a near-record low. His reaction was to reach out for a new national union, first gathering at Camp David a widely disparate collection of friends and opponents to advise him, then emerging to call the people to unify themselves behind him in the cause of energy independence.

Carter's plan involved sacrifice, the reorientation of priorities, and other discomforts. The public barely rallied, Congress yawned. The President was widely perceived—with the help of various journalist perception-makers—as lacking in "leadership,'' broadly interpreted as meaning the clout to end the trouble.

Senator Kennedy, it was suggested, had leadership. In the autumn of 1979, Kennedy floated high above Carter in the polls, a warm Irish superpolitician, handsome as Harding, apparently predestined to be wafted into the White House. On the Republican side, candidates queued up behind the early leaders— Reagan, whose soothing manner coated his radical-conservative views, and Connally, whose machismo masked a career distinguished mainly by the making of money. Predictably, the early story for the Republicans was a come-from-behind yarn starring George Bush, a newcomer contrasting nicely to the familiar front-runners.

Then came an international emergency in Iran: Americans held hostage by evil foreigners demanding the surrender of their fleeing Shah. Now, the public rallied to their President—led by the same press that, a few months earlier, had led them to see him as an inept fool.

Even before the crisis began, Kennedy's star had begun to fade, it turned out he had no convincing answers to questions about either his own checkered past or his nation's checkered future. But his fortunes dipped far lower when, driven to candor by exhaustion, he characterized the Shah as one of modern history's less admirable leaders. The President let it be known that the Senator's comments were not helpful to the delicate negotiations steadily being pressed forward. Kennedy and the Republicans were effectively muzzled as the crisis wore on. Carter, declaring "unity day" and appealing to Americans everywhere to fly their flags, soared above the pack in the greatest recovery of popular support in the history of polling.

One could expect with confidence a new series of surprises before Election Day. Less certainly, but with eight decades of evidence behind it, one could anticipate the emergence of the story of politics as conciliation as 1980's dominant theme. As its worst, that could mean another playtime of sham and evasion like 1920. At its best, it could mean the gathering of forces in tentative unities of party and nation, in preparation for the fighting election of 1984.

Brief Summaries of Four Cycles

1936: CONFLICT In 1932, hit by the Depression, the nation lost confidence and was desperate for remedies. Roosevelt, with his bright smile and forceful rhetoric, seemed to promise a binding of the nation's wounds. But the troubles did not go away, and the Republicans encouraged by the crude polls of the time, thought they had a chance to win with Governor Alfred Landon of Kansas. Roosevelt, the smiler of 1932, came across this time as a fighter, damning the "economic royalists." Demagogues of the left and right raved and ranted. FDR took every state but Maine and Vermont.

1940: CONSCIENCE After Roosevelt's second term, during which he had overreached himself by trying to pack the Supreme Court, the Republicans led off a crusade to preserve democracy, handing that flag to Wendell Wilkie. His platform for 1940 was a creed, a faith, a reprise of the sacred American promise. FDR campaigned as The President consumed with the developing war in Europe, calling on God to strengthen the cause. Despite his violation of Washington's rule against a third term, he carried the day.

1944: CONCILIATION One could say that Roosevelt won the election of 1944 on December 7, 1941—the day the Japanese attacked Pearl Harbor. For the second time in history, Americans went to the polls in the middle of a war. Roosevelt, the confident continuer, reappeared with his old jaunty humor and comforting aura of certainty, calling the nation together like a family around the dinner table. His challenger, New York Governor Thomas E. Dewey, echoed the conciliatory theme by calling for an end to New Deal bickering, but he seemed a bickerer himself as he flailed at the commander-in-chief's administrative imperfections. Once again, Roosevelt won by a safe margin.

1948: CONFLICT   Five months later, Roosevelt was dead, and Harry S. Truman was President. The year after that, the war ended, and the Republicans captured both houses of Congress as long-suppressed partisan passions revived. Dewey won through to the nomination on the third ballot at the Republican convention of 1948, but his troubles were nothing compared with Truman's. On the left, Henry A. Wallace formed a third party to fight for the Presidency; on the right, the Dixiecrats split off to support their man, Senator Richard Russell. A funereal convention nominated Truman; to nearly everyone's amazement, he won an upset victory by the closest of margins.

1952: CONSCIENCE   War broke out in Korea in 1950, and the President was held responsible for failing to beat back the Communists and end it. But perhaps as important in an age of increasingly symbolic politics, Truman's image as a scrappy politician lacking in Presidential dignity took hold. Truman saw the signs; he helped get Illinois Governor Adlai E. Stevenson to run—a man of evident high integrity, a propounder of the American conscience. The Republicans beat that move with General Dwight David Eisenhower, hero of World War II. He conducted not a campaign but a "crusade." Morals ruled the day, and the Republican diatribe against the evils of "Communism, Korea, and Corruption" won it.

1956: CONCILIATION   Eisenhower went to Korea, as he had promised, and settled the war. But in the midst of prosperity came new anxieties; the Red Scare, massive social shifts, escalating debt, demanding minorities; in 1955, the Russians exploded a hydrogen bomb. Eisenhower, meanwhile, grinned and presided. Adlai Stevenson, renominated, tried to get a fight going in 1956, but Eisenhower spoke of peace and harmony. The electorate responded to his message and kept Ike in the White House.

1960: CONFLICT   The appeal of placidity slowly waned in Eisenhower's second term; the promise of adventure beckoned again. Ike stepped aside in favor of his aggressive young Vice-President, Richard M. Nixon, who fought his way to the Republican nomination in 1960 over the challenge of New York

Governor, Nelson Rockefeller. A young Democratic war hero, John F. Kennedy, muscled aside Senator Lyndon Johnson. A partisan battle ensued as the candidates lashed out at each other, culminating in a novel confrontation: a series of televised "Great Debates." Kennedy won by a whisker. The drama of that season was combat, in a new, cool mode.

1964: CONSCIENCE   Kennedy was gunned down in Dallas, Texas, in November of 1963. His successor, President Lyndon Baines Johnson, was dedicated to Kennedy's moral purpose: justice for blacks in America. That year brought forward a new moral champion for the Republicans, who advertised his conscience as his primary qualification for the Presidency. Senator Barry Goldwater of Arizona rallied against corruption in the name of civic virtue. In the end Goldwater lost, but his moral concerns succeeded in dominating the national agenda.

1968: CONCILIATION   There followed, under Johnson, a dramatic escalation of the war in Vietnam. Those years saw the rolling up of violent racial protest and the growth of the antiwar movement. In April, 1968, Johnson bowed out of contention for renomination, the year that Martin Luther King, Jr. and Robert F. Kennedy were killed by assassins. All candidates called for peace and quiet, a revival of national unity. The Democrats, meeting in the midst of a riot in Chicago, nominated their chief apostle of brotherhood, Hubert Humphrey. The Republicans turned to a "new Nixon." He won by an eyelash—the peacemaker, the conciliator, the bringer of harmony.

1972: CONFLICT   It did not work out that way. Nixon spread the war—secretly. He got at his political enemies—secretly. In a carefully orchestrated image campaign in 1972, he presented himself as The President, negotiating with foreign powers, refusing to discuss the issues his opponents threw at him. Thus the story of politics as conflict had nowhere to go but to the Democrats, they battled their way through the national primaries to a conflict-ridden convention. Then, during the summer, Senator George McGovern worked himself out of the election by mishandling the resignation of his running mate, Senator Thomas Eagleton.

1976: CONSCIENCE   Nixon's secret war against his political enemies at last came to light, leading to his resignation. His Vice-President, Gerald R. Ford, moved into the White House amidst high hopes for moral restoration, but his pardon of Nixon raised the suspicion that he was not above a deal. The Democrats turned to an outsider from Plains, Georgia, running against the corruptions of the Capitol. Governor Jimmy Carter emerged, preaching the common American values of decency and compassion and honesty. A nation ready for moral revival voted him in.

1980: CONCILIATION   As the 1980 election approached, Carter's preacherly rhetoric began to wear thin, with a public increasingly anxious over galloping inflation and an energy crisis. In the summer of 1979, the President took note of a "crisis of confidence." Then came Iran and Afghanistan and the sudden recovery of Carter's reputation as a competent President. He called for—and got—a new wave of national unity.

3

The Candidates' Analysts

James David Barber

Journalists are clearly writers; they are also scientists insofar as they draw inferences from evidence. The line between these two high callings is not nearly so hard and fast as amateurs tend to think. The scientific method, it's true, is partly the patient, highly systematic, rule-bound accumulating of evidence. But the scientist, like the reporter, gathers selectively, guided by a theme, an hypothesis, a theory, the shape of which may be only dimly apprehended at first. Like the reporter, he starts with a potential "lead" (the opening paragraph that introduces a new development) that he must be prepared to chuck overboard as soon as it fails him.

The progress of science, examined historically, can be seen to jolt forward in leaps of creative imagination, large and small, very similar in form to the inspiration the poet knows when a verbal illumination dawns on him. The journalist as scientist is in much the same situation: if his science is to transcend the routine, he, too, will need Aristotle's touch of madness.

Now that midterm elections are over and candidates for 1980 are beginning to appear, it is a good time to take a fresh look at how journalists exercise their science in Presidential campaigns. Political scientists Christopher Arterton, William Bicker, Donald Matthews, and I were all convinced that journalists play a more decisive role in the selection of candidates now that the power of political parties is declining. We also believed that the winnowing process begins much earlier than in the past. Thus, this report is part of a larger study of campaign coverage that was carried out by the four of us. It draws on more than 200 interviews with journalists, candidates, and media managers, along with print and television accounts of the 1976 Presidential nominations and election.

If journalists had to pick a scientific home, few would opt for psychology. In 1975, David Broder of the *Washington Post* found the prospect of "journalists as amateur psychologists" a "terrifying" one. R. W. Apple, Jr., led off a series in the *New York Times Magazine* on candidate character with a valiant and incisive attempt to track down the real Henry Jackson in the streets of Everett, Washington ("They thought me mad"). He concluded, as early as Thanksgiving, 1975, that the task of lighting "fires among the suburbanites and intellectuals and young people and minorities" seemed "well beyond Scoop Jackson's capacity." Early in the piece, Apple pointed to one specifically psychological category that he apparently found helpful in assessing Jackson: the "active-negative" character type described in my book, *The Presidential Character*. But another time, he spoke for many of his colleagues when he said the whole business "makes us nervous, because most of us feel incompetent to try to do much psychological interpretation."

Jules Witcover, then of the *Washington Post*, thought there was validity to the criticism that "we don't do enough looking at the candidate and finding out what makes him tick." At the same time, Witcover said, "We are reporters; our job out there is to say what the candidate says, to analyze what he says, and, in general, to hold his feet to the fire of the campaign—to throw up issues to him that are being raised or should be raised." Witcover was loath to draw "psychoanalytical conclusions."

But like it or not, journalists are psychologists. They are right to go slow. They exercise their craft in a society obsessed with "personality," self-cultivation, and the search for uninterrupted exuberance. Their common sense sees through the vapidity of the instant psych-out. But, in fact, the journalist's work impels him to make psychological judgments, such as what a candidate means, what he is likely to do, where in his past his present behavior comes from. Those judgments may be made with one

blind eye, or vaguely, from intuitive and even absurd psychological principles. But the judgments themselves are unavoid-
able.

That is as it should and must be in Presidential-campaign
reporting. The central question is what certain human beings
would do if they were elected—a prediction about human
behavior. If a writer thinks he can get that by listening to the
candidates' issue stands, then that in itself is a psychological
proposition. If he thinks it doesn't make a tinker's damn who
gets elected President, then that, too, is a psychological proposition. Both are hypotheses subject to verification, suppositions
to be tested.

Lots of journalists think of themselves as historians of sorts,
and it is amusing to notice how quickly the journalistic product—
disdained by many academic historians while it is being produced—becomes "primary data." But venturing inside a candidate's head is riskier yet. "You don't want to play God," says
Apple of the *Times*. "It is preposterous to think you can do
psychoanalysis in daily news coverage." And there are those
who, looking back at the record, draw a negative lesson from the
apparent failures—for instance, the discovery by some journalists in the 1960s of a "new Nixon," "forged by fire," "a changed
man."

Probably the main reason journalists resist psychologizing is
that they have seen it done so badly. It can be a mask for
character assassination or for scandal-mongering. "Personality"
pieces can spill over into gossip, and reporters who go marching
into Georgia for a day or two sometimes come back with a less
than complete portrait of the Carter tribe.

But plenty of practitioners read the record as prescribing
more, not less, attention to character. Ed Kosner, editor of
Newsweek, speaks for many when he says, "Find out what kind
of person I am, and [if my character is solid] my decisions on
Portugal will come out okay." For, if character interpretation is
difficult and risky and often badly done, so is interpretation of
issues and the chance of election; and, unlike those topics,

character interpretation is directly relevant to the campaign's purpose: a choice among persons.

Journalists share with scientists at least two key attitudes, skepticism and wonder. "There can be no higher law in journalism," quoth Walter Lippmann, "than to tell the truth and shame the devil." Journalists are not always doubting Thomases, of course; in many another time, they have believed all too readily whatever the powerful were passing out. Persons who succeed at a profession are likely to be those who can adopt the appropriate stance without calculation: cool surgeons, adaptable actors, curious researchers. At least until recently, "going into journalism" was a fairly gutsy thing for a young middle-class person to do; perhaps there is a residue of rebellion in the journalistic ego. But skepticism is clearly an item in the ethos.

Richard Salant, president of CBS News, gives us a succinct example of this attitude when he says of politicians, "They are trying to sell us a bill of goods, so our job is to get behind the bullshit." Dan Crossland of CBS has also made it clear: "I don't like this government, and I didn't like the last one, and I won't like the next one." Hugh Sidey, veteran correspondent for Time, Inc., points out that negativism can go too far. He thinks the contemporary press has become "deeply suspicious of men in public life. To approve is seen as a kind of weakness."

Journalistic skepticism can find many a friend in the psychological tradition. Much of psychology grew out of pathology and curative therapy. Little wonder, then, that so much of psychology focuses on the ways people experience trouble, sorrow, need, sickness, and adversity, and that so much more seems to be approximately known about the ills than the wells.

There is a noticeable difference, though: the scientist's skepticism focuses strongly on his *own* theories, and on the adequacy of evidence. Journalists share a corner of that when they challenge the *candidate's* theories and the factuality of *his* data base. More worthy of discussion is how the day-to-dayness of journalism makes it hard to find leisure for questioning—by the active journalists themselves—of the theories and methods they use in their own work.

Precisely as the scientific researcher can't really get underway until he wrestles a thesis out of his topic and pins it down in propositions, so the journalist flounders when he cannot quite grasp what he is writing about. For example, take the so-called "campaign stress test."

On the face of it, campaigning for President is not much like being President. Presidents do not run around to shopping centers shaking hands. Presidents do not make the same speech 10 times a day. Presidents are not forever calculating how to get on the television evening news. Presidents are not followed around, day after day, by some of the nation's best reporters. Presidents wrack their brains, not their bodies.

Nevertheless, campaign life is seen to resemble White House life in the tests it poses for the person's skills, beliefs, and character. Walter Mears of the Associated Press calls the campaign "pretty good on-the-job training." Walter Cronkite thinks it "tests them in fire." But just what is being compared? In science, philosophy professors Morris Cohen and Ernest Nagel tell us, "We generally begin with an unanalyzed feeling of vague resemblance, which is discovered to involve an explicit analogy in structure or function *only by a careful inquiry*." In the journalistic accounts, specification comes hard.

The generalized assumption is that the candidate's capacity to perform under stress may be analogous to the President's capacity to perform under stress. I think careful inquiry would reveal few direct, explainable similarities—but whatever the outcome of that research, the question cannot be addressed reasonably until the supposed stresses are specified. A skeptic might ask whether the Boston Marathon, say, or a series of 48-hour "Meet the Press" sessions would not do as well.

Reporters, like classical Freudian psychoanalysts, tune their ears to hear slips that suddenly clarify something "real" about the candidate. Gaffes show the candidate to be fool or knave or both; they go way back—to Truman "considering" the use of atomic weapons in Korea, Eisenhower telling a press conference that the budget he had just given Congress could be cut, Kennedy's campaign "missile gap," Romney's confessing his brain had been washed. In 1975–76, gaffes ranged from Ford's mild malapropisms ("growth national product," "the ethnic of honest work," "our nation is resolent") to the darker implications of Carter's "ethnic purity" phrase, to Wallace's intimation that the U.S.A. might have been on the wrong side in World War II, to Reagan's plan to cut the federal budget by $90 billion. In the Ford-Carter debates, Gerald Ford, no doubt holding in mind an old Republican hope, brought a large smile to the faces of his interrogators when he put the wrong verbal twist on the idea that we should never give up on Eastern Europe—and repeated it.

Substantively, none of those gaffes amounted to a hill of beans. Ford was not about to take action to free Poland, Carter has not moved to set up pure Polish enclaves in Milwaukee. The larger—scientific—question concerns the logic of induction. The analog in science would be the single, key fact or experiment that demonstrates a truth, like Pasteur's success with sheep. In psychoanalysis, a single flash of insight may suddenly light up the minds of patient and doctor. Carter's "ethnic purity" gaffe, then, might be taken to reveal, of a sudden, that beneath all his talk of love and history of his strong stands against racism, there lurked a hateful ghost. But neither in science nor in psychoanalysis does the "key" observation, all by its lonesome, solve the puzzle. Only further tests would indicate whether the phenomenon is both representative and replicatable.

The character of the incumbent—as commonly perceived—has a profound influence on the way his potential challengers are explored. He tends to define the election's major characterological question. When Ford came in, Nixon's behavior had made the salient question: "Is he honest?" Hundreds of FBI agents combed the nation for flecks on Ford's honesty. When Ford went out, his image as honest was intact, but his behavior had raised a different question: "Is he smart?" He was beaten eventually by the image of an ethical technocrat. We jolt through history by action and reaction—Wilsonian uplift, Hardingian ease; Harding corrupt, Coolidge clean; Coolidge sleepy, Hoover vigorous; Hoover stone-hearted, Roosevelt compassionate. After the war, Truman the "influence peddler" gives way to square soldier Ike, who eventually looks lazy and is replaced by active Jack Kennedy; and so it goes.

Many an interpretative journalist did, in 1975–76, delve into the candidates' pasts for clues to their present personalities and, though mostly by implication only, to their potential Presidencies. It was a biographical year. Significant style questions were explored. Did Ford's history show him too dumb to be President? (Did Franklin Roosevelt's?) Was Jackson's lack of eloquence disqualifying? (Was Eisenhower's?) Had Carter shown himself poor at political negotiation? (Had Kennedy?) Important world-view propositions were looked into—journalists peered past campaign issue-stands to search out the basic political beliefs that had shaped the candidates' actual doings. For instance, what Carter's serious Christian commitment might mean for his politics was assessed.

The emphasis, though, was on character. One observer said that "the only real story" about Carter is "who the hell is he?" Trying to unwind what was genuine and real and operative in the tangle of manipulative artifice, journalists approached the candidates from a variety of angles familiar to psychologists.

Last season's sharpest case example featured Jerry son-of-Pat Brown, a figure of mystery who reduced Eric Sevareid of CBS to puzzlement. "I can't make him out,"the veteran Sevareid remarked. "I think something's wrong with his mind." By the same token, a "mystified" John Chancellor of NBC thought Brown had "a serious mother and father problem." Political reporter Richard Reeves found Brown "the most interesting politician in the United States" and took note of "the tortured father-son relationship."

It remained for Garry Wills to go the distance: Brown the younger mistook his own motives and Wills would explain them. In a *New York Review of Books* article called "Anti-Papa Politics," Wills salted facts with interpretations that it seems to me, owe much to psychoanalysis. Thus, according to Wills, Brown's complaints are not to be taken at face value: "He found ways to boast of the [campaign] effort's very rigors, tireless in his claim that he does not tire. He kept telling reporters how long it had been since he ate, how long since he slept." When Brown "does refer to his father, he misleads, no doubt unintentionally." Topics Brown neglects to mention may be important: he "talks easily" of much of his history, "but he never talks, if he can avoid it, of the 18 formative years in his father's house." His conversational gaps are attributable to denial: "The one debt Brown is most anxious to deny is that he is really just a politician following in his father's footsteps." And behind what Brown says lurk powerful emotional meanings: exploring the father's decision not to pardon Caryl Chessman, Wills asked Jerry "point-blank what he would do in such a position." Jerry answered, "I would make the decision and not agonize over it." The sentence is, concludes Wills, "a ringing condemnation of his father."

Wills's piece was not presented as a hatchet job. On the contrary, he explained in the article that none of what he said reflected on Jerry Brown as a politician. Indeed, Wills argued, he should be judged as a politician, and it was Brown himself who had raised the more personal issues by claiming he was not a politician in the same sense that his father was. But for the reader who doubts person and politician can be so easily dismembered, the prospect of a President given to displacing priorities to divert attention from his father is discomforting— especially when, if Wills is right, the relationship between them is loaded with intense anxiety and condemnation.

The point here is that behavior that seems mysterious on the face of it can be clarified, not only by looking inward for motive, but also by looking backward in the life history to see where the pattern came from. Again, because the purpose is not therapy but prediction, the major task is to get the pattern straight; once that is done, digging into the past is less important for political analysis. In Brown's case, understanding is advanced when we know, even roughly, that the son is reacting against his father's main identity—even if we cannot know very precisely the deep, private origins of that reaction in, say, the drama of Brown's infantile sexuality.

Of course, in interpreting the pattern of a personality, it helps if the journalist has some understanding of his own motives and biases. One of the reasons psychoanalysts must themselves be psychoanalyzed is that, to be effective, they have to understand who they are. For the patient-doctor relationship is a very intense one, at least from the patient's side. If the doctor brings to that encounter powerful unresolved conflicts, the theory goes, he may use the patient in much the same way as the patient may be trying to use him.

Political candidates often complain that they are zapped by reporters from behind a redoubt of virtual anonymity. Even though their work is usually bylined, journalists can hide their personalities; the candidate, on the other hand, is exposed. What may look like a conversation—two human beings taking turns at talk—is really a one-way test, an interrogation masked as a chat. The candidate knows that the outcome of his desperate gamble depends on how he gets reported.

But journalists tend to feel a reverse dependency. What the candidate puts out is "the same old offensive bullshit," as one journalist says, but "I have to report it." Another sees the candidates as "holding the hot hand. They've got the information. We want the information. You come to them as a supplicant."

The professional defense, on both sides, is cool detachment. Candidates rein in their feelings because they have seen how spontaneity can ruin them; press people maintain a skeptical distance. Nevertheless, columnists Robert Novak sees the danger in candidate-covering: "A reporter falls in love with him or hates him—it's hard to be neutral after so many days together."

That problem can be turned into an opportunity. Reporters can learn by taking note of their own reactions to the candidate. In the crowds and tête-à-têtes, they try to discover "what kind of guy he is." They ask questions like: "How well did he impress us?" "Does he know how to use the press?"

A natural tendency is to like the candidate who likes the press. Reporters also tend to like candidates who are like them. "Mo" Udall was a prime example. They described him as that "blithe spirit," that "chatty, funny, down-to-earth" fellow, that "fun guy to be with." Udall was rather like John F. Kennedy, who was "dear to us because he would let his hair down and just say anything." By contrast, Stanley Cloud of *Time* magazine thought the Carter the campaigner was "massively unimpressed with reporting, the triviality of it, reporters who drink and smoke too much." The point here is not that such attitudes impel to bias (they may), but that reporters should cultivate a conscious, scientific interest and understanding their own emotional reactions to the candidates they cover.

The analogy between psychoanalytic transference and campaign coverage of the candidates would be easy to overdraw. On the campaign trail, there are many doctors, not one. The candidate is seeking victory, not cure. The journalist is after a story, not a diagnosis. And the whole scene is fraught with activity, not like the quiet of the couch. Still, there is a connection, as the journalist, reaching for insight, probes inside self and other.

Like the psychologist, as we have seen, he may be inclined to probe for pathology rather than health. Like political scientists, who have been worrying for some time that Americans' reverence for their Presidents is exaggerated, he may believe it is important to "deimperialize" the Presidency. Add these trends to the journalist's own skepticism and you are likely to develop an agenda that accentuates the negative. In journalism, a contradiction of character makes a good "lead" while continuity and consistency do not. A lie told by a candidate is a story, a truth may or may not be.

Only quite recently have psychoanalytic thinkers such as Erik Erikson and Robert Coles begun to spell out what health looks like. Thus one could think of mental health, in the words of psychologist L. S. Kubie (*Neurotic Distortion of the Creative Process*, 1961), as "flexibility, the freedom to learn through experience, the freedom to change with changing internal and external circumstances, to be influenced by reasonable argument, admonitions, exhortation, and the appeal to emotions; the freedom to respond appropriately to the stimulus of reward and punishment, and especially the freedom to cease when sated.

The essence of normality is flexibility in all of these vital ways. The essence of illness is the freezing of behavior into unalterable and insatiable patterns.''

Those phrases ring true to anyone who has struggled against the bonds of various psychic slaveries, but the reader must fill in the blanks. Freedom to do what? Flexibility? What is that but the absence of solidity? And so on, down the list. Health seems peculiarly bloodless, while the blood of illness splotches vividly through our vocabulary.

Presidential power is dangerous; so is Presidential weakness. Negative virtues—peace, for example—are important; but peace needs making, not mere espousing. Journalists should reexamine not only the substantive criteria for President-choosing, but also the systems they use to research and present their findings. For instance, the division of labor some journalists would prefer—the candidate touts his virtues and the journalist grasps his defects—works only now and then.

Yet we are ineluctably dependent on journalists for these judgments. It will be a long time before candidates will sit still for scientific personality tests or psychiatric interviews. Hard problems confront scientific experts who are asked to contribute, always briefly, to candidate coverage. Lacking space to explain and particularly to present much of the pro and con evidence that would give the reader some idea of contexts and balances, the force of the author's argument comes to rest in his authority as an expert. If the expertise is psychological, the negative jargon leaps off the page. Take an example plucked unfairly out of context from a fascinating and balanced article published by *New York* magazine. Written by psychohistorian Bruce Mazlish and media critic Edwin Diamond, coauthors of a forthcoming interpretative study of Jimmy Carter's life and career, the article contains this passage (the authors' italics):

"Some translations from the confessional to the psychological mode can help at this point:

"Carter told Bill Moyers he recognized his own 'shortcomings and sinfulness. . . . ' *In psychological terms, he was depressed.*

"Carter felt filled with pride. 'I was always thinking about myself. . . . ' *The psychoanalytic term for this is 'narcissism.'*

"Carter says that he used people. *The analyst hears, 'I can't love. . . . '*

"Carter says he had 'the need to improve. . . . ' *The textbooks talk of the 'crisis of generativity.'*"

Depending on the context (and the authors supply one), these Carter confessions could be taken differently—in psychological terms. A candidate who talks easily about his former faults and failings is rare; he might be demonstrating "freedom to learn through experience." One who enters a period of intense self-concern may be taking a giant step forward in breaking through prideful resistance. One who sees that he has used people may be learning to love them. And recognition of "the need to improve" could represent an emerging achievement orientation as well as a crisis of generativity. As psychoanalyst Heinz Hartmann insisted (and I am pretty sure Mazlish and Diamond would agree), "A healthy person must have the capacity to suffer and be depressed." That is hard to hold in mind, post-Eagleton.

New journalists might join new psychologists in giving balanced attention to personal strengths and in pondering what Erikson meant when he wrote that "the patient of today suffers most under the problem of what he should believe in and who he should—or, indeed, might—be or become; while the patient of early psychoanalysis suffered most under inhibitions which prevented him from being what or who he thought he knew he was."

An inordinate proportion of the journalist's gusto goes into bookie work, such as figuring the odds on the next primary. But, insofar as he tries to see character, he is a scientist and a psychologist. That work counts, if history is any guide at all. After the fact is too late to discover that an Aaron Burr has been elected in place of a Thomas Jefferson. It will count even when—especially when—we have an election in which big issues dominate, for it is on such big issues as war and peace and the integrity of the Constitution that Presidential character is most important.

Science is one of our civilization's names for reason. It marks itself off by its intense self-consciousness—science focuses reason on reasoning itself. Even that can exaggerate itself into irrelevance, as in so many social science studies that purport to approach physics in an ability to measure and predict. But the journalist who cares whether or not his interpretations hold beyond tomorrow morning—and most good ones do—will ask himself, as he trots along what he is thinking about. He will constantly question where his hypothesis is taking him, when he will recognize the appropriate data, how to use his facts to test his thoughts, and why, in the first place he is called to this work. Like Galileo he will foster and protect in himself that odd combination of skepticism and wonder that every day's encounter with "common sense" seem to shred.

4

The Question of Presidential Character

James David Barber

The next President of the United States is the grandson of western pioneers and the son of a father out of the hell-fire-and-damnation Methodist tradition. His family endured hard times in their modest white-frame house, but eventually, as a young man in his early thirties, he won election to the House of Representatives. His parents, small-town, middle-class Republicans, were pleased when the boy turned out to be a topflight student, a champion debater, a passable pianist and play-actor, and they were content that he could live at home while attending college. Compared with his younger brother, who was forever getting into minor scrapes, he was somewhat withdrawn—especially with girls—but he found a way to popularity and was repeatedly elected president of his college class. Never much of an athlete himself, he became an avid sports fan and today enjoys watching a good pro football game on television. After service overseas in World War II and years of arduous graduate study, he tried out several different fields of work before embarking on a political career. He won his first race for Congress against apparently insuperable odds, unseating a long-term incumbent in a campaign featuring a flurry of soft-on-Communism charges. As a young congressman he became identified with the liberal wing of his party and acquired a reputation as a hard worker with a mind of his own. His political career was launched. Elected to the U.S. Senate after two terms in the House, he quickly established himself as a national figure with presidential potential.

Such was George McGovern—and Richard Nixon.

Those who think the "facts" of a man's life—his social class, professional experience, and education background—speak for themselves are going to have a hard time evaluating the 1972 presidential nominees. Their superficial biographies are just too similar to be of much help in making a choice. It is safe to predict that from next January to 1977, our President will be a middle-class ex-senator with advanced education who climbed rapidly up the traditional political ladder. Nevertheless, we sense that there are profound differences between President Nixon and Senator McGovern—differences of character—that belie these superficial resemblances.

They do differ, of course, on the issues. But the issues and the candidates' stands on them come and go. (In 1964 Johnson won election as a dove against a hawkish Goldwater; four years later Nixon's free-enterprise economics contrasted with Humphrey's support of price controls.) What persists is the slow shift of national directions, which a President can advance or retard. To move the country forward, a President must excel in the art of political leadership. Such an ability requires, first and foremost, that his character be attuned to the possibilities of the office and to the temper of the times. It requires, in short, a "presidential" character. And on the level of character, Nixon and McGovern are about as dissimilar as any two candidates could be—a fact that McGovern himself has noted. "I can't think of anyone," he recently said, "who is more of an antithesis of me than Richard Nixon."

They do, however, share certain traits. Clearly, both men are activists. They believe the President must be an energizing force and practice that belief in their daily lives. McGovern complains when his schedulers get him to an airport ten minutes early with nothing to do. Nixon's every vacation is a working one. But the term "activist" is surely too broad to tell us much about the character of our next President, especially since the demands of the office are so great today that an essentially passive man like Calvin Coolidge, who often slept eleven hours a night and still found time for a midday nap, would scarcely be able to deal with them.

History shows, however, that activist Presidents tend to divide into two opposite types, which I have termed active-positive and active-negative. Active-positive Presidents—recent examples, are Franklin D. Roosevelt, Harry Truman, and John Kennedy—experience the office as an opportunity not only to implement social reform but to fulfill themselves personally. They value productiveness highly and adopt flexible approaches toward achieving their goals. They exude confidence and the sense of enjoying the power of the presidency. And, as it happens, Presidents who *like* to do what a President *has* to do are far better able then their opposites to make the American governmental mule move forward.

By contrast, active-negative Presidents—Lyndon Johnson, Herbert Hoover, and Woodrow Wilson, for example—start out strong and flexible but wind up defeated and rigid. They experience in the office a basic contradiction between intense effort and low emotional reward for that effort. In fact, the harder they work, the worse they feel. They are the hyperambitious, compulsive, endure-today-to-enjoy-tomorrow types. Deeply unsure of themselves, they feel aggressive and suspicious toward those around them. And even though active-negative Presidents often come across as adroit political realists, they eventually endanger themselves and perhaps even the country by taking a stand on "principle" and sticking to it regardless of the consequences. Such a stand cost Wilson his League of Nations, lost Hoover his humanitarian reputation, and sent Lyndon Johnson back to his ranch prematurely.

Richard Nixon's nearly four years in office confirm, I think, his place among active-negative Presidents.

For George McGovern, of course, there is much less evidence to go on, but in my judgment his character closely resembles those of past active-positive Presidents. Both cases become clearer I think, when we step back from today's news and look at these men as whole human beings—persons like the rest of us whose basic characters were formed a long time ago.

As a law student in the Thirties, Richard Nixon was known as "Gloomy Gus." Last January, when a reporter asked Nixon whether he enjoyed being President, he replied: "Well, in terms of all the trappings of office, all the power of office, that does not appeal to me. I must say I don't particularly enjoy the struggle with the bureaucracy, the press, and all that. But what I do like about the job is the possibility, in the brief time I have, of doing something that someone else might have been able to do. . . . Just the way the cards happen to fall I may be able to do things which can create a new structure of peace in the world. To the extent that I am able to make progress toward that goal, I would very thoroughly enjoy that job. But if you put it in terms of 'Do you enjoy the job in terms of the everyday battles?'—no, not particularly. I could do without a lot of that."

There are many similar personal testimonies to the fact that Nixon experiences his political life as painful and tense, earnest but sad, worthwhile only because the effort may produce some good. At the time of his recent Moscow trip one of the television networks ran the film clip of his famous "Kitchen Debate" with Premier Khrushchev in 1959. There was Nixon, smiling and apparently serene while the Soviet premier mocked and insulted him. But, as he wrote later in *Six Crises*, Nixon was really under heavy strain: He was "walking on eggs," trying "to restrain myself time and time again from expressing views I deeply felt and wanted to get across," feeling "like a fighter wearing sixteen-ounce gloves and bound by Marquis of Queensbury rules, up against a bare-knuckled slugger who had gouged, kneed, and kicked."

As he has often said of himself, Nixon is a pessimist and a person plagued by doubt and tension when he approaches a big decision. Deciding whether to take on a crisis is "far more difficult than the test itself," an experience that "takes a heavy toll mentally, physically, and emotionally," the part that "tears your insides out." Only "tough, grinding discipline" can carry one through the test.

George McGovern is not much given to such confessions. On one occasion a reporter asked him, "Aren't you a little intimidated at the prospect of being President of the United States?" "No," he answered, "as a matter of fact, I'm thrilled at the prospect.'' The reporter pressed on: ''As exhausting physically and emotionally as it certainly is going to be, do you dread or look forward to the next fifteen months of campaigning?'' To which came the reply, ''I think it will be a very zestful experience.''

The point is not only that McGovern seems much more positive as he looks toward his future but also that, unlike Nixon, he is rarely preoccupied with the tension, pain, and doubt of life. Indeed, McGovern insists that he enjoys politics a great deal. The part of the game he finds ''the most fun'' is ''the development of ideas and issues,'' but like Harry Truman he can wind up the most grueling day of political labors—twelve hours of meetings and greetings—calm and fresh.

McGovern's good feelings about his job come out in his humor. No Adlai Stevenson, he belongs to the cornball school of political wit, though his writers occasionally invent a swift line. Significant as a sign of character, however, is the fact that he can—and often does—laugh at himself, in marked contrast to the aggressive humor of an active-negative type such as Richard Nixon or Lyndon Johnson. ''Some people say I'm too decent to be President,'' McGovern told one audience, ''but I've got members of my staff working on a list of my inadequacies.'' And in the midst of the Eagleton crisis early last month, he could remark with a smile, ''I don't say it's been a perfect campaign.'' Over and over he relates stories of his own campaign stumbles— his habit of forgetting names and places, for example. He is not above poking fun at other eminences of the political world but ends up the butt of most of his own jokes.

Again like the other active-positives, McGovern does not seem to mind sounding sentimental; as when he said after the Democratic Convention that ''the great effort to win this nomination was a concrete demonstration of the power of love . . . a labor of love.'' Neither does he hesitate to let people know that he really enjoyed (and saw repeatedly) such maudlin films as *The Sound of Music* and *Doctor Zhivago*, that he enjoys mundane tasks like cleaning out his swimming pool, that he took pleasure in retiling the kitchen floor to cheer up his wife at a time when she felt low. Both the humor and the sentimentality underline McGovern's basic self-esteem. One need not defend every little outpost of the personality if the central fortress is secure.

McGovern's cool, his frequent assertions of self-confidence (once he compared himself with Charles de Gaulle in this regard), and his undramatic public demeanor can irritate staffers concerned about some campaign crisis. And it is true that McGovern's cool can often be a kind of blindness, a typical active-positive myopia that makes such a rationally oriented man unable to see and deal with the daimonic and irrational in politics. It evidently did not occur to him that Senator Eagleton could forget or conceal his medical history, or that various, shufflings of votes at the Democratic Convention (such as the sudden shift of tactics in the credentials fight over the South Carolina delegation) could be construed as a somewhat disingenuous maneuver. Roosevelt, Truman, and Kennedy had the same trouble, leaving behind a good deal of political wreckage as they tramped blithely along. Often they had to stop at inconvenient moments and pick up the pieces.

Like his active-positive predecessors, McGovern tends to skate along the top of many a crisis, not exactly oblivious, but selective in his involvements. "I think I have a steady dependable temperament, as well as a sense of history and some degree of imagination," he says. He stresses the larger continuities in his life—his long-standing opposition to the war, for example, rather than his occasional backings and fillings on the issue, or his deeply felt indignation over poverty amidst affluence, rather than the details of his welfare plans.

That sense of continuity stands in marked contrast to Nixon's feeling that life is just one damn thing after another. He sees his experiences as an irregular series of peaks and nadirs, each a unique and novel break with the past, and describes them in superlatives ranging from "the most exciting day of my life" down to "the worst experience of my life." His political career, Nixon recalls, "has been one of very sharp ups and downs." The fact that he chose to write his book about six unconnected personal crises is a broad clue to his vision of the way life unfolds.

Nixon's political style—his penchant for surprise, for example—reflects a need to create these abrupt breaks in his career. In form, each crisis follows a serial pattern—the initial decision to become involved in it, then a time of intense preparation, then the sudden psychological release provided by some decisive act, and finally a letdown period. But the content and direction of a Nixon crisis is essentially unpredictable. If McGovern's life is a prevailing wind Nixon's is stormy weather, now from the east, now from the west.

There is another significant contrast between the two candidates' styles of leadership. A great deal of politics concerns decisions about what we (the people, the Congress, the media) should be attending to these days—and a President's character helps determine the choices he makes. Richard Nixon, much like Wilson, Hoover, and Johnson, most often has his mind focused on himself. In the midst of his speech revealing the invasion of Cambodia in 1970, Nixon took time to discuss its possible effects on his chances in an election more than two years away. He explained his course for action—taken nearly on his own—as though he were a lone ranger mounting a one man attack on an Indian camp: "I knew the stakes that were involved. I knew the division that would be caused in this country. I also knew the problems internationally. I knew the military risks. . . . I made this decision. I believe it was the right decision. I believe it will work out. If it doesn't, then I'm to blame."

Throughout his writings and speeches Nixon makes himself the central character. He saw the Haynsworth and Carswell defeats as assaults on his presidential authority, the trips to Peking and Moscow as triumphs of personal diplomacy. In these self-dramatizations Nixon becomes part of his audience, perpetually watching and correcting his own performance and managing his feelings. Here is Nixon at the airport in Caracas during his tense South American tour in 1958: "The minute I stepped off the airplane, while getting the salute, I cased the place. (I always do that when I walk out.) I looked it all over and watched the kind of crowd, thinking, where will I make an unscheduled stop, where will we move out and shake hands and so forth . . . we walked down the steps from the airplane, and I quickly made a few mental notes and decisions. As we trooped the line I decided not to wave to the crowd, but to ignore it since they were showing disrespect for their flag and their national anthem as well as ours."

It is impossible to imagine George McGovern being so self-conscious about the way he projects himself. Like Nixon, he was a college actor (Richard in the Thirties drama *Bird in Hand*, George in a play called *When Stars Shine*), but there the similarity ends. Nixon's speech in acceptance of the presidential nomination in 1968 has a long autobiographical passage about his fulfillment of "an impossible dream." McGovern's 1972 acceptance speech contains barely a whisper of self-revelation. Mc-Govern's attention moves outward from himself to the world beyond; like Roosevelt, Truman, and Kennedy, he prefers to talk about the way things are, not about who he is. Nor is he much concerned, as Nixon is, with asserting and defending his own power, dignity, and manhood. With the invasion of Cambodia, the Vietnam War became for Nixon a matter of pride versus humiliation—the "pitiful, helpless giant" theme. McGovern has said he is ready to go to Hanoi and "beg" for a settlement. McGovern stood back and smiled when Lawrence O'Brien upstaged him at a Washington press conference after the convention; partying later in the Black Hills, he was to be found over on the sidelines in a group sing. In a political crisis such as the Eagleton mess or his 1960 senatorial defeat, McGovern's habit is to get busy bucking up his staff rather than brooding over his own fate. By way of contrast, when Ike was considering dropping Nixon from the Republican ticket in 1956, the then Vice-President was, in his own words, "thrown into another period of agonizing indecision" in which "the tension dragged on" as he went through "some intense soul-searching."

Nixon's preoccupation with himself reflects to a degree, his training as a lawyer. He perceives his enemies (Voorhis, Hiss, Khrushchev, et al.) with great vividness, much as opposing adversaries must view each other in a courtroom showdown. But when he thinks of larger groups of people and their purposes, he tends toward abstraction: "Frankly most people are mentally and physically lazy." "The American people generally cast their role in the world as an idealistic role and not as a pragmatic role." "We must have the lift of a driving dream." What is missing in his response to people is a sense of the concreteness of human experience. And when Nixon does try to establish a more intimate connection with others, he often fails miserably. At the time of the antiwar demonstration in Washington following the invasion of Cambodia, he attempted to engage young demonstrators at the Lincoln Memorial with talk of football and surfing. "Have a good time in Washington and don't go away bitter," he told these student activists in parting.

Historian McGovern resists generalization. Ideologues of differing persuasions are nearly always disappointed when they try to get him to link his policy ideas together to develop a model of America and its future. Like FDR, who used to tell his wife to look at clotheslines in mining camps to determine how people were faring, McGovern focuses on the concrete experience of individuals: the farmer he knew whose land blew away, the woman wiped out by medical bills, the immigrant who wrote him that his candidacy gave her a reason to become an American citizen.

The roots of these contrasts in the characters of Nixon and McGovern can be traced back to their early days. From that long perspective, Nixon's pessimism and his crisis-haunted review of life can be partially explained by several traumatic childhood experiences, including at least three near-fatal injuries and illnesses, the sudden deaths of two brothers, the prolonged absence of his mother, and a growing awareness of the family's severe economic insecurity. Within the family young Richard developed strong ties to his mother, whose emotional restraint forbade her even the feeling of anger, much less its expression. On the other hand, his father, Frank Nixon, was, in the description of a local preacher, "brusque, loud, dogmatic, strong-willed, emotional, and impatient." The contrast thrust

Richard into a mediator role, not only in practical terms but, more importantly, in emotional terms. He took the part of the responsible son, adapting his mood now to his mother's long silences, now to his father's diatribes. In that highly charged atmosphere he struggled to pattern himself after both parents, there was little room for developing an identity of his own. It was a difficult childhood. From it Richard Nixon learned the wariness he has practiced all his life, the importance of controlling his feelings and projecting them with great care.

The crucial difference in George McGovern's early years was space—emotional space for the children to move around in. Although there was some dislocation of the general serenity in the household—the family moved to Canada when George was four, then back to South Dakota to stay—Joseph McGovern had a steady, respectable job throughout the Depression as a Methodist minister. There were rules in that family, strict ones, about proper behavior. (George's favorite sin was to sneak off to the movies, a dark, secret place much like the elaborate "cave" the children built by burrowing into the foundations of an abandoned house.) But Joseph McGovern, for all his fundamentalist beliefs, was tolerant of other viewpoints, and his wife, twenty years his junior, was even more so.

Above all else, McGovern recalls, his father taught the children the importance of "making the best use of your time. He said you couldn't make the best use of your time if you were going to live by fear. That was his message to me: "I couldn't be the kind of person who would let fear get me down." More important than any paternal instruction, however, was the fact that the children knew they were loved and approved of. They were expected to behave themselves, but old Joseph—he was in his late sixties when George was a teenager—never invaded his children's emotional territory. He never tried, for example, to push George into the ministry or even into any intense religious experience.

Like his eldest son today, Joseph McGovern was a quiet and reserved man, difficult to know. (Not until Joseph was sixty did his children learn about his first career as a traveling baseball player—an occupation he considered low-life and even a bit sinful.) "I admired him and respected him and loved him," McGovern says of his father, "but no, I was not close to him."

George McGovern's upbringing gave him an interior "landscape" similar to his early physical surroundings, the treeless plains of South Dakota, with their sense of limitless space and of life's possibilities. "Even though there were frequent droughts . . . ," McGovern recalls, "always you had the feeling that somehow the land would renew itself. They have a saying, 'It's going to be better next year.' And that's kind of a way of life out here, to feel that things are going to be better next year."

Politics was a constant topic of family conversation in the McGovern household during George's teens. In the Nixon home, aside from Frank's occasional castigations of the "thieves" in the Harding administration, there was not much talk of politics. But Richard Nixon learned his profession quickly when, shortly after his discharge from the navy in 1946, he accepted the invitation of a group of prominent Southern California Republicans to run for Congress. Up until then, he has written, "The idea that I might myself play even a minor part in practical politics never occurred to me." Nixon won that contest against very high odds, and he did it largely on his own initiative, by aggressively attacking his opponent in a series of debates that he prepared for in great detail. That victory set his political style; only then "did the meaning of crisis take on sharply expanded dimensions" for him. Nixon was then, and is now, a skilled rhetorician, who sees his strength as an ability to perform effectively in public and his weakness as an inability to relate well to other people in private. Despite his intention to share power in his administration, Nixon's lone-wolf style has become increasingly evident, while his own rhetorical talent has, if anything, improved. Success first came to Richard Nixon when he applied his immense energies to doing his homework thoroughly and skillfully projecting himself before audiences. And that's where he directs his energies today.

McGovern's style also stems from his initial political success. Long before he entered politics, school debating drew him out of his shyness. "It really changed my life. . . . It was the one thing I could do well. It became the only instrument of personal and social power that I had." Partly because of this new-found confidence in himself, he was named "Glamor Boy" of the year while at Dakota Wesleyan College.

After graduate school, wartime experience that left him with a deep detestation of killing, and short-lived jobs as a minister and a teacher, McGovern embarked on a political career. At age thirty, with four small children, he quit his safe position as a college professor to organize Democrats in South Dakota, a seemingly hopeless venture in that heavily Republican state. But in 1956 McGovern became the first Democrat elected to Congress from South Dakota in twenty years, bucking the Eisenhower tide and defeating a four-term incumbent who had been the state's top vote getter two years earlier. He did it, not through public debates, but by listening and talking to thousands of South Dakotans in visits to every corner of the state. It was a slow and quiet technique, well suited to the pace of South Dakota life. To this day a personal, conversational approach is the essence of McGovern's political style. He often comes across as dull in print and somewhat too preacherish before large audiences—"so plainly honest, kind, sincere, and good that he makes people feel rotten by comparison," wrote one reporter in describing McGovern's public manner. His most effective method of communication as a President would, I think, be an extension of his direct face-to-face approach to people—an informal conversational rhetoric similar to Roosevelt's. "There's been a lot of misreading of George's popularity," a South Dakota Republican commented recently. "It's mostly personal, not ideological."

Ideology is a bent key for unlocking the character of either Nixon or McGovern. The danger in Nixon's case is not that he will first adopt some high principle and then demand public adherence to it. Far more likely is the possibility that Nixon, following the pattern of Wilson, Hoover, and Johnson, will become emotionally exhausted by compromise and criticism, fasten on to some cause, justify it in the name of principle, and use it to effect his personal salvation whatever the social consequences. His compulsive nature—the sense of life as a series of things one must do—weighs heavily on Nixon, always tempting him to transform a passing crisis into a permanent disaster.

McGovern's supposed ideological radicalism is also a poor clue to the way he would act as President. However much critical reporters and hopeful revolutionaries press him, he simply refuses to tie his collection of policy statements into a neat philosophical bundle. Nor are any of his positions—with the exception of his stand on the war—invested with absolute moral fervor. "You never get a hundred per cent of what you wanted," he has said. "And I think the American people understand that. I think they would even support a presidential candidate who would say, 'I'm not fully certain of a particular program, but we're going to try it out. And if it doesn't work, we'll try something else.' I think the American people are willing to experiment." That statement owes much more to F. D. Roosevelt than to V. I. Lenin. A President McGovern might charge off in several directions, but not over some ideological cliff.

Particularly because neither of McGovern nor Nixon are ideologues, one or the other of their characters will be the most important factor in determining the kind of administration we shall have for the next four years. And in evaluating their characters, the chief concern is the matter of flexibility versus rigidity. Nixon's apparent readiness in his first term to shift his ideological principles might not hold true for a second term. Historically, active-negative Presidents have drifted from plasticity to rigidity as the political pressures erode their sense of personal integrity. To that danger must be added Nixon's appetite for crises; sooner or later one of them could deepen rather than disappear. Then there is Nixon's special political situation. Much of his life has been attuned to winning the next election. As a second-term President, however, there would be no next election, no need or requirement to moderate his moves to ensure widespread support. Along with God, history, and himself, the temptations of power could weigh heavily on Richard Nixon.

Would McGovern go overboard in another direction? His indecision about Eagleton, the wavering numbers in his economic proposals, and, in a different way, his readiness to believe the best about people and cheerfully accommodate their points of view—does all this indicate a presidential softie, a man too flexible to stand fast as the political ground shifts? I doubt it. They talked about FDR the same way in 1932: Harold Laski called him "a pill to cure an earthquake," and Walter Lippmann saw him as "a pleasant man . . . without any important qualifications for the office." For different reasons, Harry Truman (too corruptible) and John Kennedy (too wet behind the ears) were dismissed as raw presidential recruits who would let other politicians push them around. Each managed to establish himself as ringmaster of the presidential circus, to make it clear that he was the decisive authority. McGovern's character suggests that he might be equally effective in that way. And, if the past is any clue, character will turn out to be the political compass we should be watching this year.

5

Personalities in State Legislatures

James David Barber

Whether a man become a king or a beggar, there will always be the same
eye, dark or grey, the same mouth, prudent or rash, the same hand;
between this persistence of nature in each of us, and the endless
variations of circumstance, our history passes as it were through the
rollers of a printing press, continually receiving the two-fold impression.

ALAIN

Politicians, being human, are not just competitors, decision-
makers, wily grafters, or idealistic public servants. Like the rest
of us they have their hopes and fears, their doubts and convictions, their pleasures and pains. Like the rest of us, they vary in
the ways they work out their destinies. The stresses and strains
of a prodigious task affect them in different ways; their responses
reflect old habits, continuing needs, and in the last analysis, the
fundamentals of personality—the kinds of people they are and
think they are and wish they were. A legislator's political style is
only a segment—currently, for him, a significant segment—of
his personal style.

An Overview of the Findings

. . . Certain aspects of political behavior result from the
interplay of personal motives, resources, and opportunities, as
illustrated in the recruitment and adaptation of some state
legislators. The relationships are, of course, exceedingly complex, varying from person to person and from situation to
situation. But they appear to be reducible, in their main features,
to a limited set of patterns, which emerge when we take into
account only two variables: the person's level of activity and his

commitment to the office, the latter being indicated by his willingness to return to the legislature for an extended period of service. The activity variable separates those whose satisfactions are met primarily by acting on the environment from those whose satisfactions depend primarily on being acted upon by environmental forces. The willingness-to-return variable separates those for whom the legislature is currently perceived as meeting certain temporary or peripheral needs from those who perceive it as a source of continuing, deeper satisfactions.

The resulting fourfold division of the data reveals a number of significant regularities or patterns of interaction between the member and the institution. I have approached this material with a guiding assumption—that the individual's political behavior represents a collection of adjustive techniques or strategies by which he attempts to maximize the satisfaction of his needs. The particular strategies an individual employs depend on the special needs he brings to his political experience and the availability in that environment of satisfactions for these needs. If the needs are intense and the environment includes important sources of satisfaction, the pattern of adjustment will be modified or surrendered only in exceptional cases. To the extent that either of these factors is weak or absent, the pattern will tend toward flexibility and change. In turn, these patterns will have important effects on the legislative process insofar as they support or interfere with certain central functions that the legislature is called upon to perform.

The word "environment" has a special meaning here—the subjective environment. Although an individual will not be totally unaware of the most obvious facets of the world around him, or perceive objects which are in reality totally absent, he does pay special heed to some things and neglects others. Furthermore, he tends to react emotionally to objects he encounters, attaching positive and negative signs to things. The particular selective and value-attaching practices a person employs amounts to his reactions to the environment. Insofar as most of the real environment is common to all members of an institution, it is likely that differences in reactions are attributable to differences in the needs an individual brings to his new experience.

When we look closely at these reactions, the patterned nature of a person's adjustment begins to emerge. We appear to be dealing not with scattered relationships between this particular perception and that particular strategic device but rather with sets of these factors, sets that fit together functionally, complementing and supporting one another. This patterning leads us to suspect the presence of some underlying factor by which the perceptions and strategies are integrated. The data support the hypothesis that this integrating can be understood most clearly as a product of deeper personal needs revealed in a person's conception of himself.

The self-concept is marked by selectivity and affectivity in ways similar to perceptions of environmental objects. The individual sees himself as a certain kind of person and he reacts evaluatively to what he sees. Both these aspects of the self-concept seem to have had much to do in shaping our legislators' political behavior. For three types—the Spectators, Advertisers, and Reluctants—much of this behavior represents compensation. For three quite different reasons these individuals seek in politics opportunities for enhancing and protecting a sense of self-approval, employing strategies symptomatic of relatively low self-esteem. The Lawmakers, on the other hand, tend to evaluate themselves rather more highly and thus to be much less concerned with bolstering their egos.

Each type bases its self-estimates on different major criteria. The Spectators are concerned mainly with their unloveableness, the Advertisers with their impotence, the Reluctants with their uselessness, and the Lawmakers with their achievements. In each case the self-concept shapes and organizes the legislator's political activities.

In the following list the central characteristics of each of the four types are summarized . . .

Summary of Legislator Types

The Spectator

Defining characteristics: Low in activity, high in willingness to return.

General legislative style: Watching, being entertained.

Background and expectations: Typically a middle-aged, lower status housewife of modest achievements, limited skills, and restricted ambitions.

Nominations: Recruited in noncompetitive small-town candidate shortage. Offers negative virtues.

Reactions: Enjoys the drama and color but specially sensitive to approval and disapproval. Rewarded by admission to a prestigious, intimate group.

Self: Little sense of individuality; other-directed. Pervasive sense of personal inadequacy and unattractiveness.

Strategies: Vicarious participation, superficial socializing, submission to others.

Pattern persistence and change: Pattern meets strong needs, is supported by environment. Alternatives risky.

Legislative work: Little involvement in substantive work. Blocked by conflicting strategies. Contributes some to tension reduction.

Political future: Uncertain, depends on candidate supply at home.

The Advertiser

Defining characteristics: High in activity, low in willingness to return.

General legislative style: Exhibiting self, seeking occupationally beneficial contacts.

Background and expectations: Typically a young, upward-mobile lawyer experiencing occupational difficulties. Linked to politics mainly through occupation.

Nomination: Seeks nomination in growing, politically uncertain, larger constituency. Offers apparent skills; availability dependent on arranging time from work.

Reactions: Frustrated by environmental restrictions. Feels forced, exploited, powerless.

Self: Dominated by conflict between intense ambition and strict conscience. Anxiety, suffering. A sense of impotence.

Strategies: Indirect aggression, projection, displacement; competing and working; dwelling on own suffering; contemplating utopia.

Pattern persistence and change: Pattern meets strong needs but is punished by the environment. Leaving legislature more likely than pattern change.

Legislative work: Intense activity masks indifference to substantive work. Lowers morale, cannot accept a beginner's place in the system.

Political future: Short unless opportunities to express aggression engage strong needs.

The Reluctant

Defining characteristics: Low in activity, low in willingness to return.

General legislative style: Doing a civic duty under protest.

Background and expectations: Typically an elderly, infirm, retired person, of moderate achievements. A lifelong home-town reliable, with many friends.

Nominations: Recruited from traditional, small, rural noncompetitive town. Embodiment of community values. Helps avoid conflict.

Reactions: Bewildered by the strange cosmopolitan environment, particularly the exotic people, headlong pace, and intricate decision-making process.

Self: Strong moral sense of social responsibility, especially for preserving harmony. Feels inadequate to legislative tasks. A sense of uselessness.

Strategies: Tempted to retreat from politics, perceive harmony, withdraw to reverie or ritualism.

Pattern persistence and change: Withdrawal pattern palliates temporary anxieties, but gradual learning and minor achievement probable in the long run.

Legislative work: Hampered by provincial background, limited education, declining energies, but helps maintain important legislative norms.

Political future: Long, depending on health and constituency stability.

The Lawmaker

Defining characteristics: High in activity, high in willingness to return.

General legislative style: Attention to substantive tasks.

Background and expectations: Like Advertisers, young and mobile, but with deeper and more varied political roots and much more interest in full-time elective office.

Nominations: Seeks nomination in larger, moderately competitive, highly educated constituency. Offers interest and competence in issues.

Reactions: Concentrates on bills, decisions. Pleased at opportunity to produce desired legislation, participate in rational process, work cooperatively with others.

Self: Strong sense of individuality, personal standards. Stresses rationality; sense of the self as developing maintains and enhances self-approval.

Strategies: Conscious definition of central political roles.

Pattern persistence and change: Pattern meets strong needs for rational mastery, but environmental support varies. May turn to other arenas.

Legislative work: Makes most significant contributions, aided by congruence between personal strategies and legislative task-organization. But may neglect need for inspiration, get impatient with formal proprieties.

Political future: Long, depending on competing demands for his talents and availability of productive political institutions.

Part II.

Critique: Science or Sorcery?

Part II.

Critique: Science or Sorcery?

6

James David Barber and the
Psychological Presidency

Michael Nelson

The United States elects its president every four years, which makes it unique among democratic nations. *Time* magazine runs a story about James David Barber every presidential election year, which makes him unique among political scientists. The two quadrennial oddities are not unrelated.

Barber was 42 years old and chairman of the political science department at Duke University when the first *Time* article appeared in 1972. It was about a book he had just published through Prentice-Hall called *The Presidential Character*. The book argued that presidents could be divided into four psychological types, which Barber called "active-positive," "active-negative," "passive-positive," and "passive-negative." What's more, according to Barber via *Time*, with "a hard look at men before they reach the White House" voters could tell in advance what candidates would be like if elected: healthily "ambitious out of exuberance" like the active-positives; or pathologically "ambitious out of anxiety," "compliant and other-directed," or "dutiful and self-denying" like the three other, lesser types, respectively. In the 1972 election, Barber told *Time*, the choice was between an active-positive, George McGovern, and a psychologically defective active-negative, Richard Nixon.

Nixon won the election, but Barber's early insights into Nixon's personality won him and his theory certain notoriety, especially in the wake of Watergate. So prominent had Barber become by 1976, in fact, that Hugh Sidey used his entire *Time* "Presidency" column for October 4 just to tell readers that Barber was refusing to "type" candidates Gerald Ford and Jimmy Carter this time around. "Barber is deep into an academic study of this election and its participants, and he is pledged to restraint until it is over," Sidey reported solemnly. (Actually, Barber had told interviewers from *U.S. News and World Report* more than a year before that he considered Ford an active-positive. Carter, who read Barber's book twice when it came out, was left to tell *The Washington Post* that active-positive is "what I would like to be. That's what I hope I prove to be." And so Carter would, wrote Barber in a special postelection column—for *Time*.

The 1980 election campaign has witnessed the appearance of another Barber book, *The Pulse of Politics*, and in honor of the occasion, two *Time* articles. This is all to the good, because the first, a Sidey column in March, offered more gush than information. ("The first words encountered in the new book by Duke's Professor James David Barber are stunning: 'A revolution in presidential politics is underway. . . . Barber has made political history before.'") It wasn't until May 19 that a "Nation" section article revealed anything at all of what the new book was about, namely, Barber's cycle theory of 20th-century presidential elections. The theory holds, readers learned, that steady four-year "beats" in the public mood, or "pulse," have caused a recurring alternation among elections of what Barber calls "conflict," "conscience," and "conciliation" ever since 1900. *Time* went on to stress, though not explain, Barber's view of the importance of the mass media both as a reinforcer of this cycle and a potential mechanism for helping to break us out of it.

The kind of fame that *Time*'s infatuation with Barber has brought him comes rarely to scholars, more rarely still to political scientists. For Barber, it has come at some cost. Though his ideas now have a currency they otherwise might not have, the versions of those ideas that have circulated most widely are so cursory as to make them seem superficial or even foolish—instantly appealing to the naive, instantly odious to the thoughtful. Partly because of this, Barber's reputation in the intellectual community as *un homme sérieux* has suffered in the backrooms and corridors of scholarly gatherings. One hears "popularizer," the ultimate academic epithet, muttered along with his name.

This situation is in need of remedy. Barber's theories may be seriously flawed, but they are serious theories. For all their limitations—some of them self-confessed—they offer one of the more significant contributions a scholar can make: an unfamiliar but useful way of looking at a familiar thing that we no longer see very clearly. In Barber's case, the familiar thing is the American presidency, and the unfamiliar way of looking at it is through lenses of psychology.

II

A sophisticated psychological perspective on the presidency was long overdue when Barber began offering one in the late 1960's. Political scholars long had taken as axiomatic that the American presidency, because executive power is vested in one person and only vaguely defined in its limits is an institution shaped largely by the personalities of individual presidents. But rarely had the literature of personality *theory* even in its more familiar forms, been brought to bear. As Erwin Hargrove reflected in post-Vietnam, mid-Watergate 1974, this failure was the source of some startling deficiencies in our understanding of the office. "We had assumed," he wrote in *The Power of the Modern Presidency*, "that ideological purpose was sufficient to purify the drive for power, but we forgot the importance of character." Richard Neustadt's influential *Presidential Power*, published in 1960, was typical in this regard; it simply took for granted that "a President's success in maximizing power for himself serves objectives far beyond his own. . . . [W]hat is good for the country is good for the President, and *vice versa*."

Scholars also had recognized for some time that the attitudes Americans hold toward the presidency are psychologically as well as politically rooted. Studies of schoolchildren had found that they first come to political awareness by learning of, and feeling fondly toward, the president. There was also a sense that popular nationalistic emotions that in constitutional monarchies are directed toward the king are deflected in American society onto the presidency. Again, however, this awareness manifested itself more in casual observation (Dwight Eisenhower was a "father figure"; the "public mood" is fickle) than in systematic thought.

The presidencies of John Kennedy, Lyndon Johnson, and Nixon changed all that. Surveys taken shortly after the Kennedy assassination recorded the startling depth of the feelings that citizens have about the office. A large share of the population experienced symptoms classically associated with grief over the death of a loved one; they cried; were tired, dazed, nervous; had trouble eating and sleeping. A quick scan through history found similar public responses to the deaths of all sitting presidents, popular or not, by murder or natural causes. If Kennedy's death illustrated the deep psychological ties of the public to the presidency, the experiences of his successors showed even more clearly the importance of psychology in understanding the connection between president and presidency. Johnson, the peace candidate who rigidly pursued a self-defeating policy of war, and Nixon, who promised "lower voices" only angrily to turn political disagreements into personal crises, projected their personalities onto policy in ways that were both obvious and destructive. The events of this period brought students of the presidency up short. As they paused to consider the nature of what I will call the "psychological presidency," they found Barber standing at the ready with the foundation and first floor of a full-blown theory.

Barber's theory offers a model of the presidency as an institution shaped largely by the psychological mix between the personalities of individual presidents and the public's deep feelings about the office. Beyond that, it proposes methods of predicting what those personalities and feelings are likely to be in given instances. These considerations govern *The Presidential Character* and *The Pulse of Politics*, books that we shall examine in turn. The problem of what is to be done on the basis of all this knowledge—of how we can become masters of our own and of the presidency's psychological fates—also is treated in these books, but receives its fullest exposition in other works by Barber.

III

> The primary danger of the Nixon administration will be that the President will grasp some line of policy or method of operation and pursue it in spite of its failure. . . . How will Nixon respond to challenges to the morality of his regime, to charges of scandal and/or corruption? First such charges strike a raw nerve, not only from the Checkers business, but also from deep within the personality in which the demands of the superego are so harsh and hard. . . . The first impulse will be to hush it up, to conceal it, bring down the blinds. If it breaks open and Nixon cannot avoid commenting on it, there is a real setup here for another crisis.

James David Barber is more than a little proud of that passage, primarily because he wrote it on Jan. 19, 1969, the eve of Richard Nixon's first inauguration. It was among the first in a series of speeches, papers, and articles whose purpose was to explain his theory of presidential personality and how to predict it, always with his forecast for Nixon's future prominently, and thus riskily, displayed. The theory received its fullest statement in *The Presidential Character.*

"Character," in Barber's usage, is not quite a synonym for personality, but he clearly thinks it "the most important thing to know about a President or candidate." As he defines the term, "character is the way the President orients himself toward life— not for the moment, but enduringly." It is forged in childhood, "grow[ing] out of the child's experiments in relating to parents, brothers and sisters, and peers at play and in school, as well as to his own body and the objects around it." Through these experiences, the child—and thus the man to be—arrives subconsciously at a deep and private determination of what he is fundamentally worth. Some emerge from all this with high self-esteem, the vital ingredient for psychological health and

political productiveness; the rest face the further problem of
searching out an external, and no more than partially compen-
sating, substitute. Depending on the source and nature of their
limited self-esteem, Barber suggests, they will concentrate their
search in one of three areas: the affection from others that
compliant and agreeable behavior brings; the sense of usefulness
that comes from performing a widely respected duty; or the
deference attendant with dominance and control over people.
Because politics is a vocation rich in opportunities to find all
three of these things—affection from cheering crowds and
backslapping colleagues, usefulness from public service in a
civic cause, dominance through official power—it is not surprising that some less than secure people find a political career
rather attractive.

This makes for a problem, Barber argues: if public officials,
especially presidents, use their office to compensate for private
doubts and demons, it follows that they will not always use it for
public purposes. Affection-seekers will be so concerned with
preserving the good will of those around them that they rarely
will challenge the status quo or otherwise rock the boat. The
duty-doers will be similarly inert, though in their case, it will be
the feeling that to be "useful" they must be diligent guardians of
time-honored practices and procedures that will account for this.
The danger posed by the power-driven, of course, is the greatest. They will seek their psychological compensation not in
inaction, but action. Since such action will be motivated by the
desire to maintain or extend their personal sense of domination
and control through public channels, it is almost bound to take
destructive form: rigid defensiveness, aggression against opponents, or the like. Only those with high self-esteem are secure
enough to lead as democratic political leaders must lead, with
persuasion and flexibility as well as action and initiative. And
Barber recognizes that even they sometimes will fail us, psychological health being a necessary but not a sufficient condition for
successful political leadership.

All this—the theoretical element in Barber's character analysis—is fairly straightforward and plausible. Moving to the pre-

dictive realm is more problematic. How in the heat and haste of a presidential campaign, with candidates notably unwilling to bare their souls publicly for psychoanalytic inspection, are we to find out what they are really like?

Easy enough, argues Barber: to answer the difficult question of what motivates a political man, just answer the simpler ones in its stead: Is he "active" or "passive"? ("How much energy does the man invest in his Presidency?"); and is he "positive" or "negative"? ("Relatively speaking, does he seem to experience his political life as happy or sad, enjoyable or discouraging, positive or negative in its main effect?") According to Barber, the four possible combinations of answers to these questions turn out to be almost synonymous with the four psychological strategies people use to enhance self-esteem. The "active-positive" is the healthy one in the group. His high sense of self-worth enables him to work hard at politics, have fun at what he does, and thus be fairly good at it. Among 20th-century presidents, Barber places Franklin Roosevelt, Harry Truman, Kennedy, Ford, and Carter in this group. The "passive-positive" (William Howard Taft, Warren Harding) is the affection-seeker; though not especially hard-working in office, he enjoys it. The "passive-negative" neither works nor plays. As with Calvin Coolidge and Eisenhower, it is duty, not pleasure or zeal, that gets him into politics. Finally, there is the power-seeking "active-negative," who compulsively throws himself into his presidential chores even though the effort does not satisfy him. In Barber's view, active-negative Presidents Woodrow Wilson, Herbert Hoover, Johnson, and Nixon all shared one important personality-rooted presidential quality: they persisted in disastrous courses of action (Wilson's League of Nations battle, Hoover's depression policy, Johnson's Vietnam, Nixon's Watergate) because to have conceded that they were wrong would have been to cede their sense of control, something their psychological constitutions could not allow.

The Presidential Character caused quite a stir when it came out in 1972. Not surprisingly, it generated some vigorous criticism as well. Many argued that Barber's theory is too simple: his four types do not begin to cover the range of human complexity. At one level, this criticism is as trivial as it is true. In spelling out his theory, Barber states very clearly that "we are talking about tendencies, broad directions; no individual man exactly fits a category." His typology is offered as a method for sizing up potential presidents, not for diagnosing and treating them. Given the nature of election campaigning, a reasonably accurate short-hand device is about all we can hope for. The real question, then, is whether Barber's short-hand device is reasonably accurate.

Barber's intellectual defense of his typology's soundness, quoted here in full, is not altogether comforting:

> Why might we expect these two simple dimensions [active-passive, positive-negative] to outline the main character types? Because they stand for two central features of anyone's orientation toward life. In nearly every study of personality, some form of the active-passive contrast is critical; the general tendency to act or be acted upon is evident in such concepts as dominance-submission, extraversion-introversion, aggression-timidity, attack-defense, fight-flight, engagement-withdrawal, approach-avoidance. In everyday life we sense quickly the general energy output of the people we deal with. Similarly we catch on fairly quickly to the affect dimension—whether the person seems to be optimistic or pessimistic, hopeful or skeptical, happy or sad. The two baselines are clear and they are also independent of one another: all of us know people who are very active but seem discouraged, others who are quite passive but seem happy, and so forth. The activity baseline refers to what one does, the affect baseline to how one feels about what he does.
>
> Both are crude clues to character. They are leads into four basic character patterns long familiar in psychological research.

In the library copy of *The Presidential Character* from which I copied this passage, there is a handwritten note in the margin: "Footnote, man!" But there is no footnote to the psychological literature, here or anywhere else in the book. The casual reader might take this to mean that none is necessary, and he would be right if Barber's types really were "long familiar in psychological research" and "appeared in nearly every study of personality." But they aren't, and they don't; as Alexander George has pointed out, personality theory itself is a "quagmire" in which "the term 'character' in practice is applied loosely and means many different things." Barber's real defense of his theory—that it works; witness Nixon—is not to be dismissed, but one wishes he had explained better why he thinks it works.

Interestingly, other critics have taken Barber's typology to task for being not simple enough, at least not for the purpose of accurate preelection application. Where, exactly, is one to look to decide if down deep Candidate Schuengel is the energetic, buoyant fellow his image-makers say he is? Barber is quite right in warning analysts away from their usual hunting ground, the candidate's recent performances in other high offices. These "are all much more restrictive than the Presidency is, much more set by institutional requirements," and thus much less fertile cultures for psychopathologies to grow in. (This is Barber's only real mention of what well might be considered a third, coequal component of the psychological presidency: the rarefied, court-like atmosphere—so well described in George Reedy's *The Twilight of the Presidency*—that surrounds presidents and which allows those whose psychological constitutions so move them to seal themselves off from harsh political realities.) But Barber's alternative—a study of the candidate's "first independent political success," or "fips," in which he found his personal formula for success in politics—is not all that helpful either. How, for example, is one to tell which "fips" was first? In Barber's appropriately broad definition of "political," Johnson's first success was not his election to Congress, but his work as a student assistant to his college president. Hoover's was his incumbency as student body treasurer at Stanford. Sorting through someone's life with the thoroughness necessary to arrive at such a determination may or not be an essential task. But clearly it is not a straightforward one.

These theoretical and practical criticisms are important ones, and they do not exhaust the list. (Observer bias, for example. Since Barber provides no clear checklist of criteria by which one is to type candidates, subjectivity is absolutely inherent). But they should not blind us to Barber's major contributions in *The Presidential Character*: a concentration on the importance of presidential personality in explaining presidential behavior; a sensitivity to its nature as a variable (power does not always corrupt; nor does the office always make the man); and a boldness in approaching the problems voters face in predicting what candidates will be like if elected.

IV

The other side of the psychological presidency—the public's side—is Barber's concern in *The Pulse of Politics*, which was published by W. W. Norton midway through this year's primary season. The book focuses on elections, those occasions when because citizens are filling the presidential office, they presumably feel (presidential deaths aside) their emotional attachments to it most deeply. Again, Barber presents us with a typology; the public's election moods come in three varieties: "conflict," "conscience," and "conciliation," and this time the types appear in recurring order as well, over 12-year cycles. Again, the question he raises—what is the nature of "the swirl of emotions" with which Americans surround the presidency?—is important and original.

But again, too, the reasoning that underlies Barber's answer is as puzzling as it is provocative. Although his theory applies only to American presidential elections in this century, he seems to feel that the psychological "pulse" of conflict, conscience, and conciliation has beaten deeply, if softly, in all humankind for all time. Barber finds it in the "old sagas" of early man, and in "the psychological paradigm that dominates our age's thinking: the ego, instrument for coping with the struggles of the external world [conflict]; the superego, warning against harmful violations [conscience]; the id, longing after the thrill and ease of sexual satisfaction [conciliation]." He finds it firmly reinforced in American history: conflict in our emphasis on the war story ("In isolated America, the war-makers repeatedly confronted the special problem of arousing the martial spirit against distant enemies. . . . Thus our history vibrates with *talk* about war"); conscience in America's sense of itself as an instrument of divine providence ("our conscience has never been satisfied by government as a mere practical arrangement"); conciliation in our efforts to live with each other in a heterogeneous "nation of nationalities." In the 20th century, Barber argues, these themes became the controlling force in the political psychology of the American electorate, so controlling that every election since the conflict of 1900 has fit its place within the cycle (conscience in 1904, conciliation in 1908, conflict again in 1912, and so on). What caused the pulse to start beating this strongly, he feels, was the rise of the national mass media.

The modern newspaper came first, just before the turn of the century. "In a remarkable historical conjunction," writes Barber, "the sudden surge into mass popularity of the American daily newspaper coincided with the Spanish-American War." Since war stories sold papers, daily journalists wrote about "politics as war," or conflict, too. In the early 1900's, national mass circulation magazines arrived on the scene, taking their cues from the Progressive reformers who dominated that period. "The 'muckrakers'—actually positive thinkers out to build America, not destroy reputations" wrote of "politics as a moral enterprise," an enterprise of conscience. Then came the broadcast media, radio in the 1920's and television in the 1950's. What set them apart was their commercial need to reach not just a wide audience, but the widest possible audience. "Broadcasting aimed to please, wrapping politics in fun and games . . . conveying with unmatched reach and power its core message of conciliation." As for the cyclic pulse, the recurring appearance of these public moods in the same precise order, Barber suggests that there the dynamic is internal: each type of public mood generates the next. After a conflict election ("a battle for power . . . a rousing call to arms"), "reaction sets in. Uplift is called for—the cleansing of the temple of democracy"—in short, conscience. But "the troubles do not go away," and four years later "the public yearns for solace," conciliation. "Give that four years to settle in and the time for a fight will come around again," and so on.

In *The Pulse of Politics*, unlike *The Presidential Character*, the difficulties arise not in the predictive gloss (a calendar will do; if it's 1980, this must be a conciliating election), but in the theory itself. If anything, an even more secure intellectual foundation is needed here than with the character theory, for this time there is an assertion not only of types, but of an order of occurrence among them as well. Once again, however, there are no footnotes; if Barber is grounding his theory in external sources, it is impossible to tell—and hard to imagine—what they are. Nor does the theory stand up sturdily under its own weight: if, for example, radio and television are agents of conciliation, why did we not have fewer conciliating elections before they became our dominant political media and more since? Perhaps that is why some of the retrospective predictions Barber's theory leads to are as questionable as they are easy to make: Coolidge-Davis in 1924 a conflict election?; Eisenhower-Stevenson in 1952 conscience?; Nixon-Humphrey-Wallace in 1968 conciliating?

The most interesting criticism pertinent to Barber's pulse theory, however, was made eight years before it appeared by a political scientist who, also concerned with the public's presidential psychology, wrote of it in terms of a "climate of expectations" that "shifts and changes. Wars, depressions, and other national events contribute to that change, but there is also a rough cycle, from an emphasis on action (which begins to look too 'political') to an emphasis on legitimacy (the moral uplift of which creates its own strains) to an emphasis on reassurance and rest (which comes to seem like drift) and back to action again. One need not be astrological about it." (A year earlier this scholar had written that although "the mystic could see the series . . . marching in fateful repetition beginning in 1900 . . . the pattern is too astrological to be convincing.") Careful readers will recognize the identity between the cycles of action-legitimacy-reassurance and conflict-conscience-conciliation. Clever ones will realize that the passage above was written by James David Barber in *The Presidential Character*.

V

There is, in fact, a good deal about the public's political psychology sprinkled here and there in *The Presidential Character*, and the more of it one discovers, the curiouser and curiouser things get. Most significant is the brief concluding chapter on "Presidential Character and the Moods of the Eighth Decade" (reprinted unchanged in the 1977 Second Edition), which contains Barber's bold suggestion of a close fit between the two sides of his model. For each type of public psychological climate, Barber posits, there is a "resonant" type of presidential personality. This seems a central point in his theory of the presidency: "Much of what [a president] is remembered for," he argues, "will depend on the fit between the dominant forces in his character and the dominant feelings in his constituency." Further, "the dangers of discord in that resonance are great."

What is the precise nature of this fit? When the public cry is for action (conflict), "[i]t comes through loudest to the active-negative type, whose inner struggle between aggression and control resonates with the popular plea for toughness. . . .[The active-negative's] temptation to stand and fight receives wide support from the culture." In the public's reassurance (concili-ation) mood, "they want a friend," a passive-positive. As for the "appeal for a moral cleansing of the Presidency," or legitimacy (conscience), that mood "resonates with the passive-negative character in its emphasis on *not doing* certain things." This leaves the active-positive, Barber's president for all seasons. Blessed with a "character firmly rooted in self-recognition and self-love, [t]he active-positive can not only *perform* lovingly or aggressively or with detachment, he can *feel* those ways."

What Barber first offered in *The Presidential Character*, then, was the foundation of a model of the psychological presidency that was not only two-sided, but integrated as well, one in which the "tuning, the resonance—or lack of it" between the public's "climate of expectations" and the president's personality "sets in motion the dynamic of his Presidency." He concentrated on the personality half of his model in *The Presidential Character*, then firmed up (after "de-astrologizing" it) and filled in the other half—the public's—in *The Pulse of Politics*. And here is where things get so curious. Most authors, when they complete a multivolume opus, trumpet that fact. Barber does not. In fact, one finds in *The Pulse of Politics* no mention at all of presidential character, of public climates of expectations, or of "the resonance—or lack of it" between them.

At first blush, this seems doubly strange, because there is a strong surface fit between the separate halves of Barber's model. In the 18 elections that have been held since Taft's in 1908 (Barber did not type 20th-century presidents farther back than Taft), presidential character and public mood resonated 12 times. The six exceptions—active-negative Wilson's election in the conscience year of 1916, passive-negative Coolidge's in conflictual 1924, active-negative Hoover's and passive-negative Eisenhower's in the conciliating elections of 1928 and 1956, active-negative Johnson's in conscience-oriented 1964, and active-negative Nixon's in conciliating 1968—perhaps could be explained in terms of successful campaign image-management by the winners, an argument that also would support Barber's general point about the power of the media in presidential politics. In that case, a test of Barber's model would be: did these "inappropriate" presidents come to grief when the public found out what they really were like after the election? In every instance but Eisenhower's and Coolidge's, the answer would have been yes.

But on closer inspection it also turns out that in every instance but these two, the presidents who came to grief were active-negatives, whom Barber tells us will do so for reasons that have nothing to do with the public mood. As for the overall 12 for 18 success rate for Barber's model, it includes seven elections won by active-positives, whom he says resonate with every public mood. A good hand in straight poker is not necessarily a good hand in wild-card; Barber's success rate in the elections not won by active-positives is only five of 11. In the case of conscience elections, only once did a representative of the resonant type—

passive-negative—win, while purportedly less suitable active-negatives won three times. A final problem is born of Barber's assertion, made in the face of his prediction that Ronald Reagan would be a passive-positive president, that in the post-New Deal era of big government at home and active government abroad, the demands of the presidency—and of seeking it in the modern campaign mode—effectively will screen out passive types as would-be presidents. (In the period from 1929 to the present, the only passive president has been Eisenhower, and Barber admits that "his case is a mixed one.") Since two of his three moods—conscience and conciliation—are said to resonate with passive presidents, their elimination from contention rather trivializes the question of fit as Barber has posed it.

VI

I leave it to Barber to explain his failure to claim credit for what he has done, namely, offered and elaborated a suggestive and relatively complete model of the psychological presidency. Perhaps he feared that the lack of fit between his mood and personality types—the public and presidential components—would have distracted critics from his larger points.

In any event, the theoretical and predictive elements of Barber's theory of the presidency are sufficiently provocative to consider carefully his prescriptions for change. Barber's primary goal for the psychological presidency, it should be noted, is that it be "de-psychopathologized." He wants to keep active-negatives out and put healthy active-positives in. He wants the public to become the master of its own political fate, breaking out of its electoral mood cycle, which is essentially a cycle of psychological dependency. With presidency and public freed of their inner chains, Barber feels, they will be able to join to forge a "creative politics" or "politics of persuasion," as he has variously dubbed it. It is not clear just what this kind of politics would be, but apparently it would involve a great deal more open and honest sensitivity on the part of both presidents and citizens to the ideas of the other.

It will not surprise readers to learn that, by and large, Barber
dismisses constitutional reform as a method for achieving his
goals: if the presidency is as shaped by psychological forces as
he says it is, then institutional tinkering will be, almost by
definition, beside the point. Change, to be effective, will have to
come in the thoughts and feelings of people: in the information
they get about politics, the way they think about it, and the way
they feel about what they think. Because of this, Barber be-
lieves, the central agent of change will have to be the most
pervasive, media journalism; its central channel, the coverage of
presidential elections.

It is here, in his prescriptive writings, that Barber is on most
solid ground, here that his answers are as good as his questions.
Unlike many media critics, he does not assume imperiously that
the sole purpose of newspapers, magazines, and television is to
elevate the masses. Barber recognizes that the media are made
up of commercial enterprises that also have to sell papers and
attract viewers. He recognizes, too, that the basic format of
news coverage is the story, not the scholarly treatise. His
singular contribution is his argument that the media can improve
the way it does all of these things at the same time, that better
election stories will attract bigger audiences in more enlightening
ways.

The first key to better stories, Barber argues, is greater
attention to the character of the candidates. Election coverage
that ignores the motivations and developmental histories of its
protagonists is as lifeless as dramas or novels that did so would
be. It also is uninformative—elections are, after all, choices
among people, and as Barber has shown, the kinds of people
candidates are has a lot to do with the kinds of presidents they
would be. Good journalism, Barber argues in a 1978 Prentice-
Hall book called *Race for the Presidency*, would "focus on the
person as embodying his historical development, playing out a
character born and bred in another place, connecting an old
identity with a new persona—the stuff of intriguing drama from
Joseph in Egypt on down. That can be done explicitly in
biographical stories." Barber is commendably diffident here—he

does not expect reporters to master and apply his own character typology. But he does want them to search the candidate's lives for recurring patterns of behavior, particularly the rigidity that is characteristic of his active-negatives. (Of all behavior patterns, he feels rigidity "is probably the easiest one to spot and the most dangerous one to elect.") With public interest ever high in "people" stories and psychology, Barber probably is right in thinking that this kind of reporting not only would inform readers, but engage their interest as well.

This goal—engaging readers' interest—is Barber's second key to better journalism. He finds reporters and editors notably, sometimes belligerently, ignorant of their audiences. "I really don't know and I'm not interested," quotes Richard Salant of CBS News. "Our job is to give people not what they want, but what we decide they ought to have." Barber suggests that what often is lost in such a stance is an awareness of what voters need, namely, information that will help them decide whom to vote for. He cites a study of network evening news coverage of the 1972 election campaign which found that almost as much time was devoted to the polls, strategies, rallies, and other "horse-race" elements of the election as to the candidate's personal qualifications and issue stands combined. As Barber notes, "The viewer tuning in for facts to guide his choice would, therefore, have to pick his political nuggets from a great gravel pile of political irrelevancy." He adds that "Television news which moved beyond telling citizens what momentary collective preferences are as the next primary approaches, to telling them what they need to know—precisely on the issue of presidential choosing—might yet enlist intellectual apparatus." Critics who doubt the public's interest in long, fleshed-out stories about what candidates think, what they are like, and what great problems they would face as president would do well to check the ratings of CBS's "60 Minutes."

Barber's strong belief, then, is that an electorate whose latent but powerful interest in politics is engaged by the media will become an informed electorate, and that this will effect its liberation from the pathological aspects of the psychological presidency. On the one hand, as citizens learn more of what they need to learn about the character of presidential candidates, they will be less likely to elect defective ones. On the other hand, this process of political learning also will equip them better to act "rationally" in politics, freed from their cycle of emotional dependency on the presidency. So sensible a statement of the problem is this, and so attractive a vision of its solution, that one can forgive Barber for cluttering it up with types and terminologies.

Part III.

Comparative Tests and Case Studies: The Empirical Presidency

Part III

Comparative Tests and Case Studies:
The Empirical Presidency

7

Amnesty and Presidential Behavior: A "Barberian" Test

William D. Pederson

Although human rights organizations presumably have an impact on leaders of states holding political prisoners, little is known about why some leaders are more responsive than others to pressure groups like Amnesty International. The behavior of political leaders seems quite unpredictable in matters of civil liberties, civil rights, and human rights. For example, even though the International Committee of the Red Cross (I.C.R.C.) visited nearly a thousand prisons between 1958 and 1970 in states experiencing armed conflicts, the leaders of 14 states denied the I.C.R.C. access to their prisons.[1] Similarly, some political leaders grant amnesty quite easily, such as Prime Minister Whitlam of Australia, while others refuse, such as President Nixon; and some leaders grant more liberal forms of amnesty, such as President Carter, while others grant less liberal ones, such as President Ford. This study focuses on one aspect of the relationship between political leadership and concern for individual liberties and rights by exploring the role of American presidential behavior in granting amnesty. For purposes of analysis and discussion, the paper is divided into three parts: (1) the development of a classification scheme of presidential behavior that includes nearly every American president; (2) a comparison of the classification scheme with the entire record of presidential amnesties; and (3) some general conclusions and remarks about future research in the area of presidential behavior and individual liberties.

Classification Schemes of Presidential Behavior

Social scientists generally, and political scientists particularly, have shown some interest in the president's role in protecting individual rights and liberties,[2] and also in the general issue of amnesty,[3] but so far no attempt has been made to link the two subjects together psychologically. Recent political psychology research permits at least an exploratory effort in this direction. For example, Erwin C. Hargrove made the first step beyond individual psycho-histories of American presidents by simply dividing nine modern presidents into active and passive types.[4]

In his analysis of eleven modern presidents, James David Barber has taken the next step by forming a four-fold typology of active-positive, active-negative, passive-positive, and passive-negative presidents, based on a felt satisfaction index ("positive and negative affect") and Hargrove's political energy index (active or passive).[5] Barber presents active-positive presidents as the healthiest personality types, in contrast to the three other types that are hypothesized to be psychically deprived. Active-negatives derive little satisfaction from their accomplishments, and are likely to "rigidify" in certain situations; passive-positives are plagued with unmet love needs; and passive-negatives occupy the presidency solely out of a sense of duty without personally enjoying the office. Active-positives, on the other hand, fulfill themselves through the presidential role, and have fun in the office.

Although Barber classifies almost twice as many presidents as Hargrove (a number of early presidents are very briefly mentioned by Barber), both political scientists focus on twentieth century presidents for the basis of their classification schemes. This paper expands the number of cases even further so that nearly every president is classified, and does it in such a way to permit an independent check on the other two classification schemes.

Gary M. Maranell's questionnaire study of nearly 600 American historians is used for this purpose.[6] The historians evaluated American presidents on seven separate dimensions of prestige, strength, activeness, idealism, flexibility, and accomplishment; and then, Maranell used social psychological scaling methods to score the results. This paper has selected the dimensions of activeness ("The approach taken by each president toward his administration, an active or a passive approach.") and flexibility ("An evaluation of the flexibility or inflexibility of the approach each president took in implementing his program or policies."), and juxtaposed the rankings to form a short-cut four-fold presidential typology of active-flexibles, active-inflexibles, passive-flexibles, and passive-inflexibles.

A comparison between the classifications in the Barber typology with those in the adapted Maranell typology shows striking results. Of our ten modern presidents from Taft to Johnson, eight are in similar psychological categories in both studies (see Table 1). Hoover and Eisenhower are the two exceptions. Barber classifies Hoover as an active-negative rather than a passive-negative (inflexible), and Eisenhower as a passive-negative rather than a passive-positive (flexible). Even in the Hoover case which is the only classification of a modern president that the two studies differ on both dimensions (activeness and affect or flexibility), the Maranell ranking scores show that historians regard Hoover as the least passive of the passive-negatives (inflexibles). Hargrove's classification of Hoover as a passive president agrees with the results of the Maranell study, and it is the only classification that does not agree with Barber.

With three agreements out of five classifications of early American presidents, the correlation between Barber's and Maranell's typologies is not as high compared to the group of modern presidents, yet Barber has only made one detailed analysis of a nineteenth century president, and that is limited to the rhetorical style of Andrew Johnson.[7] Barber briefly mentions that Washington "fits best" the passive-negative type; John Adams is an active-negative; Jefferson "was clearly" an active-positive; and Madison "comes closest" to a passive-positive.

TABLE 1
PRESIDENTIAL BEHAVIOR CLASSIFICATION SCHEMES

Hargrove (1966)[a]	Barber (1972)[b]	Maranell Adaptation[c]	
Action	*Active-Positive*	*Active-Flexible*	
T. Roosevelt	Jefferson	+2.01 F. Roosevelt	+1.31
Wilson	F. Roosevelt	+1.61 T. Roosevelt	+.186
F. Roosevelt	Truman	+1.25 Truman	+.31
Truman	Kennedy	+1.06 Kennedy	+1.61
Kennedy		+.93 Lincoln	+1.50
L. Johnson		+.91 Jefferson	+1.35
		+.44 Washington	+.57
		+.03 Madison	+.576
Restraint	*Active-Negative*	*Active-Inflexible*	
Taft	J. Adams	+1.51 Jackson	−1.40
Hoover	A. Johnson	+1.39 L. Johnson	−.47
Eisenhower	Wilson	+1.05 Wilson	−2.23
	Hoover	+.59 Polk	−.19
	L. Johnson	+.34 J. Adams	−.85
	Nixon	+.20 Cleveland	−.88
		+.12 A. Johnson	−2.18
		+.01 J. Q. Adams	−1.15
	Passive-Positive	*Passive-Flexible*	
	Madison	−.06 Monroe	+1.03
	Taft	−.16 Taft	+.01
	Harding	−.24 Van Buren	+.19
		−.34 McKinley	+.49
		−.59 Eisenhower	+1.21
		−.69 Arthur	+.18
		−.74 Hayes	+.14
		−.95 Harrison	+.186
		−1.22 Fillmore	+.27
		−1.26 Buchanan	+.01
		−1.29 Pierce	+.16
		−1.37 Grant	+.59
		−1.66 Harding	+1.17
	Passive-Negative	*Passive-Inflexible*	
	Washington	−.14 Hoover	−1.01
	Coolidge	−.56 Tyler	−1.09
	Eisenhower	−.86 Taylor	−.76
		−1.37 Coolidge	−.83

Sources and Notes:
[a] Erwin C. Hargrove, *Presidential Leadership, Personality and Political Style* (New York: MacMillan, 1966).
[b] James David Barber, *The Presidential Character, Predicting Performance in the White House* (Englewood Cliffs, N.J.; Prentice-Hall, 1972), and James David Barber, "Adult Identity and Presidential Style: The Rhetorical Emphasis," *Daedalus*, Vol. 97, No. 3 (Summer, 1968), 938-68.
[c] Adapted from Gary M. Maranell, "The Evaluation of Presidents: An Extension of the Schlesinger Polls," *Journal of American History*, Vol. 57, No. 1 (June, 1970), 109-10. Maranell's study was conducted during March, 1968, so it does not include an evaluation of Nixon. Two Presidents, William Henry Harrison and . . . Garfield, were excluded since both served less than a year in office.
The numbers to the left of each name indicate degree of activeness; a high positive score is active, a high negative score is passive. The numbers to the right of each name indicate the degree of flexibility; a high positive score is flexible, a high negative score is inflexible.

Barber's two boldest assertions classifying America's first four presidents agree with the Maranell study, but his two weaker statements regarding Washington and Madison disagree with the adapted Maranell typology which puts them into the active-positive (flexible) category. There may be some justification for considering Madison as a passive-positive, since Maranell's ranking scores show that Madison is the least active of the active-flexibles, but Washington's presence among the passive-negatives is probably due to modern views of the presidency carried over to another age, as well as Barber's lack of research on early American presidents.

Yet overall, 75 percent of Barber's 16 judgments correlate with similar categories in the adapted Maranell typology, and 80 percent of Barber's 12 detailed analyses correlate with Maranell. Only the classifications of Hoover and Washington disagree on both dimensions of activeness and affect (flexibility) in both studies. Most importantly, there seems to be a rather strong consensus among Hargrove, Barber, and Maranell concerning which presidents are the active-positives (flexibles). All twentieth century presidents in the group of active-positives (flexibles) agree in both classification schemes, and except for two of America's first four presidents (Washington and Madison), the earlier active-positives (flexibles) correlate. The high correlation between Barber's typology and the adapted Maranell typology may indicate that Barber was actually evaluating presidential flexibility-inflexibility to a greater extent than he realized.[8]

Just as Barber's analysis nearly doubled the number of presidents classified in Hargrove's study, the adaptation of the Maranell study into a rough "Barberian" typology more than doubles the number of presidents classified by Barber, so that except for Presidents William Henry Harrison and Garfield who served for less than a year, and for our last three presidents who assumed office after the study was conducted, every president is classified.[9] The strong agreement among the classification schemes makes it easier to determine if active-positive presidents are more likely to grant amnesties, and whether they grant more liberal types of amnesties than other types of presidents.

TABLE 2
COMPARISON OF PRESIDENTIAL TYPE WITH AMNESTY RECORD*

President	Amnesty	President	Amnesty
Active-Positive		*Active-Negative*	
F. Roosevelt	1	Jackson	1
T. Roosevelt	1	L. Johnson	0
Truman	4	Wilson	2
Kennedy	0	Polk	0
Lincoln	6	J. Adams	1
Jefferson	1	Cleveland	1
Washington	5	A. Johnson	9
Madison	4	J. Q. Adams	0
	(55.0%) 22		(35.0%) 14
Passive-Positive		*Passive-Negative*	
Monroe	0	Hoover	0
Taft	0	Tyler	0
Van Buren	0	Taylor	0
McKinley	0	Coolidge	1
Eisenhower	0		(2.5%) 1
Arthur	0		
Hayes	0		
Harrison	1		
Fillmore	0		
Buchanan	1		
Pierce	0		
Grant	1		
Harding	0		
	(7.5%) 3		

Sources:
* Here amnesty refers to a formal proclamation or executive order given to a group of individuals. They are found in James D. Richardson, ed., *A Compilation of the Messages and Papers of the Presidents* (New York: Bureau of National Literature, 1897), and Morris Sherman, *Amnesty in America. An Annotated Bibliography* (Passaic, New Jersey: New Jersey Library Association, 1974).

Comparison of Presidential Personality Types with Amnesties

Presidential amnesty behavior ranges from public proclamations to more private types of clemency acts. Although this study relies primarily on the number of formal amnesties granted by means of proclamation or executive order (see Table 2),[10] an additional effort was made to supplement the formal record by exploring less public presidential behavior toward the power of executive clemency. As far as can be determined, both the formal and informal behavior of presidents toward amnesty seems consistent with each other.

Approximately forty formal amnesties have been issued by American presidents. Nine have been granted in the twentieth century (excluding the Ford and Carter administrations), and thirty-one in the nineteenth and late eighteenth centuries. Thus, if the amnesties were distributed evenly among the presidents, each would have authored an amnesty, but the record shows that two presidents (Abraham Lincoln and Andrew Johnson) granted nearly 40 percent of them, while roughly half of the presidents granted no amnesties, and eleven presidents granted only one each. Yet instead of concluding that amnesty is not part of the American tradition,[11] a comparison of amnesties with the twenty presidents who have given formal and informal amnesties, suggests that amnesty is a tradition that depends on presidential character.

Not surprisingly, the sixteen active presidents (positive and negative) have granted 90 percent of the amnesties, and the eight active-positives have granted the most amnesties of the four types of presidents. Indeed, the active-positives issued more than half of all the formal amnesties, averaging nearly three per president. Only one of the eight active-positives did not issue an amnesty, and he (Kennedy) served the shortest period in office. Abraham Lincoln leads the group with six amnesties; George Washington with five; James Madison and Harry Truman with four each; and Thomas Jefferson, Theodore Roosevelt, and Franklin Roosevelt with one each.

The three other groups, even if combined together (25 presidents), granted fewer amnesties than the group of eight active-positives. The eight active-negatives with a total of 14 amnesties granted more than three times the number of amnesties of the entire group of 17 passive presidents (positive and negative). Five of the eight active-negatives granted amnesties in comparison to three of the thirteen passive-positives, and one of the four passive-negatives.

In addition to the statistics of amnesty, a closer examination of individual presidential behavior seems to also reflect the general statistical patterns. For example, while active-positives simply grant more amnesties, they also seem to show more willingness to use their clemency power in broader ways. George Washington's behavior during and after the American revolution seems to reflect this tendency of the active-positives. As early as Spring, 1775, he considered amnesty a wise policy, and by April, 1782, he recommended that Congress should pardon the Loyalists who had served with the British.[12] Although Washington did not push Congress in regards to pardoning the Loyalists, during the Whiskey Rebellion he made repeated efforts through public proclamations and empowering his negotiators to extend amnesty to the rebels. Later active-positives seem to follow in this tradition of private and public willingness to use the power of executive clemency.

The active-negatives exhibit a more extreme range of amnesty behavior in contrast to the other types of presidents, ranging from Andrew Johnson's historical record of nine amnesties to none during the administrations of John Quincy Adams, James Polk, and Lyndon Johnson.[13] Most of the amnesties of the active-negative represent special cases. For example, Wilson granted two, but one proclamation was only a clarification of an earlier one; Cleveland granted one during his second split term, but not until after passive-positive Harrison had granted the first one to the Mormons. The compulsive behavior of active-negatives is reflected in Andrew Johnson's behavior that nearly cost him his office. A tendency toward vindictiveness even in the act of clemency is sometimes noticeable in the language of amnesties granted by active-negatives. For example, even though John Adams acted against the advice of his associates in granting an amnesty to the participants in Fries Rebellion, he could not help referring to the rebels as the "ignorant, misguided, and misinformed." Similarly, active-negative Jackson refers to deserters in his proclamation as "degraded materials." This is in sharp contrast to other presidents such as active-positive George Washington, who refers to the Whiskey rebels in his amnesty as "citizens," and expresses his desire "to mingle in the operations of Government every degree of moderation and tenderness which national justice, dignity, and safety may permit."

The restrained clemency behavior of passive-positive presidents is perhaps illustrated best in the case of the Mormons and polygamy.[14] The persecution of Mormons occupies the period between the administrations of two active-positives, Abraham Lincoln and Theodore Roosevelt. The first conviction of a Mormon polygamist took place in 1875 during the Grant administration; Hayes issued the first individual pardon five years later; Arthur withheld further pardons; and then active-negative Cleveland granted 46 individual pardons during his first term in office.

Finally, Benjamin Harrison granted the first amnesty to the Mormons after two decades had elapsed, but proceeded in a typical slow passive-positive fashion. First, after he had issued one more individual pardon than Cleveland, Harrison took the unique step of granting an unconditional amnesty to one person in 1891, then retreated somewhat the next year by only granting a conditional amnesty for one person. During his last month in office, Harrison granted a regular amnesty in 1893, but not until after seeking the legal advice of his solicitor-general.[15]

Although much of the restraint shown by the passive-positives during the years after the Civil War can be traced to the excessive behavior of Andrew Johnson, later passive-positives continue to show hesitancy in using the power of executive clemency, and narrowing the scope of clemency as much as possible when it is used. For example, passive-positive McKinley acted with little public notice by granting the largest number of individual pardons to deserters up to that time in American history, rather than making a public proclamation. Even then, most of the pardons were less than full pardons.[16] Similarly, passive-positive Warren Harding, who initially favored amnesty during the 1920 presidential campaign, quickly reversed himself after detecting opposition among his more conservative supporters.[17] While in office he managed to avoid a formal amnesty by granting a number of individual pardons, and selective commutation of sentences of imprisoned World War I radicals.[18] Another case of the more private use of executive clemency by passive-positives is reflected in Eisenhower's decision not to prosecute Korean war "traitors."

Calvin Coolidge, the only passive-negative to grant an amnesty, did not act until after forming the first clemency commission whose final decision he had agreed to in advance.[19] Even this action still left other victims of World War I hysteria and oppression. Active-positive Franklin Roosevelt went against the advice of his pardon attorney by granting an amnesty to these victims during the first days of his presidency. Roosevelt's action contrasts with the behavior of passive-negative Herbert Hoover, who despite the recommendation of his pardon attorney, failed to extend clemency to World War I victims of injustice.[20] Yet Hoover's behavior is similarly reflected in the other two passive-negatives. For example, Zachary Taylor granted no amnesties, and although John Tyler privately recommended to the governor of Rhode Island to pardon the participants in Dorr's rebellion, Tyler refused further action.[21]

Amnesty and Beyond

In summary, then, there is data to support the notion that active-positives produce better clemency records than other types of presidents. The amnesty record and the evaluations of a sampling of American historians tend to support Barber's typology of presidential character. Barber's effort to sensitize the American public to patterns in presidential style, world view, and character may be further enhanced by assessing a candidate's overall degree of flexibility and inflexibility. If historians can make similar judgments about past presidents without psychological expertise, informed citizens can just as well determine a candidate's character.

Political candidates and presidents who realize they are being judged for their flexibility may even show a greater degree of concern for human rights and individual liberties than they might otherwise.[22] This may suggest which political leaders should receive the most attention by those interested in achieving the most immediate results in the area of amnesty. Of course, more research is needed on amnesty in other countries particularly, and much more needs to be known about presidential involvement in other aspects of individual liberties and human rights. It is hoped that the "Barberian" test used in this paper will contribute to better indexes for predicting presidential performance.

References

[1] Jacques Froymond, "Confronting Total War: A 'Global' Humanitarian Policy," *American Journal of International Law*, Vol. 67, No. 4 (October, 1973), 681.

[2] For example, Richard P. Longaker, *The Presidency and Individual Liberties* (Ithaca, New York: Cornell University Press, 1961).

[3] Everett S. Brown, "The Restoration of Civil and Political Rights by Presidential Pardon," *American Political Science Review*, Vol. 34, No. 2 (April, 1940), 295–300; Harry M. Scoble and Laurie S. Wiseberg, "Human Rights and Amnesty International," *The Annals*, Vol. 413 (May, 1974), 11–26; Dan W. Brock, "Amnesty and Morality," *Social Theory and Practice*, Vol. 3, No. 2 (Fall, 1974), 131–48; and Wallace D. Loh, "National Loyalties and Amnesty: A Legal and Social Psychological Analysis," *Journal of Social Issues*, Vol. 31, No. 4 (Fall, 1975), 157–170.

[4] Erwin C. Hargrove, *Presidential Leadership. Personality and Political Style* (New York: MacMillan, 1966).

[5] James David Barber, *The Presidential Character. Predicting Performance in the White House* (Englewood Cliffs, N.J.: Prentice-Hall, 1972).

[6] Gary M. Maranell, "The Evaluation of Presidents: An Extension of the Schlesinger Polls," *Journal of American History*, Vol. 57, No. 1 (June, 1970), 104–13.

[7] James David Barber, "Adult Identity and Presidential Style: The Rhetorical Emphasis," *Daedalus*, Vol. 97, No. 3 (Summer, 1968), 938–68.

[8] A part of his definition of an active-positive is "an ability to use style flexibly," and a passive-negative lacks "flexibility to perform effectively." Barber, *Presidential Character*, pp. 12–13. Barber's dimension of "positive and negative affect" (a kind of felt satisfaction index) seems to be harder to measure than flexibility. For an empirical study that claims flexibility is a necessary and sufficient condition of support for civil liberties, see Stephen Crocker, "Personality and Civil Liberties: A Re-examination and a New Model" (Unpublished Ph.D. dissertation, University of California, Berkeley, 1972).

[9] For Barber's speculation about Ford and Carter, see *U.S. News and World Report*, Vol. 77, No. 10 (September 2, 1974), p. 25; and Alan C. Elms, "Psychological Candidates," *Human Behavior*, Vol. 5, No. 10 (October, 1976), p. 28.

Hereafter Barber's nomenclature for presidential types is used in place of the terms flexible and inflexible, because of the high correlation between the Barber and Maranell typologies, and in order to avoid confusion of new names.

10 The text of most amnesty proclamations may be found in James D. Richardson, ed., *A Compilation of the Messages and Papers of the Presidents* (New York: Bureau of National Literature, 1897). The first comprehensive effort to determine the number of presidential amnesties is John C. Etridge, *Amnesty: A Brief Historical Overview* (Washington, D.C.: Library of Congress, Legislative Reference Service, 1972). Nearly every legal analysis of the amnesty issue for Vietnam war resisters has used the Etridge study, but it is incomplete. For example, it neglects amnesties granted by Buchanan and Grant, as well as the informal McKinley "amnesty." It also distorts the total number of amnesties granted by each president.

For the most useful bibliographies on amnesty, see Morris Sherman, *Amnesty in America. An Annotated Bibliography* (Passaic, New Jersey: New Jersey Library Association, 1974); and David Lamkin, *The "Amnesty" Issue and Conscientious Objection. A Selected Bibliography* (Los Angeles: Center for the Study of Armament and Disarmament, California State University, 1974).

11 William A. Rusher, "Amnesty? Never!," in Arlie Schardt, William A. Rusher, and Mark O. Hatfield, *Amnesty? The Unsettled Question of Vietnam* (Lawrence, Mass.: Sun River Press, 1973), p. 57.

12 Wilbert H. Siebert, "George Washington and the Loyalists," *American Antiquarian Society Proceedings*, New Series, Vol. 43; Pt. 1 (April 19, 1933), 47–48.

13 In fact, during Lyndon Johnson's last year in office and Richard Nixon's first year, the two active-negatives "set some sort of modern (at least) record for non-clemency" by denying requests for pardons, and granting no pardons or commutation of prison sentences. Glendon Schubert, *Judicial Policy Making* (Glenview, Ill.: Scott, Foreman and Co., 1974), pp. 63–64.

14 The amnesty record of the presidency relating to Mormons and polygamy is found in U.S. Department of Justice, *Annual Reports of the Attorney General of the United States* (Washington, D.C.: Government Printing Office, 1870–1894).

15 William Howard Taft, "Amnesty. Power of the President," *Official Opinions of the Attorney General, 1894–1895*, Vol. 20 (Washington, D.C.: Government Printing Office, 1895), 330–45.

16 U.S. Department of Justice, *Annual Report of the Attorney General of the United States* (Washington, D.C.: Government Printing Office, 1898), p. 190.

17 Horace C. Peterson and Gilbert C. Fite, *Opponents of War 1917–1918* (Madison: University of Wisconsin Press, 1957), pp. 273–74.

18 William Preston, Jr., *Aliens and Dissenters: Federal Suppression of Radicals, 1903–1933* (Cambridge: Harvard University Press, 1963), pp. 259–61.

[19] *Ibid.*, pp. 265–66.

[20] *Ibid.*, pp. 271–72.

[21] Bennett M. Rich, *The Presidents and Civil Disorder* (Washington, D.C.: The Brookings Institution, 1941), p. 58.

[22] Especially President Carter whose favorite political text is Barber's *Presidential Character*. Walt Anderson "Looking for Mr. Active-Positive," *Human Behavior*, Vol. 5, No. 10 (October, 1976), p. 20.

Bibliography

Anderson, Walt. "Looking for Mr. Active-Positive." *Human Behavior*, Vol. 5, No. 10 (October, 1976), 16–21.

Barber, James, David. "Adult Identity and Presidential Style: The Rhetorical Emphasis." *Daedalus*, Vol. 97, No. 3 (Summer, 1968), 938–68.

——. *The Presidential Character. Predicting Performance in the White House.* Englewood Cliffs, N.J.: Prentice-Hall, 1972.

——. "Some Strategies for Understanding Politicians." *American Journal of Political Science*, Vol. 18, No. 2 (May, 1974), 443–67.

Brock, Dan W. "Amnesty and Morality." *Social Theory and Practice*, Vol. 3, No. 2 (Fall, 1974), 131–48.

Brown, Everett S. "The Restoration of Civil and Political Rights by Presidential Pardon." *American Political Science Review*, Vol. 34, No. 2 (April, 1940), 295–300.

Crocker, Stephen. "Personality and Civil Liberties: A Re-examination and a New Model." Unpublished Ph.D. dissertation, University of California, Berkeley, 1972.

Dolan, Edward F., Jr. *Amnesty. The American Puzzle.* New York: Franklin Watts, 1976.

Donley, Richard E. and David G. Winter. "Measuring Motives of Public Officials at a Distance: An Exploratory Study of American Presidents." *Behavioral Science*, Vol. 15, No. 3 (May, 1970), 227–36.

Dorris, Jonathan T. *Pardon and Amnesty under Lincoln and Johnson. The Restoration of the Confederates to Their Rights and Privileges, 1861–1898.* Chapel Hill: University of North Carolina Press, 1953).

Elms, Alan C. "Psychological Candidates." *Human Behavior*, Vol. 5, No. 10 (October, 1976), 25–28.

Etheredge, Lloyd S. "Personality and Foreign Policy: Bullies in the State Department." *Psychology Today*, Vol. 8, No. 10 (March, 1975), 37–43.

Etridge, John C. *Amnesty: A Brief Historical Overview.* Washington, D.C.: Library of Congress, Legislative Reference Service, 1972.

Freymond, Jacques. "Confronting Total War: A 'Global' Humanitarian Policy." *American Journal of International Law*, Vol. 67, No. 4 (October, 1973), 672–92.

Friedlander, Saul and Raymond Cohen. "The Personality Correlates of Belligerence in International Conflict," *Comparative Politics*, Vol. 7, No. 2 (January, 1975), 155–86.

Fund for New Priorities in America. *Amnesty. An Unresolved National Question*. New York: Fund for New Priorities in America, 1976.

George, Alexander L. "Assessing Presidential Character." *World Politics*, Vol. 26, No. 2 (January, 1974), 234–82.

Habibuddin, Syed M. "Theodore Roosevelt's Attitude Toward Civil Rights and Civil Liberties." Unpublished Ph.D. dissertation, University of Pennsylvania, 1968.

Hargrove, Erwin C. "Presidential Personality and Revisionist Views of the Presidency." *American Journal of Political Science*, Vol. 17, No. 4 (November, 1973), 819–35.

———. *Presidential Leadership. Personality and Political Style*. New York: MacMillan Company, 1966.

Humbert, W. H. *The Pardoning Power of the President*. Washington, D.C.: American Council on Public Affairs, 1941.

Kirchheimer, Otto. "The Quality of Mercy On the Role of Clemency in the Apparatus of Justice." *Social Research*, Vol. 28 (Summer, 1961), 151–70.

Lamkin, David. *The "Amnesty" Issue and Conscientious Objection. A Selected Bibliography*. Los Angeles: Center for the Study of Armament and Disarmament, California State University, 1974.

Levy, Leonard W. *Jefferson and Civil Liberties. The Darker Side*. Cambridge: Belknap Press, 1963.

Loh, Wallace D. "National Loyalties and Amnesty: A Legal and Social Psychological Analysis." *Journal of Social Issues*, Vol. 31, No. 4 (Fall, 1975), 157–70.

Longaker, Richard P. *The Presidency and Individual Liberties*, Ithaca, New York: Cornell University Press, 1961.

Maranell, Gary M. "The Evaluation of Presidents: An Extension of the Schlesinger Polls." *Journal of American History*, Vol. 57, No. 1 (June, 1970), 104–13.

———, and Richard A. Dodder. "Political Orientation and the Evaluation of Presidential Prestige: A Study of American Historians." *Social Science Quarterly*, Vol. 51, No. 2 (September, 1970), 415–21.

McClelland, David C. "Love and Power: The Psychological Signals of War." *Psychology Today*, Vol. 8, No. 8 (January, 1975), 44–48.

Peterson, Horace C. and Gilbert C. Fite. *Opponents of War, 1917–1918*. Madison: University of Wisconsin Press, 1957.

Preston, William, Jr. *Aliens and Dissenters: Federal Suppression of Radicals, 1903–1933*. Cambridge: Harvard University Press, 1963.

Rich, Bennett M. *The Presidents and Civil Disorder*. Washington, D.C.: The Brookings Institution, 1941.

Richardson, James D., ed. *A Compilation of the Messages and Papers of the Presidents*. New York: Bureau of National Literature, 1897.

Schardt, Arlie, William A. Rusher, and Mark O. Hatfield. *Amnesty? The Unsettled Question of Vietnam*. Lawrence, Mass.: Sun River Press, 1973.

Scheiber, Harry N. *The Wilson Administration and Civil Liberties, 1917–1921*. Ithaca, New York: Cornell University Press, 1960.

Schubert, Glendon. *Judicial Policy Making. The Political Role of the Courts*. Glenview, Ill.: Scott, Foreman, and Company, 1974.

Scoble, Harry M. and Laurie S. Wiseberg. "Human Rights and Amnesty International." *The Annals*, Vol. 413 (May, 1974), 11–26.

Sherman, Morris. *Amnesty in America. An Annotated Bibliography*. Passaic, N.J.: New Jersey Library Association, 1974.

Siebert, W. H. "George Washington and the Loyalists." *American Antiquarian Society Proceedings*, New Series, Vol. 43, Pt. 1 (April 1933), 34–48.

Taft, William H. "Amnesty, Power of the President." *Official Opinions of the Attorney General, 1894–1895*. Vol. 20, Washington, D.C.: Government Printing Office, 1895.

U.S. Department of Justice. *Annual Reports of the Attorney General of the United States*. Washington, D.C.: Government Printing Office, 1870–1970.

U.S. News and World Report. "Ford: Will He Turn Tough? Analysis by James David Barber." Vol. 77, No. 10 (September 2, 1974), 22–25.

Westin, Alan F. and Trudy Hayden. "Presidents and Civil Liberties from FDR to Ford: A Rating by 64 Experts." *The Civil Liberties Review*, Vol. 3, No. 4 (October-November, 1976), 9–32.

Winter, David G. "What Makes the Candidates Run." *Psychology Today*, Vol. 10, No. 2 (July, 1976), 45–49ff.

8

The President and the White House Staff

William D. Pederson and Stephen N. Williams

Although members of the White House Office do not normally receive the same degree of publicity as cabinet officers and congressmen, they sometimes exert more influence in the government than nearly anyone apart from the President himself. Indeed, on occasion key White House assistants become substitute Presidents! The most important members of the White House staff are typically drawn from the dozen or so senior political advisers to the President known today as the "inner circle," but who in the past were called "the kitchen cabinet," "the tennis cabinet," "the poker cabinet," and "the brain trust." Although membership in this exclusive circle depends on each President, it usually includes individuals such as the White House chief of staff, the assistant for national security affairs, the assistant for domestic affairs, the White House counsel, the appointments secretary, the assistant for legislative affairs, the press secretary, and the assistant for public relations, whom Garry Trudeau has more accurately dubbed "the Secretary of Symbolism."

The White House Office is a development of the modern presidency that grew out of the Second World War. In 1936, Franklin Roosevelt created the President's Committee on Administrative Management headed by Louis Brownlow, a successful city manager, to study the problem of presidential assistance. The following year the Brownlow Committee issued its report that concluded with the words "the President needs help." The Congress subsequently passed the Reorganization Act of 1939 which created the Executive Office of the President, the general managerial arm of the modern presidency.

The White House Office needs to be distinguished from the larger Executive Office of the President. The latter includes several thousand employees who are housed in two large office buildings near the White House, while the former includes several hundred employees located on the ground floor and in the basement of the White House. The "inner circle" is usually composed of the assistants who occupy the offices nearest the President's Oval Office. Its members are among the most powerful bureaucrats of the five million employees who make up the executive branch of the United States.

The White House Office is organized as the President wants. He appoints his staff without Senate approval. While serving him, they are not subject to congressional interrogation, and they are assigned and removed at his pleasure. Flexibility is the major structural characterization of the White House Office, particularly as shown in its expansion and organization.

Presidents have always felt quite independent in staffing the White House. George Washington took the initiative to hire an aide at his own expense after the Congress refused to provide him secretarial assistance. Subsequent Presidents continued the practice until Andrew Jackson broke the tradition by "borrowing" a bureaucrat from one of the departments to work for him in the White House at government expense. The Jacksonian precedent continues in the modern presidency as an ordinary practice. Although federal law limited the number of assistants to fourteen, for more than forty years Presidents were using hundreds of employees in the White House until the Congress finally legalized a vastly enlarged staff during the Carter administration.

In a sense, the recurrent problems associated with the modern presidency are related to the phenomenal increase in the size of the White House Office. Although the Brownlow Committee called for six presidential assistants, the number reached more

than six hundred full-time employees during the Nixon administration. A White House bureaucracy has been created which
stands between the President and the departments. Flexibility in
its size and organization has created dangers. The "plumbers"
unit, which conducted wiretaps and burglaries, was established
in the Nixon White House to plug alleged national security
"leaks." Less alarming, but illustrative of the structural flexibility in the White House, was Rosalyn Carter's appointment of
a chief of staff for the First Lady when her staff expanded to
more than twenty persons.

Three persistent problems remain in the White House which
have not been solved by the expansion of the White House staff:
(1) loyalty, (2) centralization, and (3) external relations. In order
to understand each of these problem areas, it is necessary to
understand how the personalities involved with the White House
Office interact with each other.

The Problems of Excessive Loyalty: Palace Guard Politics

Although the White House Office allows for flexibility in terms
of expansion and organization, there are a number of factors
which push it toward rigidity and isolation. Woodrow Wilson
believed the American political system, with its numerous
checks and balances, cuts the President off from the support of
the cabinet, the Congress, and political parties. Presidents
inevitably turn toward their "inner circle" for ego support,
particularly during times of crisis. As will be shown, presidential
aides have a similar tendency to become dependent on their
boss. The most dangerous problem of the modern presidency
concerns the excessive mutual dependence that develops between Presidents and their aides. The personalities of "the inner
circle" and the President become crucial in determining the
degree of isolation of the Oval Office from outsiders.

The mutual dependence of Presidents and their aides is often
strengthened by the "marginality" of both. Marginal persons
leave their old ties behind and establish new ones to achieve
greater success. They do not feel that they fully belong in their

new surroundings, but cannot return to their old ones. They develop a strong need for approval and acceptance, and place great value on loyalty and conformity (James C. Davies, *Human Nature in Politics*, John Wiley, 1963).

Presidents and their aides have risen to the top of American political life. Once in Washington, however, they often feel alienated from what they perceive to be the reigning "Washington Establishment." This reaction was extremely strong with Richard Nixon and his conservative West Coast aides. But the same reaction has characterized all recent Presidents to some degree including President Carter and his Georgian staff. Thus, even Presidents and their aides may feel a lack of "belongingness" in Washington, and retreat behind a shield of excessive loyalty and conformity.

In selecting their staff, Presidents usually seek out likeminded men. Patricia Florestano has presented evidence indicating that no matter who is President, certain background characteristics are preferred in White House aides. Presidents apparently feel more comfortable with aides who are middle-age or younger, white males (96 percent), college educated (86 percent) in private schools (58 percent), and recruited from the private sector (60 percent) while working on the East Coast (77 percent).

The preferences of individual Presidents become more specific. John Kennedy liked football players and World War II veterans and Richard Nixon favored nonpracticing lawyers and military men. Six of the seven highest aides in the original Carter administration came from Georgia, so that the press tagged it "the Georgia Mafia," in the tradition of "the Missouri Gang" during the Truman administration, and "the Irish Mafia" during the Kennedy administration.

If the process of presidential selection of aides often leads to excessive conformity and loyalty, the needs of the aides themselves strongly reinforce these qualities in the form of submission to the President. The overriding need of the White House staffer is to keep his or her job. Submission, therefore, is hardly surprising in view of the fact that presidential assistants owe their jobs completely to one person. For many, their entire professional association has revolved around the career of the politician they serve in the Oval Office. Moreover, the awe of that office, if not the individual himself, encourages deference. These factors work together to produce submissive assistants who obey the President without question.

Submissiveness is often shown by an aide's attempt to make himself over in the likeness of the President. For example, William Loeb, Jr., the lower-class top aide to Theodore Roosevelt, began wearing pince-nez spectacles, a mustache and the same hair style as the President. Although reserved by nature, he adopted Roosevelt's assertiveness in the White House; although a high school drop out, he adopted Roosevelt's reading habits; and although in poor physical shape initially, he became more athletic. He wanted to be Roosevelt! More recently, Theodore Sorenson, John Kennedy's top aide, displayed similar behavior. Although a native of Nebraska, he began speaking with a Boston accent, and adopted so many of Kennedy's gestures and other mannerisms that he was able to receive White House calls by impersonating the President.

A dilemma for White House aides is learning how to conform and be submissive, yet at the same time be noticed and promoted by the President. Too great a show of independence can lead to certain demotion. Aides, therefore, are often reduced to gimmicks or subterfuges to achieve their ends.

Gaining proximity to the President's Oval Office, for example, becomes very important. Daniel Moynihan clearly recognized this during the Nixon administration when he gave up the chance for a spacious office in the Old Executive Office Building next door to the White House for a tiny office in the White House basement. Similarly, assistants realize they have fallen from grace when they lose their ground floor offices in a transfer to the basement, the fate of Midge Costanza, a public liaison assistant, before leaving the Carter White House.

Presidential assistants may also try to prove their worth by the size of their personal staffs, a factor contributing to the expansion of the modern presidency. But the primary means to prove one's loyalty is through the use of flattery and "brown-nosing."

Longevity in the White House Office often seems to require nearness to the President when good news is announced and one's absence when bad news breaks. Unpleasant thoughts uttered in the proximity of some Presidents become taboo. For a President whose primary value is loyalty, this is the ideal setting to become captured by one's staff. Rather than receiving an accurate portrayal of reality, such a President encourages his own isolation by keeping aides around him who promote the imaginary view of the world.

The sort of aide who might save a President from this folly is unlikely to get into the Oval Office. Thus, what has been called the "selection-submission-subterfuge system" used to staff the modern presidency promotes excessive loyalty and isolation. With no outside references, the President becomes a prisoner of his staff. President Johnson could not understand why young people identified with Dustin Hoffman in "The Graduate." Richard Nixon could not understand "the bums" who protested against his Vietnam policy. Both Presidents turned the White House into a bunker staffed with clean-cut clones of themselves. Crisis situations further intensify the demand for loyalty among aides. Even if Presidents use outside advisers, the tendency is to ignore their advice. For example, President Nixon publicly refuted the findings of both the National Commission on Obscenity and Pornography and the National Commission on Drug Abuse.

Centralization: A Matter of Organization and Presidential Personality

In every presidency, there are powerful forces encouraging submissiveness and conformity among members of the President's staff. The organizational structure of the White House, however, can either undergird these forces or act as a counterweight against them. There are two contrasting models of staff organization. The first is represented by Franklin Roosevelt's decentralized staff. It is an informal, unstructured, subordinate-centered model that tends to encourage competition, tension, and dissent in decision making. The second is Dwight Eisenhower's highly centralized model. It is structured like a pyramid. Rather than reporting directly to the President, most assistants report through a formal hierarchy to a chief of staff who then deals with the President. It is a boss-centered model that discourages open conflict.

Franklin Roosevelt acted as his own White House chief of staff. He surrounded himself with generalists rather than specialists in order to avoid dependence on a single source of information. John Kennedy's staff organization maximized the benefits of the decentralized model. Emphasis was placed on increasing the President's sources of information and obtaining opinions different from his own. Assistants received equal consideration so that a minimum of filtering of communication occurred. The main difference between the two administrations from a staffing perspective was that Roosevelt introduced greater competition among his aides than Kennedy. For example, Franklin Roosevelt once remarked, "There is something to be said for having a little conflict between agencies. A little rivalry is stimulating you know. It keeps everybody going to prove that he is a better fellow than the next man. It keeps them honest too" (Arthur M. Schlesinger, Jr., *The Age of Roosevelt*, Houghton Mifflin, 1958, p. 535). Although some viewed the Roosevelt White House as utter chaos, the system was intended to give the maximum amount of information to the President.

The greatest similarity between the Roosevelt and Kennedy administrations was the accent on equality within the White House, which is at the heart of the decentralized model. This emphasis was most clearly present in the Kennedy administration. With a person-centered orientation, John Kennedy was sensitive to those who worked for him and was able to convey his respect for them. Theodore Sorenson, Kennedy's most influential aide, recalls, "There was a rapport between the President and his staff. He was informal without being chummy, hard-driving but easy-mannered, interested in us as people without being patronizing. He treated us more as colleagues or associates than employees" (Theodore Sorenson, *Kennedy*, Harper and Row, 1965, p. 41).

Kennedy's preference for an atmosphere of equality among his advisers was reflected in his restrictions on protocol during decision making. The President learned an important lesson about the dangers of protocol early in his term. In a meeting of the National Security Council during the planning of the Bay of Pigs fiasco, Chester Bowles was prevented from voicing his strong objection to the invasion plan. At the time, Bowles was an under secretary of state filling in for the secretary of state. Protocol required silence for those "filling in" unless called on to speak. Bowles was not called upon.

After the Bay of Pigs fiasco, Kennedy decided to overcome the restrictions that protocol placed on his advisers. To encourage dialogue and dissent, he set up an office in the State Department, known as the Operations Center, where his top advisers could meet without the President and engage in dialogue as equals. This new system was tested a year later during the Cuban Missile crisis. Theodore Sorenson captures the spirit of the change:

> . . . one of the remarkable aspects of those meetings was a sense of complete equality. Protocol mattered little when the nation's life was a stake. Experience mattered little in crisis that had no precedent. . . . We were fifteen individuals on our own, representing the President and not different departments. Assistant Secretaries differed vigorously with their Secretaries. I participated much more freely than I ever had in a NSC [National Security Council] meeting; and the absence of the President encouraged everybody to speak his mind (Theodore Sorenson, *Kennedy*, Harper and Row, 1965, p. 679).

Apparently, Kennedy had sensed some of the loyalty problems of the modern presidency. He purposely was absent from some of the meetings in order to encourage dissent. Respected outsiders were invited to attend the meetings for the same reason. A robust debate followed that gave the President carefully considered alternatives for dealing with the crisis.

In addition to feeling he did not need to be the center of every discussion, Kennedy was able to tolerate the public recognition of his senior aides. For example, rather than reacting angrily to the press notice of McGeorge Bundy's important role as his national security adviser, Kennedy commented dryly, "I will continue to have some residual function." In a similar vein, during his first official trip to Paris he introduced himself as the husband of Jacqueline Kennedy, rather than as President of the United States.

In contrast to Roosevelt and Kennedy, the Eisenhower staffing system was highly centralized along elitist lines. President Eisenhower carried his military backgound into the Oval Office by instituting a vertical chain of command in the White House. The formality of the staffing system was suggested by the fact that his top aide was designated the first White House "chief of staff," rather than the "secretary to the President" as the post was called during the first half of the twentieth century, or the even less impressive title of "President's private secretary" as the post was called in the nineteenth century. Sherman Adams, the chief of staff during most of the Eisenhower administration, became the most powerful man next to the President. Adams handed out assignments himself, as well as deciding who and what would gain entry to the Oval Office. This suggests a built-in flaw of the centralized elitist model; its tendency to isolate the President from a variety of sources of information.

The Nixon administration carried the Eisenhower model to its logical extreme, and in the process revealed its major limitations and inherent dangers. H. R. Haldeman, Nixon's chief of staff, also controlled everybody and everything that went into the Oval Office. If a staff member attempted to circumvent the system, or go beyond his specific role, he was severely reprimanded. For example, Jeb Magruder found this out after he proposed a new idea in a memo and forwarded it to Haldeman for the President to read. The chief of staff immediately stopped the memo in his office, and quickly returned it with the abrupt comment, "Your job is to do, not to think" (Lewis Paper, *The Promise and the Performance*, Crown: 1975, p. 120).

The strong emphasis placed on order and division of labor in the elitist organization hinders dialogue. If reports and memos were to have any chance of gaining the attention of President Eisenhower, they had to be no longer than one page. Similarly, if ideas were to have any chance of penetrating the Oval Office during the Nixon administration, they had to be put on paper. President Nixon disliked dialogue and refused to engage in the give and take that is characteristic between a President and his aides in a decentralized system.

A formal chain of command and protocol discourages conflict in a staffing system. Yet a President's personality can be just as oppressive as these structural devices for maintaining order. For example, Lyndon Johnson's staffing system illustrates its kinship with the centralized-elitist model. Rather than relying on a permanent chief of staff, he used his domineering personality to exert control over the smallest matters during his administration; rather than letting his staff have some access to the media, he alone dealt with the press; and rather than establishing rapport with his assistants he kept them continually off guard, thereby creating "an atmosphere of permanent intimidation" (Doris Kearns, *Lyndon Johnson and the American Dream*, Harper and Row, 1976, pp. 238–242).

A former presidential assistant during these years aptly captures the master-serf relationship that Johnson's personality established in the White House:

> The President would berate his aides in lashing language. Sometimes he did this collectively, as when he exploded at three of them in his office, "How can you be so goddamn stupid! Why can't I get men with the brains of the Kennedy bunch?" More often, he would turn on a single staff member. On a number of occasions I saw an aide emerge from a presidential session white-faced and shaking, swearing that he could not stand it another day. (Eric F. Goldman, *The Tragedy of Lyndon Johnson*, Knopf, 1969, pp. 120–121.)

Johnson used his intimidating personality to stifle dissent. He had an obsession for making decisions by consensus in his dominating presence. As in the Nixon administration, those who challenged policies during the Johnson administration were let go or lost access to the President. Such Presidents view others as objects rather than as equals. Both administrations erred in an attempt not just to maintain order, but to assert absolute control over subordinates.

The ever-expanding size of bureaucracy and the desire of Presidents to govern their administrations has led the modern presidency in the direction of centralization. Although there seems to be a near ritual requiring new Presidents to voice a desire to return to a decentralized staffing model, most recent Presidents have inevitably discovered the need for hierarchy. For example, both Gerald Ford and Jimmy Carter stressed at the outset of their administrations that they intended to have decentralized staff systems to avoid the pitfalls of the Nixon administration. Both discovered that a great deal of confusion and chaos resulted from their attempts at decentralization. Finally, both moved to centralize their staff organizations, but not to the same degree as had Presidents Eisenhower and Nixon.

It is probable that if Franklin Roosevelt were faced with the huge executive bureaucracy of today, he would be forced to adopt a more centralized system than he used in the 1930s. The lesson of the Ford and Carter presidencies would seem to be that time and efficiency require some hierarchy in a large bureaucracy, such as the modern presidency. The problem is to have enough order to avoid chaos, without so much order as to turn aides into obedient serfs.

There is some evidence that psychologically healthy Presidents are best able to achieve the balance between centralized and decentralized staff systems that is needed in providing leadership for the modern presidency. James David Barber has classified Franklin Roosevelt, Harry Truman, John Kennedy, Gerald Ford, and Jimmy Carter, as the healthiest Presidents of the modern presidency, based largely on their high degree of self-esteem and flexibility, in contrast to the lower self-esteem and greater inflexibility of Dwight Eisenhower, Lyndon Johnson, and Richard Nixon. There is also evidence to suggest that the elitist staff systems required by Presidents with relatively low self-esteem contribute to low morale among White House staffers. The highest turnover rate among the staffs of recent presidents occurred in the Johnson and Nixon administrations, suggesting greater employee dissatisfaction working under an elitist system. The only two dissmissals of chiefs of staff because of scandals (Sherman Adams and H. R. Haldeman), also occurred in elitist staff systems. Moreover, the President and the two chiefs of staff who subjected their aides to the worst personal abuse (Lyndon Johnson, Sherman Adams, Eisenhower's chief of staff, and H. R. Haldeman), operated similar systems.

On the other hand, our healthiest Presidents seem better able to attract the most gifted aides, for example, the cases of Franklin Roosevelt and Harry Hopkins, John Kennedy and Theodore Sorenson, and Gerald Ford and Richard Cheney. Surely the most important aide of the entire postwar presidency, in terms of positive contributions to a number of Presidents, has been Clark Clifford, who began as special counsel to Harry Truman. The Truman-Clifford association, based on equality and mutual respect, represents a model of the type of relationship that is possible in a relatively decentralized staffing system.

It is difficult, at the conclusion of one four-year term, to state with certainty whether Jimmy Carter's White House staff conforms more closely to a highly centralized, or to a less centralized pattern of staff organization.

Carter initially vowed to avoid a hierarchical, highly centralized system. Yet James Fallows, chief White House speechwriter during President Carter's first two years in office, complained that the White House staff was, first and foremost, an entrenched hierarchy. He observed that everyone in Carter's White House had a fixed place "from God and the angels, through kings, noblemen, and serfs, down to animals, plants, and stones. . . ."

Fallows also observed among Carter's White House staffers the low morale often found in highly centralized staff systems. He agreed with journalist Jeff Greenfield's characterization of the Carter team as "the President's Sad Young Men." (Fallows, *Atlantic Monthly*, June 1979, pp. 76, 79.)

Although James David Barber has classified Jimmy Carter as

a modern President possessing high self-esteem in marked contrast to others such as Johnson and Nixon, there has been a great deal of skepticism about this assessment of Carter. Professor Fred I. Greenstein, for example, spoke for many political observers when he stated that beneath Carter's great composure "is a personal lack of confidence in being able to do the job" (*National Journal*, July 28, 1979, p. 1239). James Fallows similarly observed in Jimmy Carter an "insecurity at the core of his mind and soul." (*Atlantic Monthly*, May 1979, p. 46). There is no doubt that Carter sincerely wanted at the outset of his presidency to avoid the pitfalls of excessive hierarchy and centralization in his White House staff organization. But it may well be that he lacked the high self-esteem necessary, not only to live with, but to effectively manage the conflicts and discomforts which are a natural product of less centralized and less hierarchical staff systems.

External Relations: Building Bridges or Barricades?

The "insiders" within the White House Office who are closest to the President's Oval Office have experienced a variety of problems with those outside of it during the modern presidency. In fact, these problems have spread from the traditional critics of administrations, such as members of the Congress and the media, to those within "the President's branch of government," particularly in the executive departments. Presidential assistants in the White House "inner circle" have increasingly come to view themselves as an extension of the President's personality whose proper role is to guard him and his policies from outsiders who might have priorities different from those of the President. As a result, mutual tensions are generated between insiders and outsiders that may develop into a rivalry or even a hostile relationship.

There are structural factors in the modern presidency that contribute to these difficulties. The expansion of the White House Office from a staff of forty-five during Franklin Roosevelt's administration to an impersonal bureaucracy of more than five hundred full-time employees during recent administrations, inevitably fuels suspicions between the insiders and outsiders. White House staffers tend to be young amateurs devoted to the success of a single individual in the Oval Office, in contrast to the older, more established professionals in the cabinet and the Congress who are dependent on a variety of sources for their success. Furthermore, the insiders tend to think and work within a relatively short time frame of four to eight years, while the outsiders are more likely to have a much different perspective since they are likely to be in Washington longer than one or two persidential terms.

A bureaucracy inside the White House encourages the President to challenge and perhaps even dominate the views of outsiders much more readily than in the past. This adds to the suspicions of those who have lost in the power shift as policymaking has moved from the departments to the White House during the modern presidency. For example, relations between the State Department and the White House ebbed during the Nixon administration when he turned his national security adviser, Henry Kissinger, into the de facto secretary of state who made American foreign policy. Secretary of State William Rogers was often kept in the dark regarding policy changes until after Kissinger had made the decisions. Foreign service officers in the State Department became flunkies in the policymaking process.

This departure from the traditional role of the State Department in the formulation of foreign policy spread further suspicions to the Congress which had no power to confirm, and lost its power to question the new White House policymakers. President Nixon refused to permit any of his insiders to testify before the Congress. This was the first time a President established an absolute prohibition against testifying under the guise of executive privilege, a customary practice used by Presidents to withhold information from the Congress regarding activities within the executive branch of government. Congress clearly was threatened with losing much of its investigatory power under Nixon's policy.

Presidents have the choice to increase or decrease the suspicions that have developed in the modern presidency by the tone they set for their administrations. Generally, the personalities of Presidents seem to influence the degree to which they are willing to build bridges to outsiders or construct barricades around the White House. As policymaking has moved into the White House, healthy Presidents are most likely to recognize the need for personal negotiation and compromise with outsiders, as well as the necessity of tension and conflict in democratic politics.

The political styles of Richard Nixon and John Kennedy, particularly in their dealings with cabinet officers, suggest the difference between psychologically healthy and unhealthy Presidents. A clear pattern of closure emerged during the Nixon administration. For example, he began his administration with a 1968 television extravaganza promoting the virtues of each of his cabinet members, but four years later ended up collectively emasuclating them during a mandatory mass resignation ritual. A suspicious President wanted to purge those whom he saw as disloyal department heads. Nixon's treatment of his cabinet officers is also suggested by his lack of personal contacts with the majority of them. For example, Walter J. Hickel, secretary of the interior, complained in 1970 that he had seen the President only twice during his sixteen months in office. Rather than personally negotiating with outsiders, Nixon spent more than sixty percent of his time alone with H. R. Haldeman, his chief of staff (John Kessel, *The Domestic Presidency*, Duxbury, 1975, p. 114).

In contrast to Nixon's penchant to control outsiders from behind "the Berlin Wall" around the White House, Kennedy continually looked outside the government for advice and was sensitive to the needs of the departments and other outsiders. Indeed, he tried to make outsiders feel like insiders. For example, although he appointed a powerful national security adviser in the White House, he also involved his secretary of state in policy development. Kennedy allowed greater independence for his cabinet officers who were allowed to run their departments on their own. He allowed his secretary of defense to fill all the important positions in the Pentagon with his own men. Rather than relying on a chief of staff to shield him from cabinet members, Kennedy acted as his own chief of staff and allowed a high degree of personal access to cabinet members. The differences in the Nixon and Kennedy treatment of cabinet members are indicative of how they generally handled other outsiders, such as members of the Congress and the news media.

At the outset of his presidency, Jimmy Carter veered sharply from the Kennedy pattern toward the Nixon pattern of dealing with his cabinet. During his first months in office, he seemed determined that his cabinet members be treated like true insiders and have the power of insiders. He vowed that during his presidency, there would never be an instance where members of his White House staff would dominate or act superior to the members of his cabinet.

By the spring of 1978, however, President Carter had clearly become less trustful of the loyalty of his cabinet members. He therefore shifted the balance of power away from them toward the trusted members of his White House staff.

Then in July of 1979, the most dramatic and sudden shift of power occurred. Carter asked for the resignations of all his cabinet members and accepted almost half of them. The inner group of White House staffers, sometimes called "the Georgia mafia," emerged untouched and dominant after the great cabinet shakeup.

Carter's sudden and massive move against his cabinet was more reminiscent of Nixon's approach to "outsiders" in his administration than Kennedy's. *Newsweek* magazine noted that the danger in the sudden "purge" of cabinet members was that it might produce "a garrison mood" in the Carter White House in which "dissent is perceived as disloyalty and the whisper of the [White House] courtiers is mistaken for the voice of America." (*Newsweek*, July 30, 1979, p. 28.)

Fundamentally, a President sets the mood for his adminsitration in its dealings with outsiders. Because healthy Presidents have flexible personalities, their personal relationships with insiders and outsiders are likely to promote understanding.

Robert Kennedy's account of the Cuban missile crisis captures an essential characteristic of his brother's personality:

> The final lesson of the Cuban missile crisis is the importance of placing ourselves in the other country's shoes. During the crisis, President Kennedy spent more time trying to determine the effect of a particular course of action on Khrushchev or the Russians than any other phase of what he was doing. What guided all his deliberations was an effort not to disgrace Khrushchev, not to humiliate the Soviet Union, not to have them feel they would have to escalate their response because their national security or national interests so committed them. (Robert Kennedy, *Thirteen Days*, Norton, 1968, p. 102.)

Flexible personalities tend to have the empathetic skills that are necessary for democratic politics. Kennedy's ability to empathize, even with his opponents abroad during a crisis, sharply contrasts with Nixon's treatment of his opponents at home: "One day we will get them—we'll get them on the ground where we want them. And we'll stick our heels in, step on them, crush them, show no mercy." (Charles Colson, *Born Again*, Chosen Books, 1976, p. 72.) The mood that Richard Nixon set for his administration is eerily reminiscent of George Orwell's *1984*, "If you want a picture of the future, imagine a boot stamping on a human face—forever."

Some Tentative Conclusions

The three main problems of the modern presidency in relation to staffing are linked to the phenomenal growth in the White House Office. The loyalty problem arises out of the tendency of individuals to associate with persons like themselves. The pressures of the White House reinforce this tendency to such an extent that Presidents may end up talking to themselves. A possible solution to the loyalty problem is to use a decentralized staffing system, yet there seems to be an inevitable need for hierarchy in large organizations. The trend toward centralization is complicated by the fact that Presidents use the type of staff system that best fits their personalities. Unfortunately, the least healthy personalities select systems that further isolate them from political reality. Finally, the problem of establishing and maintaining successful relationships with outsiders has become more difficult as policymaking has been moved into the White House bureaucracy, but once again, it seems that the personality of the President and his empathetic skills strongly influence the relationships that are likely to emerge.

Suggested Readings

The standard works on White House staffing include Patrick Anderson, *The President's Men* (Garden City, New York: Doubleday, 1968); Richard T. Johnson, *Managing the White House* (New York: Harper and Row, 1974); and Stephen Hess, *Organizing the Presidency* (Washington, D.C.: Brookings Institution, 1976.) A fascinating new work is Michael Medved, *The Shadow Presidents* (New York: Times Books, 1979). Two books which thoughtfully examine the pressures toward submission and conformity in the White House environment are George Reedy, *The Twilight of the Presidency* (New York: World, 1970) and Irving Janis, *Victims of Groupthink* (Boston: Houghton Mifflin, 1972).

The best study of the psychological aspects of presidential performance is James David Barber, *The Presidential Character*, 2nd ed. (Englewood Cliffs, N.J.: Prentice-Hall, 1977). The first empirical test of Barber's theory is William D. Pederson, "Amnesty and Presidential Behavior," *Presidential Studies Quarterly*, Vol. 7, No. 4 (Fall 1977), pp. 175–183. The modern classic that relates psychology to politics is James C. Davies, *Human Nature in Politics* (New York: John Wiley, 1963).

An article that puts White House staffing in a comparative politics perspective is Russell Baker and Charles Peters, "The Prince and His Courtiers," *Washington Monthly*, Vol. 4 (February 1973), pp. 30–39. Two important empirical studies are Michael G. Fullington, "Presidential Staff Relations," *Presidential Studies Quarterly*, Vol .7, Nos. 2–3 (Spring-Summer 1977), pp. 108–114; and Patricia S. Florestano, "The Characteristics of White House Staff Appointees," *Presidential Studies Quarterly*,

Vol. 7, No. 4 (Fall, 1977). pp. 184–191. Recent works on staffing in the Carter administration are James Fallows, "The Passionless Presidency," *Atlantic* (May and June 1979), pp. 33–48, 75–81; and Bruce Adams and Kathryn Kavanagh-Baran, *Promise and Performance* (Lexington, Massachusetts: Lexington Books, 1979). Excellent articles concerning relations between Carter's White House staff and his cabinet have appeared in the *National Journal*, (See November 18, 1978, p. 1852; July 28, 1979, p. 1236; August 18, 1979, p. 1356.)

9

Putting Gippergate into Perspective

William D. Pederson

None of the national commentary on "Gippergate" has put the crisis in historical perspective. This is curious, for two significant events took place shortly before its revelation. The first concerns the publication of *Chief of Staff* (University of California Press). It is the transcript of a dialogue among eight former White House Office chiefs of staff. Of even more portent was the little-noted death of Sherman Adams, President Eisenhower's first chief of staff and the most powerful one until Donald Regan, the present chief.

The modern White House Office (WHO) was created during Franklin Roosevelt's administration. He needed administrative help to perform his job. Public administration experts and the Congress agreed. Eventually, help grew from six persons to 600. Despite rhetoric against big government, President Nixon employed the largest staff in American history. The justification was his effort to use WHO to gain control over the rest of the federal bureaucracy.

These roughly 600 presidential assistants are located in the White House itself, and in the adjacent Old Executive Office Building. Presidents are free to organize them as they see fit. Public administration theory provides two staffing models for the chief executive. Some presidents use a decentralized, subordinant-centered, loosely structured staffing arrangement which encourages equality, discussion and dissent. Franklin Roosevelt, John Kennedy and Gerald Ford used this organization model to great advantage—especially Kennedy during the 1962 Cuban Missile Crisis.

Other presidents prefer a centralized, boss-centered, chain-of-command arrangement which emphasizes hierarchy and discourages dissent. Dwight Eisenhower, Richard Nixon and Lyndon Johnson preferred this staffing model. Subordinates report to a chief of staff who determines entry to the Oval Office. President Johnson substituted his domineering personality for a powerful chief of staff.

Most recent presidents have found a chief of staff useful. Jimmy Carter began without one and finally was forced to appoint one after an excess of democratic chaos. The Reagan administration also underwent an abrupt change in its staffing system. During his first term the president used a modified form of the decentralized staffing model with a competitive troika, (Edwin Meese, James Baker and Michael Deaver) serving as a kind of collective chief of staff. The arrangement acted as a check and balance on the White House Office. The unique feature of the Reagan administration in terms of staffing is that the president allowed his chief of staff to be picked by others who in turn imposed the opposite staffing model on the White House during the second term. Donald Regan became the most powerful chief in the history of the White House Office.

A centralized staffing system with an unchecked chief of staff is an invitation to disaster. The first scandal involving a WHO chief of staff occurred during the Eisenhower administration. Sherman Adams was forced to resign during Ike's second term after the relatively innocuous vicuna coat episode. Adams, like Regan, was an ex-Marine. Whereas Adams was a former politician who tried to maintain a sense of modesty, Regan had little political identity (except as the former Treasury secretary), and even less modesty. In addition to the name similarity with the president, there are indications that Donald Regan saw himself as Ronald Reagan—a fairly common psychological phenomenon in the Oval Office. For example, Teddy Roosevelt's chief assistant changed his life to such an extent that he began to dress and look like the president. John Kennedy's chief assistant similarly began to walk and talk like the president. Even if the Sherman Adams scandal was overblown, his power was so immense as "the assistant president" that his modesty could not prevent him from being dubbed "the Abominable No Man" by those denied entry to the Oval Office.

The other major scandal in the White House Office, of course, is Nixon and Watergate. H. R. Haldeman, President Nixon's "German Shepherd" chief, also lacked elected political experience. He guarded the president so well that Nixon eventually spent the majority of his time isolated in the Oval Office with Haldeman. From an administrative viewpoint, Gippergate seems to be a replay of earlier mismanagement disasters involving too much power in the hands of the chief of staff.

An administrative solution to the current crisis might involve the retention of a strong White House chief of staff with awareness that the chief executive and the chief of staff need to monitor each other. When chiefs of staff acquire so much power that they become *de facto* chief executive officer, they clearly intrude on the managerial responsibility of the president. Sherman Adams died in October just after *Fortune* magazine featured President Reagan in a cover story as a managerial hero. Perhaps Gippergate will mark the final eclipse of an administrative style followed too often in the office on the ellipse.

10

The Behavior of Lawyer-Presidents: A "Barberian" Link*

Thomas M. Green and William D. Pederson

Lawyer-politicans are a predominant force in American politics with a monopoly of the judicial branch of the state and federal government, as well as with a majority or plurality in the legislative and executive branches. For example, in the presidency more than half (56%) of all American presidents have practiced the law before entering the White House. Although political scientists continue to research the role of lawyers in the judicial and legislative branches of government with mixed results in the case of the latter branch,[1] little systematic research has been directed toward lawyer-politicians in the executive branch,[2] and even less on the presidency. The purpose of this paper is to start to fill this gap with an exploration of lawyer-presidents in the White House.

The presidential record on human rights suggests that the grossest violations of civil liberties have taken place during the administrations of lawyer-presidents.[3] The indictment of twenty-five lawyers in the Watergate affair is merely the most recent illustration.[4] Earlier episodes include Franklin Roosevelt and the removal of Japanese-American citizens into "concentration camps," Woodrow Wilson and the suppression of dissent, Abraham Lincoln and the suspension of the right of habeas corpus, and John Adams and the Alien and Sedition Acts. These

* This essay is based upon a paper presented at the Annual Meeting of the Louisiana Political Science Association New Orleans, March 12–13, 1982

abuses of presidential power raise the question whether there is a relationship between the personality of lawyer-presidents and the violation of democratic values.

For purposes of exploring this question further, this paper is divided into four main sections: (1) a psychological framework is presented so that comparisons may be among the presidents; (2) a check of the degree of legal background of each president is made, as well as the commitment of lawyer-presidents to the legal profession or to political life; (3) a discussion of the findings; and (4) some conclusions about legal background and presidential behavior.

A Comparative Framework

Presidents like most groups of human beings are likely to contain some individuals who are psychologically healthier than others. Although there is a natural resistance to classification systems of human beings, it seems fairer to make explicit such a system than to operate on an implicit one that does the same thing but is more difficult to detect or impossible to judge. James David Barber's typology of American presidents is the boldest psychological classification of healthy and ill personalities to date,[5] yet it is also the clearest to empirically test.[6] For the latter reason, Barber's theory of presidential behavior forms the basis for attempting to determine whether lawyer-presidents are psychologically more or less healthy than non-lawyer-presidents.

Barber derives his four-fold typology of active-positive, active-negative, passive-positive, and passive-negative presidents from a political energy index ("active" or "passive" depending on the degree of energy a president puts into his performance), and a felt satisfaction index ("positive or negative affect" depending on the degree of personal enjoyment a president derives from his work). Of the four personality types, the active-positive presidents are the healthiest. With high self-esteem, they are able to have fun fulfilling themselves through the presidential role. In contrast, the other three personality types are posited with suffering from low self-esteem for a variety of reasons: (1) the active-negatives are compulsive power-seekers who expend great energy but derive little personal satisfaction from the work, and are likely to "rigidify" in certain situations; (2) the passive-positives are compliant persons plagued with unmet love needs which tend to encourage them to give in too easily to those around them; and (3) the passive-negatives are withdrawn personalities who feel useless, but occupy the presidency out of a sense of duty and public service.

The findings of a survey-questionnaire study are adapted for this paper in order to extend Barber's original classification of eleven modern presidents to include nearly every president in American history.[7] In a recent chapter of the "presidential rating game," Gary M. Maranell asked nearly 600 American historians to rank the presidents on seven separate dimensions of prestige, strength, activeness, idealism, flexibility, and accomplishment; and then he scored the results through the use of social-psychological scaling methods.[8] This paper uses the dimensions of activeness ("The approach taken by each president toward his administration, an active or a passive approach.") and flexibility ("An evaluation of the flexibility or inflexibility of the approach each president took in implementing his program or policies."), in order to form a short-cut "Barberian" typology from the juxtaposed rankings (see Table 1).

A check between Barber's classifications and those in the modified and expanded typology shows remarkable congruity. Most important, both schemes agree as to who are the active-positives (flexibles) in the twentieth century, so there is some ground for asserting which of our presidents are psychologically the healthiest. Among the three other categories, only Hoover and Eisenhower do not completely match. Barber classifies Hoover as an active-negative rather than a passive-negative (inflexible), and Eisenhower as passive-negative rather than passive-positive (flexible), but since neither president were lawyers, the classifications are not of immediate importance to this paper.

The particularly high correlation (82%) between Barber's

156   *The Behavior of Lawyer-Presidents*

TABLE 1
MODIFIED AND EXPANDED "BARBERIAN" CLASSIFICATION*

Activeness	President	Flexibility	Activeness	President	Flexibility
Active-Positive		*(Flexible)*	*Active-Negative*		*(Inflexible)*
+2.01	F. Roosevelt	+1.31	+1.51	Jackson	−1.40
+1.61	T. Roosevelt	+.186	+1.39	L. Johnson	− .47
+1.25	Truman	+ .31	+1.05	Wilson	−2.23
+1.06	Kennedy	+1.61	+ .59	Polk	− .19
+ .93	Lincoln	+1.50	+ .34	J. Adams	− .85
+ .91	Jefferson	+1.35	+ .30	Cleveland	− .88
+ .44	Washington	+ .57	+ .12	A. Johnson	−2.18
+ .03	Madison	+.576	+ .01	J. Q. Adams	−1.25
Passive-Positive		*(Flexible)*	*Passive-Negative*		*(Inflexible)*
− .06	Monroe	+1.03	− .14	Hoover	−1.01
− .16	Taft	+ .01	− .56	Tyler	−1.09
− .24	Van Buren	+ .19	− .86	Taylor	− .76
− .34	McKinley	+ .49	−1.37	Coolidge	− .83
− .59	Eisenhower	+1.21			
− .69	Arthur	+ .18			
− .74	Hayes	+ .14			
− .95	B. Harrison	+.186			
−1.22	Fillmore	+ .27			
−1.26	Buchanan	+ .01			
−1.29	Pierce	+ .16			
−1.37	Grant	+ .59			
−1.66	Harding	+1.17			

Sources and Notes:
* Adapted from Gary M. Maranell, "The Evaluation of Presidents: An Extension of the Schlesinger Polls," *Journal of American History*, Vol. 57, No. 1 (June, 1970), 109–110. The numbers to the left of each name indicate the degree of activeness: a high positive score is active, a high negative score is passive. The numbers to the right of each name indicate the degree of flexibility: a high positive score is flexible, a high negative score is inflexible.

classification and those in the modified typology may indicate that Barber places more weight on presidential flexibility and inflexibility in determining psychological health than he realizes. For example, a part of his definition of active-positives is "an ability to use style flexibly," and passive-negatives lack "flexibility to perform effectively."[9] In any case, the high correlation permits some confidence to extend the classification scheme to earlier presidents, so that except for the two presidents who served in office for less than a year (William Harrison and James Garfield), every president is classified.[10] Moreover, the high correlation between Barber's classification and those in the

"Barberian" typology enhances the possibility to detect patterns among the lawyer-presidents, as well as between them and the non-lawyers. For the sake of avoiding additional and awkward terms, Barber's nomenclature is used for the remainder of the paper.

A "Barberian" Link

A president's legal background consists of the degree of training, practice, and service in the law. Two primary objective indexes are used to measure legal background for this paper. First, the professional lawyer is distinguished from the non-lawyer in the traditional sense of determining which presidents have completed state certification to practice the law (see Table 2). To supplement this data an effort is made to distinguish between informal training (independent study) and formal training (office apprenticeship, law school); and between private practice and public service (public prosecutor, law enforcement officer, judge, professor). Second, the factor of time spent in private practice and public legal service requires attention. Although it is easy to determine the date a lawyer's formal career began (admission to the bar), it is difficult to determine when it ended or was suspended for political life. For this reason, a "legal commitment index" is presented to mark the time between bar admission and when a lawyer first seeks political office outside the field of law (see Table 3). This index appears to roughly measure the change from a legal to a political career.

If the active presidents (positive and negative) are compared to the passive presidents (positive and negative), the data shows that the active presidents generally are less likely to be lawyers (58%) then the passive presidents (67%). Four other areas distinguish the actives from the passives; (1) almost twice as many actives attended law school than passives; (2) almost all the law school dropouts are actives; (3) the actives generally have shorter careers in private law practice than the passives; and (4) only the actives have waged campaigns against the legal

TABLE 2
LAWYER AND NON-LAWYER PRESIDENTS*

President	Status	President	Status
Active-Positive		*Active-Negative*	
1. F. Roosevelt	Lawyer	Jackson	Lawyer
2. T. Roosevelt	Non-Lawyer	L. Johnson	Non-Lawyer
3. Truman	Non-Lawyer	Wilson	Lawyer
4. Kennedy	Non-Lawyer	Polk	Lawyer
5. Lincoln	Lawyer	J. Adams	Lawyer
6. Jefferson	Lawyer	Cleveland	Lawyer
7. Washington	Non-Lawyer	A. Johnson	Non-Lawyer
8. Madison	Non-Lawyer	J. Q. Adams	Lawyer
9. Ford**	Lawyer	Nixon**	Lawyer
10. Carter**	Non-Lawyer		
Passive-Positive		*Passive-Negative*	
1. Monroe	Lawyer	Hoover	Non-Lawyer
2. Taft	Lawyer	Tyler	Lawyer
3. Van Buren	Lawyer	Taylor	Non-Lawyer
4. McKinley	Lawyer	Coolidge	Lawyer
5. Eisenhower	Non-Lawyer		
6. Arthur	Lawyer		
7. Hayes	Lawyer		
8. B. Harrison	Lawyer		
9. Fillmore	Lawyer		
10. Buchanan	Lawyer		
11. Pierce	Lawyer		
12. Grant	Non-Lawyer		
13. Harding	Non-Lawyer		
14. Reagan**	Non-Lawyer		

Notes:

* A lawyer is defined as a person who has fulfilled state requirements and is licensed to practice the law.

** The classifications of Nixon through Reagan are based only on Barber's personal assessments since Maranell's study was conducted during March, 1968. Two presidents were excluded from that study. W. Harrison (Non-Lawyer) and Garfield (Lawyer), because both served terms of less than a year.

profession.[11] The meaning of these patterns become more evident when the four personality types are examined.

Active-Positives. The most striking finding is that the healthiest presidents are the least likely to be lawyers (40%) of the four personality groups, and even if they are lawyers, they are the first to abandon law for politics. The active-positives are from three to seven times faster than the other personality groups to run for political office outside the field of law at the level of the state legislature or above. A similar pattern emerges if the period

TABLE 3

LEGAL COMMITMENT INDEX OF LAWYER-PRESIDENTS

President	Yrs. to Political Office*	Position Sought
Active-Positive		
F. Roosevelt	3	State Legislature
Lincoln	–5	State Legislature
Jefferson	2	State Legislature
Ford	7	Congress
	(2 yr. average)	
Passive-Positive		
Monroe	–4	State Legislature
Taft	29	President
Van Buren	9	State Legislature
McKinley	9	Congress
Arthur	26	Vice-President
Hayes	19	Congress
B. Harrison	22	Governor
Fillmore	5	State Legislature
Buchanan	2	State Legislature
Pierce	2	State Legislature
	(12 yr. average)	

President	Yrs. to Political Office*	Position Sought
Active-Negative		
Jackson	9	State Legislature
Wilson	28	Governor
Polk	3	State Legislature
J. Adams	15	State Legislature
Cleveland	23	Governor
J. Q. Adams	12	Congress
Nixon	9	Congess
	(14 yr. average)	
Passive-Negative		
Tyler	2	State Legislature
Coolidge	9	State Legislature
	(6 yr. average)	

Notes:
* Period from the time of fulfillment of state requirement to practice the law until first running for a state or national political office that did not require bar admission. Lincoln and Monroe ran for public office before they were licensed to practice the law.

measured is from bar admission to the first political office sought
above the state legislature level (governor, congress, vice-
president): active-positives run for these higher offices twice as
early (7 year average) than the other personality groups (13–15
year average). Moreover, in contrast to the other personality
groups, none of the active-positives held or sought legal-oriented
public offices (public prosecutor, sheriff, attorney general,
judgeship).

Franklin Roosevelt perhaps best illustrates the career pattern
of the active-positive lawyer. He found school dull, failed two
law courses at Columbia Law School, and dropped out his third
year after he passed the New York bar. Although Roosevelt
found the practice of law more stimulating, it too became dull
after a while, so he ran for state legislature.[12] Although Gerald
Ford was a better law student than Roosevelt, as well as having
the distinction as the only active-positive law school graduate,
he ran for Congress after less than three years of private law
practice.[13]

Nineteenth-century active-positives show a similar preference
for politics over law. For example, although Thomas Jefferson
was an outstanding student of nearly everything, including the
law, his private practice served only as a second vocation.[14]
Abraham Lincoln's behavior suggests a similar preference for
the political arena over the law office. He ran for national office
earlier in his life than any other lawyer-president—five years
before becoming a lawyer.[15] Although a successful lawyer, "it is
fair to conclude that if Lincoln had died in 1860 no one would
have ever heard of him again as an attorney."[16]

Even the active-positive non-lawyers suggest a similar pattern. James Madison studied public law at home, but never
intended to practice the law or qualify as a lawyer.[17] Two went
slightly further, but then quit. Theodore Roosevelt studied at
Columbia Law School, "but with no clear or certain intention of
one day becoming a practicing attorney," so he dropped out
before obtaining a degree.[8] Similarly, Harry Truman dropped
out of evening law school after two years. Although he was
referred to as a "judge" in Missouri, the office Truman occupied

is known in other states as a county commissioner (an administrative rather than a judicial office).[19] George Washington, John Kennedy, and Jimmy Carter never seriously considered law as a career. In short, the active-positive presidents tend to be career politicians rather than career lawyers.

Passive-Positives. An opposite picture from the active-positives emerges during an examination of the passive-positive presidents. The passive-positive tends to be a career lawyer rather than a career politician. In fact, if any personality group as a whole personifies the career lawyer or judge, it is the passive-positive. Ten of the fourteen passive-positives are lawyers (71%). They tend to have the longest and most successful legal careers, at least in terms of financial success.[20] Of the four personality groups, the passive-positives have the most legal experience outside of private practice (64%). Indeed, seven of the ten passive-positive lawyers served as public prosecutors or judges before seeking public office. Moreover, the passive-positives contain the most presidents who attended law school, as well as the most who graduated from law school, and the only law professors.

The model passive-positive lawyer and judge is best portrayed by Barber in his case study of William Howard Taft, who emerges as a far happier judge than president.[21] After his presidency, Taft taught law school and later was appointed as Chief Justice of the U.S. Supreme Court by the only passive-positive legal dropout, Warren Harding. The passive-positives have several other distinctions that reflect a preference for law. Rutherford Hayes was the first president to attend Harvard Law School; Benjamin Harrison was the first president to teach law school prior to the presidency; and Franklin Pierce resigned his position as a U.S. Senator to return to the practice of law. In short, with the exception of James Monroe, who is ranked as the least passive of the passive presidents (positive and negative), the behavior of the passive-positives reflect an enjoyment of law over politics.

Active-Negatives. Of the four personality groups, the active-negatives contain the most lawyers (78%).[22] Only two of the active-negatives are non-lawyers, and of these one is a law school dropout. Moreover, as a group they contain the second most lawyers who have had additional legal experience outside of private practice (27%). On the other hand, the active-negatives tend to have the shortest careers in the law, as well as delaying the longest before turning from law to politics. They are neither career politicians in the sense of the active-positives, nor career lawyers in the sense of the passive-positives.

The discontent of the active-negatives is illustrated in the brief legal career of Woodrow Wilson. He was "terribly bored" by law school, so after dropping out to study independently on his own, Wilson completed his legal training at home and was admitted to the bar after a year and a half. Unlike most of the other lawyer-presidents in the other groups, Wilson found the practice of law equally as distasteful as law school, so after a year he decided to do graduate study in political science.[23] In contrast to Wilson, Andrew Jackson entered politics to pursue a legal career as a judge. He has the distinction of instigating his first duel against a prominent attorney who had refused to accept him as a legal apprentice. After an early position as a public prosecutor, Jackson entered politics as a U.S. Senator but quickly resigned his position because of a dislike of legislative life. He soon returned to the law as a judge.[24]

Grover Cleveland served as a district attorney and county sheriff who acted as his own hangman in two murder cases that took place during his term of office, even though he could have easily delegated that duty. Richard Nixon also served as a city attorney and public prosecutor. Unlike passive-positives, the active-negatives, who had longer legal careers than Polk, seem to display a similar habit of intense effort in the law. For example, John Adams suffered a breakdown during his early legal career from working so hard.[25]

Lyndon Johnson and Andrew Johnson are the only non-lawyers among the active-negatives, though the former enrolled briefly in law school and the latter presumed to know more constitutional law than his opponents. In brief, the active-negatives seem to be a marginal career group in contrast to the career politicians among the active-positives and the career lawyers among the passive-positives.

Passive-Negatives. There are too few passive-negatives to make any generalizations about them. Two of the four were lawyers (Coolidge and Tyler), who became accidental presidents.

High and Low-Brow Chief Executives

Louis W. Koenig makes a useful distinction between democratic presidential personalities ("high-democracy types") and those with undemocratic tendencies ("low-democracy types"). He associates Barber's active-positives with the former type and the latter with the active-negatives (presumably the passives fall between the two types).[26] There is some research already to support this distinction. Active-positives are hypothesized to be more concerned about civil-liberties and the amnesty record of presidents reflects this.[27] Active-positives are hypothesized to be more flexible and open and this is reflected in the way they organize the White House staff with less need for structure and hierarchy.[28] In fact, even the active-positives' lack of much concern over secret service protection is suggestive of secure personalities.[29] The active-positives appear to operate on a higher level of human needs than most presidents, so they place greater emphasis on democratic values. They self-actualize in politics more than law.[30] For that reason, they become models of presidential leadership.[31]

In contrast, the "low-democracy" presidents operate on a lower level of human needs (security, love, status, power, etc.). It may be that the legal profession helps to compensate for past deprivations in these areas. Law offers an orderly and secure substitute for a less than orderly world. Low-democracy presidents grant fewer amnesties for they find it hard to justify them in a dichotomous world. A "law and order" disposition is reinforced by the added legal experience of these presidents. This helps to explain the major violations of human rights by active presidents. In a crisis situation, the legal background of

lawyer-presidents reinforces a tendency to perceive a dichotomous world of either legality or illegality, of either peace or war,
and of either right or wrong. Nixon and his low-brow associates
really perceived a wartime situation in peacetime.[32] In "psycho-
moral" terms,[33] low-democracy presidents operate at a pre-
conventional level ("Law-and-Order" stage, according to Lawrence Kohlberg), in contrast to the high-democracy presidents
that lean toward a post-coventional orientation (universal hu-
man-rights stage). Even the high-democracy presidents are
prone to human rights violations in extreme crisis (such as the
American Civil War or World War II).

Conclusions

The findings of this paper correct some historical errors and
increase knowledge about the behavior of lawyer-presidents.[34]
Beyond the generally known fact that more presidents are
lawyers, the "Barberian" typology shows that (1) the active-
positives are more likely to be career politicians than lawyers;
(2) the passive-positives (and perhaps the passive-negatives) are
more likely to be career lawyers than politicians; and (3) the
active-negatives are more likely to be caught between the law
and politics without enjoying either career.

The gross violation of civil liberties by active lawyer-presidents does not augur well for the role of the lawyer-president as
a de facto mechanism for protecting democratic values within a
constitutional context. Increased public awareness of presidential behavior is likely to be the best check against tyranny. The
fact that the percentage of American lawyer-presidents has
drastically fallen from seventy percent in the nineteenth century
to forty percent in the twentieth century, and to only twenty-five
percent since World War II may be seen as an optimistic trend.[35]
Special caution is justified when evaluating lawyer-candidates
for the the presidency. It's no accident that good lawyers
generally make lousy presidents and poor civil libertarians.

References

* *Research supported by the National Endowment for the Humanities at New York University during the 1981 Summer Seminar on the Presidency directed by Louis W. Koenig. Professor James R. Klonoski at the University of Oregon, and Lorna Mitchell at Westminister College in Missouri provided early assistance in the project.*

¹ For example, see Richard L. Engstrom and Patrick F. O'Connor, "Lawyer-Legislators and Support for State Legislative Reform," *Journal of Politics*, Vol. 42, No. 1 (February, 1980), 267–276; Albert P. Melone, "Rejection of the Lawyer-Dominance Proposition: The Need for Additional Research," *Western Political Quarterly*, Vol. 33, No. 2 (June, 1980), 225–232; Walter Weyrauch, *The Personality of Lawyers* (New Haven: Yale University Press); and Paul L. Hain and James E. Pierson, "Lawyers and Politics Revisited," *American Journal of Political Science*, Vol. 19, No. 1 (February, 1975), 41–51.

² Henry Kissinger has noted a tendency of lawyer-diplomats to focus too much on short-range goals, Henry A. Kissinger, *American Foreign Policy* (New York: Norton, 1977), pp. 30–32; Erwin Hargrove speculates that this behavior contributed to American involvement in Vietnam, Erwin C. Hargrove, *The Power of the Modern Presidency* (New York: Knopf, 1974), p. 152. Also see, Laurin A. Wollan, Jr., "Lawyers in Government—The Most Serviceable Instruments of Authority," *Public Administration Review*, Vol. 38, No. 2 (March, 1978), 105–112.

³ For a readable summary of these episodes, see Nat Hentoff, *The First Freedom* (New York: Delacorte Press, 1980).

⁴ Jethro K. Lieberman, *Crisis at the Bar* (New York: Norton, 1978), p. 35.

⁵ James David Barber, *The Presidential Character. Predicting Performance in the White House* (Englewood Cliffs, NJ: Prentice-Hall, 1972).

⁶ For the first empirical test, see William D. Pederson, "Amnesty and Presidential Behavior: A 'Barberian' Test," *Presidential Studies Quarterly*, Vol. 7, No. 4 (Fall, 1977), 175–183.

⁷ For the most recent criticism of Barber's typology, see Jeffrey Cohen, "Presidential Personality and Political Behavior," *Presidential Studies Quarterly*, Vol. 10, No. 4 (Fall, 1980), 588–599.

⁸ Gary M. Maranell, "The Evaluation of Presidents: An Extension of the Schlesinger Polls," *Journal of American History*, Vol. 57, No. 1 (June, 1970), 104–113.

⁹ James David Barber, *Presidential Character*, pp. 12–13.

¹⁰ The classifications of presidents after Lyndon Johnson are based on Barber's personal evaluations, as found in the second edition of *Presidential Character* (1977), and James David Barber, "Worrying about Reagan," *New York Times*, September 8, 1980.

¹¹ The first was active-negative Andrew Johnson during his fifth congressional campaign in 1851 against a lawyer-opponent: "Observing that his

opponents had almost all been lawyers, Johnson attacked the domination of the government by that profession. 'There are two hundred and twenty-three Congressmen,' he pointed out, 'and of this number all are lawyers except twenty-three. The laboring man of America is ignored, he has no proportionate representation, though he constitutes a large majority of the voting population. . . . For my part, I say let the mechanic and the laborer make our laws than the idle and vicious aristocrat.' " Lately Thomas, *The First President Johnson* (New York: Morrow, 1968), p. 77; the second was Jimmy Carter during his 1976 presidential campaign, "I am not from Washington, I'm not a lawyer and I will not lie to you," even though he subsequently appointed lawyers in his Cabinet and top White House staff positions. Thomas E. Cronin, *The State of the Presidency*, 2nd edition (Boston: Little, Brown, 1980), pp. 96; 213; 255. Both Southerners won their elections.

[12] James MacGregor Burns, *Roosevelt: The Lion and the Fox* (New York: Harcourt Brace Jovanovich, 1956), pp. 28–29.

[13] Jerald F. terHorst, *Gerald Ford and the Future of the Presidency* (New York: Third Press, 1974), pp. 43–44.

[14] Caleb P. Patterson, *The Constitutional Principles of Thomas Jefferson* (Austin: University of Texas Press, 1953), p. 9.

[15] Albert A. Woldman, *Lawyer Lincoln* (New York: Houghton Mifflin, 1936), p. 23.

[16] John P. Frank, *Lincoln as a Lawyer* (Urbana: University of Illinois Press, 1961), p. 171.

[17] Ralph Ketcham, *James Madison. A Biography* (New York: Macmillan, 1971), p. 56.

[18] David H. Burton, *Theodore Roosevelt* (New York: Twayne Publishers, 1972), p. 35.

[19] Harold F. Gosnell, *Truman's Crisis. A Political Biography of Harry S. Truman* (Westport, Connecticut: Greenwood Press, 1980), pp. 33–34; 69.

[20] Harry J. Lambeth, "Lawyers Who Become Presidents," *American Bar Association Journal*, Vols. 63–64 (October, 1977–February, 1978), pp. 1430–1433; 1578–1581; 1732–1735; 78–82; 222–226.

[21] James David Barber, *Presidential Character*.

[22] Barber found a similar pattern in his early study of state legislators. The equivalent category to the active-negatives among legislators ("Advertisers") contained the highest percentage of lawyers. These were the legislators who showed low commitment to legislative life, but high activity, see James David Barber, *The Lawmakers: Recruitment and Adaptation to Legislative Life* (New Haven: Yale University Press, 1965), pp. 68; 215.

[23] Arthur S. Link, *Wilson. The Road to the White House* (Princeton: Princeton University Press, 1947), p. 10.

[24] James C. Curtis, *Andrew Jackson and the Search for Vindication* (Boston: Little, Brown, 1976), pp. 16–18; 31–34.

[25] Peter Shaw, *The Character of John Adams* (Chapel Hill: University of North Carolina, 1976), pp. 39; 64–65.

[26] Louis W. Koenig, *The Chief Executive*, 4th edition (New York: Harcourt Brace Jovanovich, 1981), pp. 341–346.

[27] William D. Pederson, "Amnesty and Presidential Behavior."

[28] William D. Pederson and Stephen N. Williams, "The President and the White House Staff," in Edward N. Kearny, ed., *Dimensions of the Modern Presidency* (St. Louis: Forum Press, 1980), pp. 139–155.

[29] Dwight L. Tays, "Presidential Reaction to Security: A Longitudinal Study," *Presidential Studies Quarterly*, Vol. 10, No. 4 (Fall, 1980), 600–609.

[30] For the first effort to systematically apply the work of Abraham Maslow to politics, see James C. Davies, *Human Nature in Politics* (New York: John Wiley, 1963). For a related work that is built upon this work, see James MacGregor Burns, *Leadership* (New York: Harper and Row, 1978).

[31] For example, see James MacGregor Burns, *Presidential Government* (Boston: Houghton Mifflin, 1973).

[32] See David Frost, *"I Gave Them a Sword." Behind the Scenes of the Nixon Interviews* (New York: Morrow, 1978), pp. 296–297; Thomas E. Cronin, *State of the Presidency, 1980*, p. 191; and Arthur M. Schlesinger, Jr., *The Imperial Presidency* (Boston: Houghton Mifflin, 1973), pp. 264–267. Although one study of first-year law students finds them more trustful than the general public, those found to be "Machiavellian" were "statistically more likely to be more 'cynical' of people in general." These individuals were significantly more likely to come from those who label themselves "Republicans" and "conservatives," see Alan N. Katz and Mark P. Denbeaux, "Trust, Cynicism, and Machiavellianism Among First-Year Law Students," *Journal of Urban Law*, Vol. 53, No. 3 (February, 1976), 397–412.

[33] See Richard W. Wilson, "Political Socialization and Moral Development," *World Politics*, Vol. 33, No. 2 (January, 1981), 153–177; John W. Patterson, "Moral Development and Political Thinking: The Case of Free Speech," *Western Political Quarterly*, Vol. 32, No. 1 (March, 1979), 7–20; and Robert P. Steed, "Moral Development and Attitudes Toward the Presidency within a Democratic Context," *Presidential Studies Quarterly*, Vol. 8, No. 4 (Fall, 1978), 365–377.

[34] For example, the historical error that James Madison and Theodore Roosevelt were lawyers as found in Thomas A. Bailey, *Presidential Greatness: The Image and the Man from George Washington to the Present* (New York: Appleton-Century, 1966), p. 235.

[35] Lawyer-Legislators have also decreased, see Rita Jameson, "Study Shows Drop in Lawyer-Legislators," *Trial*, Vol. 16, No. 8 (August, 1980), 8–9.

11

Presidential Reaction to Security: A Longitudinal Study

Dwight L. Tays

An area that has been neglected in political analysis is the aspect of Presidential reaction to the extraordinary security measures taken to protect the Chief Executive. The occupant of the White House is constantly bombarded with threats upon his life. President Ford received about a hundred per month.[1] Millions of dollars are spent solely for the protection of the President and his family. Every member of a President's family has a detail of Secret Service agents assigned to them. These specially trained people know exactly where every member of the First Family is at every moment. In the White House there are boxes with little display screens and each person being protected is assigned a number or code name. When the person changes locations the change is registered on the computer. To illustrate, Gerald Ford was assigned number 1. If the screen read, 1: Oval Office, then the President was there. If he left to go to the Capitol the screen would read, 1: Capitol.[2] If the President or a member of his family wished to dine in a restaurant, the agents are eating at the next table. Of course the kitchen, also, is thoroughly checked. In short the First Family is constantly shadowed by protective personnel. Humorous incidents do occur. For example, when a member of the Presidential Family goes to the lavatory on an airplane, an agent is diligently standing on guard just outside the door. Once, Mrs. Ford was in the restroom when a plane was about to land and the weather was rather turbulent as the aircraft was descending. The Secret Service agent, Frank Domenico, yelled through the door; "Sit down, Mrs. Ford, please sit down," and she shouted back, "I *am* sitting down."[3]

Naturally, one may wonder how have Presidents reacted to these uncommon protective measures? The following hypotheses will provide the framework for exploring Presidential reaction to security precautions.

(1) Different Presidential styles can be identified in relation to security.

(2) The President does have an effect on security measures used in his administration.

(3) Personality is an influencing factor in the President's attitude toward security.

The methodology utilized for the analysis includes surveying critical incidents, examining the President's comments and actions concerning security, and incorporating the observations of other individuals.

In regard to the first hypothesis, a conceptual framework may be formulated for classifying the Presidents according to "style" or ways they have reacted to security. The first category includes discounting the need for strict precautions and continuing one's activities with as little regard for security as possible. The Presidents in this less-restrictive category enjoy their freedom and ready access to the public.

The second classification would be passive-cooperative. While not really seeing the need nor wanting strict security the President in this category would, nevertheless, go along with the measures without much opposition.

The third type would encompass the supportive-preference group. The members in this classification are more receptive and defensive of security measures. They are not opposed to secrecy and tend to shy away from public exposure. Furthermore, the public appearances which are made tend to be in select and well controlled areas. As with any hypothetical model it is difficult to formulate iron clad categories. Certainly there are incidents which do not conform precisely to the given model. Nevertheless, there can be observations made as to the propensity of a given President. With these theoretical models in mind we will now turn our attention to individual cases.

According to Colonel Edmund Starling of the Secret Service, FDR was "utterly fearless, contemptuous of danger, and full of desire to go places and do things, preferably unorthodox places and unorthodox things—for a President."[4] The precautions imposed on him by law, and faithfully executed by the Secret Service bored and irritated him. Roosevelt thought little about personal safety. He had no physical fear except for one thing—fire. He hated and feared it.[5] Of course, this was reasonable since he was a paraplegic. If he were trapped in a sudden fire, he would be completely helpless. As a precaution FDR would crawl across the floor practicing his escape from a possible fire.[6] In addition he was never allowed to travel except with a portable rig. The apparatus was helpful to get him out of wherever he was if a fire broke out.[7]

Roosevelt presented some unique problems to the Secret Service. He could not move quickly and he continually insisted on exposing himself to great crowds. Although he was crippled, Roosevelt appeared at public gatherings, on the back platforms of trains, and in open cars without seemingly being concerned with danger. Regardless of the risk, FDR spent a lot of time trying to elude his guardians. He knew the countryside around Warm Springs very well. In fact he knew the area better than did the Secret Service agents. When driving, he would speed down back roads making sudden turns until he lost the agents. He then would drive back to the resort to await their return.[8]

An avid swimmer, Roosevelt enjoyed the relaxing waters of Warm Springs. He also found the pools a means to play tricks on the ever somber Presidential guards. There were three pools with connecting channels. When Roosevelt would catch the Secret Service men looking off, he would drive deep, duck through a channel and surface in the privacy of another pool. His guards, not seeing the President, would frantically jump fully clothed into the water to find him.[9]

The Roosevelt years were not void of physical danger. Roosevelt got threats on his life fairly often. These would come through the mail and indirectly over the telephone. Also, there were attempts made on his life. In February of 1933 Guiseppe Zangara, an unemployed bricklayer, attempted to assassinate FDR. Roosevelt remained calm during the whole affair. There was, Ray Moley observed, "not so much as the twitching of a muscle, the mopping of a brow, or even the hint of a false gaiety."[10] According to James Roosevelt, his father was a fatalist concerning assassination. FDR stated, "Since you can't control these things, you don't think about them."[11] His attitude may in part be attributed to the fact that for three years he had rolled in the gutter with death. Having overcome polio he may have truly believed, "I'll outlast my enemies."

Despite dangers, Roosevelt loved losing his Secret Service detail. A couple of times Gus Gennerich, FDR's body guard, was the target of Roosevelt's pranks. He had the agent on some pretext climb upon the roof at Warm Springs or Hyde Park. He then ordered a hired hand to quickly remove the ladder, leaving the bewildered agent stranded.[12]

There was also a good-natured running battle between FDR and the Secret Service concerning food precautions. Roosevelt had a fondness for exotic fish and game. These delicacies flowed to the White House from all over the world. Roosevelt objected strenuously to having his oysters or pheasants sent to a laboratory for analysis. To save him the ordeal of objecting the Secret Service would just destroy or consume the questionable food gifts.[13]

The summer of 1933 further illustrates FDR's determination to rid himself of his protectors. He announced to the Service that he would spend his vacation sailing up the coast of New England in a yawl. The boat would sleep five people. He also informed the Secret Service that all of the places were taken so there would not be room for any agents. That was the way it would be—like it or lump it.[14] So the Service prepared to go along in other boats. These boats were larger than the yawl. FDR knew the coast and would sail his smaller boat in places the larger ones could not go. There he maintained his privacy from his protective guards.[15]

Also, there were other restrictions placed upon the Service. FDR had a few superstitions and he would not permit the Secret Service to set up a traveling schedule that called for his departure on a Friday. Thus, many trains would leave at 11:59 p.m. on Thursday or 12:01 a.m. on Saturday.[16]

Before the outbreak of World War II President and Mrs. Roosevelt had tried to build up interest in the White House. They were happy to see it gradually growing. However, after the war started the Secret Service refused to allow the public to go through the first floor. These restrictions upon the public were "irritating" to FDR.[17] The Secret Service in general was irritating to Mrs. Roosevelt. She strongly resented protection. Eleanor was so opposed to it and made it so unpleasant for those who tried to stay with her that the Service finally gave in. They then tried another tactic. The Service provided her with a gun and coached her in the handling of it. Mrs. Roosevelt was to keep it on her at all times while in public. However, Eleanor, being a woman of her own mind, put it in a dresser drawer and never took it out.[18] Without Mrs. Roosevelt knowing it, the Service, usually had agents in the audience when she made public appearances.[19]

Again showing indifference to security measures, President Roosevelt refused to allow an air raid shelter to be built even after World War II had started. However, he finally did give in when it was pointed out that needed office space could be built on top. Thus, the East Wing would serve as office space and the basement would be the air raid shelter.[20]

An incident at Hyde Park will serve as a final illustration of the Roosevelt attitude toward security. While driving in the countryside, FDR turned his small car completely around in the narrow road and headed back to the house. The larger Secret Service vehicles were temporarily stuck. At the residence, the President gleefully remarked, "Ed, I have lost the Secret

Service boys. I cannot find them anywhere. Do you know where they are?'' When the detail finally got back to the house, the President told them he was sorry and he hoped they would not get lost again. With that he drove off with a mischievous grin on his face.[21]

Roosevelt's successor, Harry S Truman, also disliked having his privacy and personal freedom restricted. He simply resented the fuss over protection.[22] Furthermore, Truman literally gave the Secret Service a run for their money. In fact some agents actually lost weight trying to follow him around.[23]

As Vice-President, Truman had an office in the Capitol. One day he noticed a man had been sitting outside his office most of the day. He asked General Vaughn, "Who is that young fellow who's been out there, does he want to see me?" "No he doesn't want to see you," said General Vaughn. "Who is he?" "Secret Service." "Well, what the hell is this," Truman said, "When did this happen?" "It started a day or two ago." Truman walked over to the young man, shook hands, and told him, "I don't see much sense in this but if you fellows are detailed to do it, I'll give you all the cooperation I can." According to his daughter, "this was the beginning of our long, often hectic, but never unfriendly relations with the Secret Service."[24]

Truman would walk through the underground corridors to his Senate office and at times the Secret Service, not knowing his plans would lose him. This was the case when Truman learned that Roosevelt had died. When he received the call to come to the White House he immediately did so without notifying his security guard. Thus, the new President, completely unguarded, rode to the White House with his chauffeur, Tom Harty.[25]

Before moving to the White House, Truman was concerned about how the tight security would affect others. It bothered him that his neighbors could not come and go as they pleased. To enter their own home they had to be identified and cleared by the Secret Service.[26]

Truman had a habit of doing little things that created havoc for the Secret Service. Like any other average American he decided to take a stroll to his bank. Off he went followed by the completely aghasted Secret Service. Needless to say, a terrific traffic jam and mob was created by Truman's "stroll" to the bank.[27]

The Truman walks from the White House to the Blair House also created tremendous security problems. To help cope with the situation the Secret Service had the traffic lights fixed so they would turn red in all directions. When Truman observed that all the traffic was stopped just for him he immediately ordered the practice to cease. "I'll wait for the light like any other pedestrian," stated Truman. The Secret Service was so nervous over the situation that Truman finally gave in and was driven by car.[28]

The Secret Service was given a workout during Truman's visit to Mexico. Truman, delighted by the crowds, started mingling with the people. In addition, being the active person he was, he thoroughly enjoyed climbing up and down the pyramids and temples outside Mexico City. As might be expected the Secret Service agents were completely exhausted by this Presidential trip.[29]

Like Roosevelt, Truman also was a target of an assassination attempt. Two supporters of the Nationalist cause for Puerto Rico, Collazo and Torresola, stormed the Blair House trying to get to Truman. Truman remained calm. He stated, "A President has to expect such things," and kept a speaking engagement that afternoon.[30]

Truman may well have summed up his attitude toward security with this statement, "Kind and considerate as the Secret Service men were in the performance of their duty, I couldn't help feeling uncomfortable."[31] His actions support his statement. During 1965, the law was changed to state that the Secret Service "will" protect a former President during his lifetime unless such protection is declined. After a short time Truman declined such protection except on trips away from his Missouri home.[32]

Dwight and Mamie Eisenhower, upon leaving the hotel after learning of the election results, became aware through a simple occurrence, of a complex change in their lives. As they walked out to Park Avenue and bent to get into their car, they found instead of their own driver, two complete strangers. From that moment on they like their predecessors were to be transported, guarded, and protected by the Secret Service. A group, which Eisenhower stated, "turned out to be one of the finest and most efficient organizations of men I have ever known."[33]

Ike's detail, headed by James J. Rowley, tried to impose only minimum restrictions on the President. They allowed him to practice golf at the White House and tried not to restrict his golfing outings. However, Ike was never permitted to paint a picture on the White House lawn. Sitting or standing still before an easel would be too easy a target for someone to hit. Ike, being understanding, went along with the requirement.[34]

While at residence at the official White House, the President is very near to being a prisoner in his own house. When he would leave his residential quarters to go to another part of the White House, bells would go off alerting the White House guards. However, Eisenhower's other residences were not as rigid as the White House as far as security went.[35]

Eisenhower did not worry about his safety and regarded the elaborate precautions of the Secret Service as something of a waste of time and effort. He believed that if an assassin was seriously planning to kill him, it would be almost impossible to prevent it. One night while in Denver he pointed to the fire escape outside his hotel room window and told his aide, Sherman Adams, "If anybody really wanted to climb up there and shoot me, it would be an easy thing to do. So why worry about it?"[36]

After Ike's 1955 heart attack the Secret Service carried along a supply of oxygen and special medicines. It always impressed Ike when agents had to be away from their homes at Christmas time. Even though Eisenhower tended to discount the need for such careful surveillance he generally would acquiesce to the wishes of the Secret Service. He stated that at times he "apparently worried these protectors by my unthinking disregard of their advice."[37] It is important to note Eisenhower's use of the word "unthinking" disregard.

John F. Kennedy maintained that about all the Secret Service could do was to protect a President from unruly or overexcited crowds. JFK stated, "But if someone really wanted to kill a President, it was not too difficult; put a man on a high building with a telescopic rifle, and there was nothing anybody could do to defend the President's life." Kenneth O'Donnell, Special Assistant to JFK, said that Kennedy regarded assassination as a risk inherent in a democracy and that it didn't disturb him at all.[38]

Kennedy paid little attention to warnings concerning his safety. He would shrug off the possibility of assassination and quip, "Jim Rowley is most efficient. He has never lost a President." JFK traveled 200,000 miles in a dozen foreign countries where anti-American frantics or publicity-seeking terrorists could always be found. Despite the risk he would wade into uncontrolled crowds of foreign handshakers.[39]

This became a trademark of Kennedy at home as well as abroad. JFK's appearance at Muscle Shoals, Alabama, as part of a T.V.A. celebration, illustrates the Kennedy propensity to plunge into crowds. After finishing his speech, which was delivered outside, Kennedy came off the platform and into the sea of people. It should be noted that JFK was not the most popular person in Alabama. However, this did not stop Kennedy.

On that dismal day in Dallas, the President's party arrived at Love Field. The President was supposed to go directly to his limousine from the Motorcade. Typical of the Kennedy style, he and the First Lady walked along the fence, shaking hands with the spectators. About ten minutes later they went to their car. The Presidential limousine is equipped with small running boards, but Kennedy had instructed the agent not to ride on them unless absolutely necessary. He also had requested that the flanking motorcycles be kept back from the sides of his car.[40] This clearly shows Kennedy's wish to maintain visual contact with the public and not to be overly protected.

At times the security of a President is in conflict with the customs of another country. This was the case with LBJ's visit to Mexico. It had been taken for granted that Johnson would ride in his own armor-plated limousine with its bullet-proof glass and bomb-proof underside. However, it was learned just before Johnson arrived that the Mexican President must ride in an open car. An ancient and unbreakable rule of Mexican politics is that the President never appear in public with anything barring him from his people. A closed car is a barrier and therefore unacceptable. Remembering the recent Kennedy assassination, the Secret Service termed this a crisis. A Johnson aide, Jack Valenti, called Johnson to inform him of the situation. In no uncertain terms Johnson told him that he didn't care what kind of car he rode in. LBJ stated, "I will even ride a burro if that is the only way to get into the city." With that Johnson hung up the phone. Valenti, still not convinced, called J. Edgar Hoover. After conferring with Hoover the open car motorcade was agreed upon.[41]

At the beginning of his administration LBJ was not overly receptive to request by the Secret Service. When the Service asked for additional space in the Executive Office Building, LBJ wrote, "No, Hell No. Secret Service would absolutely have no hesitancy in occupying my bedroom!" That settled that.[42]

LBJ's approach to campaigning in 1964 was, "I have to press palms and feel the flesh." On some of his trips he would clasp so many hands that at the end of the day his hands would be scarred with cuts from rings and fingernails.[43] He was reluctant to turn away from any friendly political crowd. He had his "bubble" top limousine equipped with tiny outside microphones so he could gauge the reaction of his greeters.[44]

In Pittsburgh on April 24, 1964, Johnson violated an unwritten rule that had been observed since Dallas. He abandoned his enclosed limousine and stepped into the Secret Service convertible. He stood there waving and inviting people to move close enough to touch. He also used the bullhorn. He would stop the cavalcade every block or so and make a few remarks over the bullhorn.[45]

During a New England campaign swing Johnson would order his Secret Service driver to stop so he could hop out and press the flesh. At one point he walked one-half mile. Johnson seemingly, was trying to prove he had charisma and that he could get crowds to respond like John Kennedy.[46]

LBJ had certain habits that security personnel had to be alerted to. He was not bashful concerning attending to bodily functions. Newly assigned agents to the Johnson ranch had to be warned: "If you hear a rustling in the bushes near the Old Man's bedroom door during the night, don't shoot. It's probably him taking a leak."[47]

By 1966 things had changed tremendously from the exciting flesh-pressing campaign against Goldwater. Johnson's public appearances decreased even though he did manage a few campaign-style appearances. His travel was often shrouded in secrecy. When he went to New York for the funeral of Congressman Celler's wife the precautions taken to safeguard the President were unprecedented for peacetime. The reporters didn't know where LBJ was going until after the plane was airborne. Newsmen and photographers were barred from the ramp during his arrival and departure. This had never been done before during peacetime. In addition a White House spokesman indicated the secrecy that surrounded the New York visit would be the pattern for future trips.[48]

As opposition to the Vietnam War increased plans were also devised to save Johnson from embarrassment as well as harm. Before Johnson delivered a speech at the University of Rhode Island the Secret Service learned that an economics professor was going to leave the platform to protest. As the man left two nurses rushed up to him as if he were ill. They had been recruited by the White House.[49]

As his tenure in office increased and his popularity decreased Johnson would appear more and more at military bases.[50] These installations offered platforms safe from the growing anti-war ranks. In fact there was a 14 month span that Johnson did not make any old-fashioned political appearance. At one point Johnson told the press plainly, "I think you're going to find most of my trips are going to be without much advance notice."[51] The questions were coming up as to how Johnson would campaign in secret or show himself to the voters. Of course, he chose not to.

In analyzing Richard Nixon's reactions to security we will first look at his Vice-Presidential trip to South America. During the tour he insisted on minimum force to be used. However, due to anti-American riots and rumors of intended assassination, beefed-up security forces were used in Venezuela. The Nixon party had to plow their way through rock-throwing and spitting demonstrators. They rushed the car shouting, "Death to Nixon." The Nixon party finally managed to get inside the U.S. Embassy. After the ruling Junta pleaded, Nixon agreed to attend one function outside the Embassy. Neither the Vice-President nor the Secret Service wanted to risk another long automobile ride across Caracas. So a plan was devised to use a small airplane. However, Admiral Larragabal prevailed upon Nixon to go by car so the Venezula government could prove that it could protect foreign dignitaries.[52]

Nixon, had been an anomaly among his fellow politicians, and once inside the White House there were all kinds of barriers to seal him off.[53] Even though Nixon said he was "fatalistic" about assassination he did defend the elaborate and costly security measures at Key Biscayne and San Clemente.[54] No other President had "security" improvements on the scale that Nixon did for "maximum security." In addition, many of the projects did not originate with the Secret Service but with the President or his representatives. Examples would include the installation of a fireplace exhaust fan at San Clemente and the enlargement and replacement of windows with bullet proof glass in Nixon's den.[55]

Those within the Nixon White House became disliked by members of the Secret Service. Those dutiful body guards who are schooled to behave at all times with decorum and to avoid the slightest hint of personal or political bias could not help but show their dislike for Haldeman and Ehrlichman. As early as 1970, a Secret Service man confided to a friend: "You know what we say to each other now, don't you?" "No, what?" "Come the revolution, be sure and save two bullets: one for Haldeman and one for Ehrlichman." When asked if there was only one bullet, the response came immediately, "Haldeman.

Definitely. The other guy has moments when he's not so bad. But Haldeman, never."[56]

Nixon used the Secret Service to help regulate the crowds. During the 1970 mid-term election he instructed the Secret Service men to allow just enough hecklers to provide a foil for his denunciations.[57] As his time in office increased Nixon like Johnson increased his unannounced trips. His plans would be kept secret for "security reasons." Many of his appearances would be in controlled areas such as military installations. For example, President Nixon went to Nashville to welcome Mrs. Nixon back from a good will mission to Latin America. The appearance was at the airbase located at the National Guard Armory. Only members of the public with a special pass were permitted inside the area to greet the President. This select public was scrutinized closely as they filed through the entrance of the hanger where Nixon was to speak. Air Force One taxied to the hanger and the President deboarded to be greeted enthusiastically by this pro-Nixon audience. The President delivered a well-received speech in which he declared that one year of Watergate was enough. The audience was behind a roped area and when Nixon concluded his remarks he walked briskly to the edge of the roped enclosure and shook hands with a few of his supporters. Despite the selectivity of the crowd and their warm welcome, the President's handshaking was extremely limited and he refrained from plunging into the crowd as had been the propensity of JFK. As Nixon's troubles increased he became more and more secluded. He would slip off in an unmarked Lincoln with Bebe Rebozo. They would prowl the California freeways with the Secret Service following. His contact and mingling with the public became less and less frequent.[58]

In the aftermath of Watergate, Gerald R. Ford assumed the Presidency as America's first non-elected President. He immediately began to establish direct contact with the American people. On September 4, 1975 President Ford flew to the West Coast to give several speeches. The following day the President delivered an address on the subject of crime to a joint session of the California legislature. As he was walking across the Capitol grounds toward the office of Governor Jerry Brown, the President paused to shake hands with the people who had lined the sidewalk. As he reached to shake hands with a woman clad in a bright red dress he "looked into the barrel of a .45 caliber pistol" which was pointed directly at him. An alert Secret Service agent, Larry Buendorf, grabbed Lynette Alice ("Squeaky") Fromme's hand and wrestled her to the ground. Other agents hustled the President into the Capitol and Ford calmly concluded his business with Governor Brown without even mentioning the assassination attempt.[59]

In less than three hours after the attempt on his life President Ford stood before TV cameras and stated, "This incident under no circumstances will preclude me from contacting the American people as I travel from one state to another and from one community to another. In my judgement, it is vitally important for a President to see the American people, and I am going to continue to have that personal contact and relationship with the American people."[60] However, President Ford did demonstrate more caution and allowed more protective measures to be taken as he completed his traveling schedule immediately after Sacramento.[61]

Nevertheless, he was not to be deterred from access to the public and demonstrated exactly what he meant when he went to New Hampshire on September 11 to campaign for Republican Senatorial hopeful Louis C. Wyman. For eleven hours from Keene to Portsmouth Ford repeatedly jumped from his open limousine, plunging into crowds and grasping hands. He stopped in fourteen towns. At several points along the way he would stop and stand on the car's runner and speak to the crowd. Of course, this position was an easy target for a would-be assassin. Seemingly, the only added security precaution taken was that Ford was wearing a bullet-proof vest.[62] However, Ford discarded it after only one day.[63]

Ford continued his hectic round of speaking tours and was in St. Louis and Dallas the following week. In a building in St. Louis where the President was to speak the police spied but did not apprehend a man with a gun.[64] The third week of September found President Ford returning to California for several engagements. On September 22, he traveled to San Francisco. While here the President did adhere to the Secret Service's request that he not venture into street crowds.[65] However, as the President was walking toward his armored Lincoln Continental, Sara Jane Moore fired a shot at the President. A bystander, Oliver Sipple, who was a former Marine veteran of Vietnam, noticed the gun in Moore's hand and reached out and deflected her aim. The slug passed a few feet to the left of Ford. Secret Service agents Jack Merchant and Ron Pontius forced Ford down behind the car and then opened the door and pushed him inside. The agents and Donald Rumsfeld then piled on top of the President. As they sped to the airport Ford, good-naturedly, said, "Hey, will you guys get off? You're going to smother me."[66]

Despite two attempts on his life Ford continued public appearances in uncontrolled areas and conducted a highly visible campaign in 1976. For example, after the second debate with Jimmy Carter, President Ford campaigned in Dallas from an open limousine in a preannounced parade route waving to the people constantly.[67]

From the preceeding information it seems evident that Presidents Roosevelt, Truman, Kennedy, and Ford demonstrated characteristics of the less-restrictive type. They generally discounted the need for strict precautions and enjoyed their freedom and ready access to the public. The passive-cooperative type of President would not emphasize security but on the other hand would cooperate and not intentionally make security more difficult. Eisenhower exemplifies the cooperative, less resistant President. Of the Presidents surveyed Nixon was the most supportive and defensive of Presidential security. He did not enjoy or cherish his contact with the public but preferred isolation. Johnson, also, would fall into the supportive-preference classification even though at the beginning of his administration he demonstrated characteristics of the less-restrictive group. These traits, however, were short-lived. As his administration developed Johnson definitely took up features of the supportive-preference model. Thus, it may be concluded that Presidents have distinctive styles in relation to security.

According to law, the President must be allowed protective assistance. However, the degree of security agreed to is dependent upon the individual. The Secret Service can not prohibit a President from making public appearances wherever he chooses. The President may publicize his travel plans or keep them secret. He may ride in an open or closed limousine or even decide to walk. The President may instruct security personnel not to obstruct the public's view. On the other hand certain measures may be initiated by the administration for "security" reasons as during the Nixon years. A President may consult the Secret Service as to whether an appearance in a particular city or country would be advisable or he may simply state that he is going and never ask the Service for their opinion. Whether or not a President plunges into crowds is dependent upon the President's wishes. While security would be easier if he did not, the Secret Service is not at liberty to prohibit such action. Thus, the individual President has a rather broad leeway concerning security measures.

Lastly, the question of personality arises. Personality characteristics of Presidents seemingly are an influencing factor on their view of security. There is a congruence between the three divisions of the security model and the Barber Presidential Character Model.[68] Roosevelt, Truman, Kennedy, and Ford have similar personality traits which James Barber classifies as active-positive. By the same token Eisenhower falls into the "passive" category with both Johnson and Nixon demonstrating characteristics of the active-negative President.

In conclusion from the study of these preceding Presidents it appears evident that there are distinct typologies concerning Presidential reaction to security. While the security model may not be infallible, hopefully it will be a catalyst for future thought and analysis.

References

[1] Gerald R. Ford, *A Time to Heal* (New York: Harper & Row and Reader's Digest Assoc., 1979), p. 310.

[2] Betty Ford with Chris Chase, *The Time of My Life* (New York: Harper & Row and Reader's Digest Assoc., 1978), p. 176.

[3] *Ibid*, p. 177.

[4] Edmund W. Starling, *Starling of the White House*, ed. Thomas Sugrue (New York: Simon and Schuster, 1946), p. xviii.

[5] John Gunther, *Roosevelt in Retrospect* (New York: Harper, 1950), p. 30.

[6] James Roosevelt and Bill Libby, *My Parents A Differing View* (Chicago: Playboy Press, 1976), p. X.

[7] Gunther, p. 30.

[8] Roosevelt, p. 90.

[9] *Ibid*.

[10] *Ibid.*, p. 196.

[11] *Ibid.*, p. 201.

[12] *Ibid.*, p. 201.

[13] Michael F. Reilly, *Reilly of the White House*, ed. William J. Slocum (New York: Simon and Schuster, 1947), p. 17.

[14] Starling, p. 308.

[15] *Ibid.*, p. 309.

[16] Reilly, p. 52.

[17] Eleanor Roosevelt, *This I Remember* (New York: Harper and Brothers, 1949), p. 248.

[18] J. Roosevelt, p. 216.

[19] Reilly, p. 81.

[20] *Ibid.*, p. 37.

[21] Starling, p. 312.

[22] Margaret Truman, *Harry S. Truman* (New York: William Marrow Co., 1973), p. 201.

[23] Gunther, p. 144.

[24] Truman, p. 201.

[25] *Memoirs of Harry S. Truman*, Vol. 1, (Garden City, N.Y.: Doubleday & Co., Inc., 1955), p. 4.

[27] M. Truman, p. 228.

[28] *Ibid.*, p. 228.

[29] *Ibid.*, p. 373.

[30] *Ibid.*, p. 373.

[31] *Memoirs*, p. 27.

[32] Michael Dorman, *The Secret Service Story* (New York: Delacorte Press, 1967), p. 166.

[33] Dwight D. Eisenhower, *Mandate for Change 1953–1956* (Garden City, N.Y.: Doubleday & Co., Inc., 1963), p. 75.

[34] Sherman Adams, *Firsthand Report* (New York: Harper, 1961), p. 84.

[35] Arthur Larson, *Eisenhower: The President Nobody Knew* (New York: Charles Scribner's Sons, 1968), pp. 178–179.

[36] Adams, p. 85.

[37] Eisenhower, p. 269.

[38] Arthur M. Schlesinger, Jr., *A Thousand Days* (Boston; Houghton Mifflin Co., 1965), p. 1024.

[39] Theodore C. Sorensen, *Kennedy* (New York: Harper & Row, 1965), p. 749.

[40] Dorman, p. 179.

[41] Jack Velenti, *A Very Human President* (New York: W. W. Norton & Co., Inc., 1975), p. 120.

[42] Valenti, p. 175.

[43] Frank Cormier, *LBJ: The Way He Was* (Garden City, N.Y.: Doubleday & Co., Inc., 1977), p. 72.

[44] *Ibid.*, p. 116.

[45] *Ibid.*, p. 73.

[46] Cormier, p. 115.

[47] *Ibid.*, p. 136.

[48] *Ibid.*, p. 220.

[49] *Ibid.*, p. 221.

[50] *Ibid.*, p. 260.

[51] *Ibid.*, p. 262.

[52] Dorman, p. 156.

[53] Dan Rather and Gary Paul Cates, *The Palace Guard* (New York: Harper & Row, 1974), p. 23.

[54] *RN: The Memoirs of Richard Nixon* (New York: Grosset & Dunlap, 1978), p. 253.

[55] J. Anthony Lukas, *Nightmare—The Underside of the Nixon Years* (New York: Viking Press, 1976), pp. 350–352.

[56] Rather, p. 227.

[57] Lukas, p. 4.

[58] *Ibid.*, p. 4.

[59] G. Ford, p. 310.

[60] John Osborne, *White House Watch: The Ford Years* (Washington, D.C.: New Republic Books, 1977), p. 189.

[61] *Ibid.*, p. 191.

[62] Jules Witcover, *Marathon; The Pursuit of the Presidency 1972–1976* (New York: The Viking Press, 1977), p. 61.

[63] *Ibid.*, p. 191.

[64] *Ibid.*, p. 61.

65 *Ibid.*, p. 62.
66 G. Ford, p. 311.
67 Witcover, p. 637.
68 For a detailed study of personality characteristics of the Presidents see James David Barber, *The Presidential Character; Predicting Performance in the White House* (Englewood Cliffs, N.J.: Prentice-Hall, 1972).

Bibliography

Adams, Sherman. *Firsthand Report*. New York: Harper, 1961.

Barber, James David. *The Presidential Character; Predicting Performance in the White House*. Englewood Cliffs, N.J.: Prentice-Hall, 1972.

Cormier, Frank. *LBJ The Way He Was*. Garden City, N.Y.: Doubleday & Co., Inc., 1971.

Dorman, Michael. *The Secret Service Story*. New York: Delacorte Press, 1967.

Eisenhower, Dwight D. *Mandate for Change 1953–1956*. Garden City, N.Y.: Doubleday & Co., Inc., 1963.

Ford, Betty with Chase, Chris. *The Time of My Life*. New York: Harper & Row and Reader's Digest Assoc., 1978.

Ford, Gerald R. *A Time to Heal*. New York: Harper & Row and Reader's Digest Assoc., 1979.

Gunther, John. *Roosevelt in Retrospect*. New York: Harper, 1950.

Larson, Arthur. *Eisenhower: The President Nobody Knew*. New York: Charles Scribner's Sons, 1965.

Lukas, J. Anthony. *Nightmare—The Underside of the Nixon Years*. New York: Viking Press, 1976.

Memoirs by Harry Truman, 2 Vols., Garden City, N.Y.: Doubleday & Co., Inc., 1955–1956.

Osborne, John. *White House Watch; The Ford Years*. Washington, D.C.: New Republic Books, 1977.

Rather, Dan, and Cates, Gary Paul. *The Palace Guard*. New York: Harper & Row, 1974.

Reilly, Michael F. *Reilly of the White House*. Edited by William J. Slocum. New York: Simon and Schuster, 1947.

RN: The Memoirs of Richard Nixon. New York: Grosset & Dunlap, 1978.

Roosevelt, Eleanor. *This I Remember*. New York: Harper and Brothers, 1949.

Roosevelt, James, and Libby, Bill. *My Parents. A Differing View*. Chicago: Playboy Press, 1976.

Schlesinger, Arthur M. Jr. *A Thousand Days*. Boston: Houghton Mifflin Co., 1965.

Sorensen, Theodore C. *Kennedy*. New York: Harper & Row, 1965.

Starling, Edmand W. *Starling of the White House*. Edited by Thomas Surgrue. New York: Simon and Schuster, 1946.

Truman, Margaret. *Harry S. Truman*. New York: William Morrow Co., Inc., 1973.

Valenti, Jack. *A Very Human President*. New York: W.W. Norton & Co., Inc., 1975.

Witcover, Jules. *Marathon; The Presidency 1972–1976*. New York: The Viking Press, 1977.

12

Truman's Seizure of the Steel Mills as an Exercise of Active-Positive Combat

Frank Schwartz

When on April 8, 1952 President Truman was faced with the certainty of a strike in the steel industry the following day, he could have taken any of a number of possible courses of action. We all know that ultimately Truman chose to seize the steel mills pursuant to what he believed to be his inherent executive powers. In so doing, he precipitated a constitutional crisis, until on June 2, 1952 the Supreme Court declared the seizure to be unconstitutional. President Truman immediately returned the mills to their private owners, thereby ending the crisis.[1]

While it is common knowledge as to what Truman did, it is not so well known why he did it. Most often his action is explained as a result of his general pro-labor stance and his antipathy toward the Taft–Hartley Act, which he vetoed in a strongly-worded message to Congress when it was presented to him for his signature in 1947.[2] However, I do not think either explanation is satisfactory. After careful analysis of the situation I do not see President Truman's actions as resulting from a disagreement with a particular act of Congress or his general pro-labor stance, but rather as stemming from his presidential character, described by James David Barber as one of Active-Positive Combat.[3] I believe Truman's personality, combined with the unique factual context confronting Truman during the steel dispute of 1952, best explains why he chose to seize the mills on April 8, 1952. This paper will present an argument for this thesis and hopefully add a better understanding of President Truman's motivations when he ordered the seizure.

Three important objectives will be realized by this research effort. First, Barber's paradigm for the prediction of presidential performance can be tested for its explanatory power in the present and in the future in as far as it can help to explain an instance of presidential behavior in the past. If presidential character is of no consequence in helping to explain past presidential practice, there is little reason to believe it can be helpful in explaining present or predicting future presidential performance.

Secondly, this paper will show how President Truman's presidential character, when combined with the factual context of a specific instance, resulted in his choosing a particular course of action from among the many alternatives open to him. Such a look into the workings of the Truman administration will give us a closer understanding of the man behind the Presidency. Truman, although often portrayed as rash and unpredictable, is when viewed from the perspective of his presidential character, nothing if not consistent.

Thirdly, this paper will attempt to dismiss the most often preferred explanations as to why Truman chose to seize the mills. As mentioned earlier, Truman's decision is popularly ascribed to his well known hostility towards the Taft–Hartley Act. However, I do not believe that such antipathy for the Taft–Hartley Act had a significant, let alone determinative impact upon Truman's ultimate choice of seizure. I will marshall my arguments for this position later in the paper.

Before establishing the presidential character of Harry Truman so that it can be applied to help explain his actions in the steel dispute, a brief introduction to Barber's scheme of analysis is necessary for those unfamiliar with his methodology and terminology.

Presidential Character as a Means of Forecasting Presidential Performance[4]

In order to understand and predict presidential performance, James David Barber has taken the general premise that a person's behavior is at least partially a product of his personality and applied it to political situations in which a president finds himself. Barber has identified three elements of a person's personality which impact upon political behavior; style, world view, and character. "To understand what actual presidents do and what potential presidents might do, the first need is to see the man whole . . . as a man trying to cope with a different environment. To that task he brings his own character, his own view of the world, his own political style."[5]

Character is defined by Barber as "the way the President orients himself towards life—not for the moment, but enduringly. Character is the person's stance as he confronts experience."[6] A person's character is developed primarily through childhood experiences. Barber asserts that the core of whatever character is developed is the degree of self-esteem engendered by early experiences in the home and with others. Certain types of interactions seem to develop a high degree of self-esteem, and others to engender low feelings of self-esteem. As for the impact of character upon Presidential decision-making, Barber writes, "Every story of presidential decision making is really two stories: an outer one in which a rational man calculates, and an inner one in which an emotional man feels."[7]

Barber sees presidents as simultaneously performing three different political roles; "rhetoric, personal relations, and homework." Rhetoric is the manner in which the President presents himself to the public via speeches and personal appearances. The personal relations role refers to how a president conducts himself when interacting with individuals or small groups of people on a non-public basis. Homework is how the president chooses to familiarize himself with the nearly endless flow of information and detail necessary to perform in office. Some presidents love detail and to read and will spend hours studying reports during decision-making. Other presidents prefer to be briefed by advisors. Still others eschew detail entirely and are interested only in the "big picture."

Each president will develop characteristic ways of fullfilling these three roles which Barber refers to as a president's "style."

"Style is the President's habitual way of performing his three political roles . . . Not to be confused with 'Stylishness,' charisma, or appearance, style is how the President goes about what the office requires him to do."[8]

In addition to character and style, a President also holds a particular "world view" according to Barber's paradigm. "A President's world view consists of his primary, politically relevant beliefs, particularly his conception of social causality, human nature, and the central moral conflicts of the time. This is how he sees the world, and his lasting opinions about what he sees. Style is his way of acting; world view is his way of seeing."[9] A president who perceives the world to be a place of opportunity in which men are basically good and able to change the course of events will conduct an administration quite different in tone from a president who sees the world as a hostile place where people cannot be trusted.

Barber is careful to note that a president's personality does not determine any particular behavior, but rather acts as a guide to general patterns of performance while in office. One aspect which operates alongside personality, and which can further determine a particular course of action, is the "power situation" confronting a president with regard to an issue. Key elements in the "power situation" are the level of popular support the President has, the degree of Congressional support the President can marshall on Capitol Hill (both generally and in regard to a particular action), the enthusiasm of the bureaucracy for a particular policy, and sometimes, especially when constitutional issues might be raised, the opinion of the courts as to the constitutionality of a particular option.

The more favorable the power situation is for the President, the more autonomy he can exercise in the decision-making process. Of the relationship between personality and power situation, Barber writes, "A President's personality interacts with the power situation he faces and the 'national climate of expectations' dominant at the time he serves. The tuning, the resonance—or lack of it—between these external factors and his personality sets in motion the dynamic of his presidency."[10]

In order to compare Presidents and their performance in relation to their character, Barber establishes four presidential types according to two criteria. The first baseline is that of activity/passivity and asks the question, "How much energy does the man invest in his presidency?" Presidents have varied on this measure from Calvin Coolidge who, in sleeping 11 hours and taking a midday nap was not a very energetic President, to a Truman or a Johnson, who regularly put in sixteen-hour days.

Active presidents perceive themselves to be problem solvers or crisis managers and are not afraid to "grab the bull by the horns." Passive presidents on the other hand are more likely to take a "wait and see" attitude toward problems in the hope that they will go away of their own accord. Hoover's handling of the Depression was an example of presidential passivity, while F.D.R.'s treatment of the same issue was indicative of an active president.

The second baseline measure Barber uses is that of positive/negative affect, " . . . that is, how he feels about what he does. Relatively speaking, does he seem to experience his political life as happy or sad, enjoyable or discouraging, positive or negative in its main effect."[11] According to the affective tenor of statements made, both public and in private, by presidents regarding their political life, Barber assigns presidents to one or the other category.

Using these two baseline measures, Presidents fall into one of four presidential types; active-positive, active-negative, passive-positive, and passive-negative. Barber has shown that there are significant differences in behavior patterns between types, differences which, he asserts, can help to generally predict presidential performance. However, Barber is also careful to point out differences among presidents in the same category. Each President is indeed unique, but their uniqueness should not blind us to their overall similarities which make comparison possible.

Now that the terminology of Barber's system of analysis of presidential character is understood we can move to an application of the typology to Harry Truman's presidency. Then we will follow a discussion of how Truman's presidential character helps to explain why he took the actions he did during the steel dispute of 1952.

Harry Truman and Active-Positive Combat

Barber places Harry Truman in the category of an active-positive president. Describing active-positive presidents Barber writes, "There is a congruence, a consistency between much activity and the enjoyment of it, indicating relatively high self-esteem and success in relating to the environment. . . . There is an emphasis on rational mastery, on using the brain to move the feet. This may get him onto trouble . . . not everyone he deals with sees things his way and he may find it hard to understand why. . . . Active-positive presidents want most to achieve results."[12]

When faced with a problem Truman was most comfortable when he was in action. He was not one to sit around waiting for problems to disappear lest he be overwhelmed by the multitude of issues demanding his attention. In speaking of the need for decision-making in the presidency Truman said, "Within the first few months I discovered that being President is like riding a tiger. A man has to keep on riding or be swallowed. . . . A President is either constantly on top of events, or, if he hesitates, events will soon be on top of him. I never felt I could let up for a moment."[13] While Truman much preferred action to inaction, he also favored offensive action to defensive stances and did not shy away from "bold strokes" when he thought the benefits would be worth the risks.

Truman was not only an active President, but he enjoyed what he was doing as well. One aspect of his character which helped him to take some joy as well as pride in a very tough job was his ready sense of humor. "Harry Truman's first memory was of laughter,"[14] and he laughed easily throughout his political career. "He grinned his way through the most trying times. . . . He often got angry, but rarely depressed."[15]

Truman expressed his opinion as to the rewards of political life in general when he addressed the Jefferson–Jackson Day Dinner on March 28, 1952. "I like political meetings and I like politics. Politics—good politics—is public service. There is no life or occupation in which a man can find a greater opportunity to serve his community or his country. I have been in politics for thirty years, and I know nothing else could have given me greater satisfaction."[16] In discussing his attitude toward the Presidency in particular Truman told a gathering of friends, after first addressing the difficulties of the Office, that " . . . don't tell anybody, but just between you and me, I like it."

This positive attitude, which was kept in spite of the fact that for most of his presidency Truman's personal popularity remained at very low levels, allowed Truman to experience the vicissitudes of the presidency and to accept the often harsh personal criticisms of his handling of the office without building up a sense of frustration and resentment.

Certainly the aspect of Truman's presidential character which is most widely known is his rhetorical style, which at best can be described as aggressive and at worst combative and abrasive. Known for his "plain speaking," Truman would voice exactly what was on his mind. "Truman was a spontaneous man, ready to say what he felt and thought rather than hold it back. And he never mastered the politician's rhetorical talent for dissembling."[17] Barber saw Harry Truman's rhetorical style as a reflection of his father's very aggressive manner. For his honesty and enthusiasm Truman often paid a high price. Perhaps this was because, as Alfred Steinberg suggests, Truman's style did not seem sufficiently "presidential" to a majority of the American people.[18]

Truman's hardhitting rhetorical style was reflected in his mode of decision-making. "Truman's style in decision making had two large elements. One was close attention to detail. . . . Truman as President could and did study hard. . . . The other element was decisiveness—the habit of nearly impulsive assertion of definite answers. . . ."[19] This is not the same as saying, as many are apt to do, that Truman's decision-making was the result of a hasty process. Truman asked for advice readily from across the spectrum of opinion. However, after due consideration of the options, Truman would announce his decision and stick with it. He rarely looked back, and therefore was not given to second guessing himself or changing his mind. Simply stated, he thought out decisions, but once made, refused to agonize over them. Truman characterized his decisiveness in the following way. "All my life whenever it comes time to make a decision I make it and forget about it and go to work on something else . . . and you don't want to look back. If you make a mistake in one of those decisions, correct it by another decision, and go ahead."[20]

Harry Truman's world view was shaped by his family experiences as an adolescent and by his assiduous reading of history, especially the history of the world's leaders. Wrote Truman in his *Memoirs*, "My debt to history is one which cannot be calculated, I know of no other motivation which so accounts for my awakening interest . . . in the principles of leadership and government."[21] From his readings of Alexander, Attila, Napoleon, Washington, Lee and many others Truman developed what Barber called the "religion of the deed." Truman firmly believed that individual men could alter the course of events: Throughout his lifetime Truman developed a great sense of personal efficacy.

Truman saw the world as an invigorating challenge, not as a frightening and hopeless struggle of man against insurmountable odds. This world view allowed him to venture forth in efforts which would hopefully gain the results he desired. However, Truman was also aware that life was a gamble, that sometimes you win and sometimes you lose. (He had witnessed his family lose its fortune during his childhood.) But win or lose in a particular instance, Truman was encouraged by a world view that interpreted his world as basically good, inhabited by trustworthy men of good faith.

In many ways Truman's world view complemented his active character. His world view promoted feelings of personal and political efficacy which in turn allowed him to be more active and positive about the actions he took.

One of the most powerful aspects of Truman's character was

his highly developed sense of national responsibility. When faced with a decision I believe Truman, to a degree greater than the vast majority of public servants, drew his conclusions on the basis of what he believed was best for the country. Throughout his political career Truman exhibited a keen sense of responsibility to the national welfare. On many occasions Truman remarked that the President was the representative of all the people, and as such, should not resolve issues on the basis of what was good for special interest groups or the advancement of any individual's political career, his own included. Truman's abiding preoccupation was with the country's well-being and not with his personal welfare. His attitude towards the proper motivation of political leaders is reflected in a remark he made concerning famous historical personages. "I was not very fond of Alexander, Attila, Genghis Khan, or Napoleon because while they were great leaders of men they fought for conquest and personal glory. The others [Hannibal, Wellington, Washington] fought for what they thought was right and for their countries. They were patriots and unselfish. I could never admire a man whose only interest was himself."[22]

This aspect of Truman's presidential character is I believe crucial to an understanding of why he acted as he did during the steel dispute of 1952. Many of his actions during that time can be best interpreted by considering his very highly developed sense of national responsibility. We now move to a consideration of President Truman's performance during this dispute in view of his presidential character.

Truman's Presidential Character as Applied to the Steel Strike of 1952

When the possibility of a steel strike during 1952 first presented itself to the Truman administration, two concerns were paramount: the avoidance of any stoppage in steel production which would be harmful to the Korean defense effort, and the prevention of any large increase in the price of steel which could begin an inflationary spiral and thereby wreck Truman's economic stabilization policies. Consequently, when negotiations between industry and labor broke down on December 20, with a strike called upon the expiration of the current contract on December 31, Truman began to seek a way to satisfy both concerns.

On December 22, Truman decided to refer the dispute to the Wage Stabilization Board, Truman's plan of action was made clear in his statement to the country regarding the involvement of the WSB in the dispute. "The Wage Stabilization Board is made up of representatives of labor, management, and the public. The Board will give both sides an opportunity to present the facts and arguments they think the Board should consider. . . . The Board will consider the case promptly on its merits and make recommendations for a fair settlement, consistent with sound stabilization policies."[23] It was hoped that once the WSB's recommendations were released that both industry and labor would feel compelled by public pressure to adopt the recommendations of such an impartial body as a basis for settlement.

Furthermore, in order to prevent the stoppage of steel production, Truman requested that the union call off the strike set for January 1, pending the Board's proceedings. This the Union agreed to do and steel production continued unbroken.

On March 20, 1952, the WSB, having completed its investigation, made public its recommendations for settlement. The Board recommended an eighteen-month contract with a 12 1/2 cents per hour wage increase retroactive to January 1; an additional 2 1/2 cents per hour increase effective June 30, 1952; and another 2 1/2 cents per hour increase to begin January 1, 1953.[24] Along with the wage increases the Board recommended certain fringe benefits and the industry-wide adoption of the union shop.

Reaction to the WSB's proposals was swift from both sides involved in the dispute. The union agreed immediately to use the WSB guidelines as a basis for settlement even though they granted less wage and fringe benefit increases than the union had originally wanted. The union also agreed to further postpone any strike until April 9, 1952.

The steel industry quickly denounced both the Board and its recommendations. Steel company spokesmen said the public members of the Board were pro-labor, and hence they had not received a fair hearing. They characterized the guidelines as "unfair and unreasonable" and said they would ". . . if complied with, completely wreck the Government's stabilization program."[25] The companies announced that if the WSB recommendations were made the basis for a settlement they would need price relief of $12 per ton. Such a price increase would certainly have wrecked Truman's economic stabilization plan.

At this point whether or not a settlement could be reached before the April 9 deadline set by the Union seemed to be largely up to the companies. The main sticking point was with prices though, not wages per se. The companies refused to negotiate over wage demands until they were first assured of "adequate" price increases by the government. Truman wanted no price concessions until a wage settlement had been reached.

In a letter to Charles Wilson accepting his resignation as Director of Defense Mobilization, Truman enunciated his own belief on the issue of price relief. He believed none was necessary above that legally required ($2 to $3 per ton) by the Capehart Amendment.[26] ". . . [It] seems to me quite natural and important that the profits of the steel industry are continuing at extraordinarily high levels—that their profits amount to a good many times as much as any increased costs they would incur under the recommendations of the Wage Stabilization Board."[27]

By April 7, two days before the strike deadline, it was clear to all parties that no settlement would be reached. Since the WSB had announced its guidelines on March 20th the steel companies had refused to negotiate in good faith. After two earlier postponements amounting to ninety-nine days, the union was in no mood for any further work while waiting for collective bargaining to bear fruit. A break in steel production, beginning at midnight April 8 seemed a certainty unless some further action was taken by the government. As the strike deadline approached

Truman and his advisors discussed the options open to them for dealing with the dispute.

Truman's Options

On the eve of the strike Truman could have chosen any one or a combination of seven alternative courses of action: (1) he could allow the strike to begin and hope that further collective bargaining would yield a settlement, (2) he could yield to the price demands of the steel industry, thereby removing the major impediment to a settlement, (3) he could invoke the emergency provisions of the Taft–Hartley Act to enjoin the union from striking, (4) he could begin proceedings to seize the steel mills under the provision of Title II of the Defense Production Act of 1950, (5) he could begin proceedings to seize the mills under Section 18 of the Selective Service Act of 1948, (6) he could ask Congress to immediately pass emergency legislation specifically authorizing the President to seize the mills, or (7) he could seize the mills under his own authority pursuant to inherent powers vested in the President by the Commander in Chief clause of the Constitution. We all know that Truman chose the last of these seven options. Why he chose this option over the others is not well known and will be explained in terms of the resonance between his presidential character and the power situation confronting him at the time the decision was made.

The first two options, to let the strike begin and or yield to the price demands of the steel companies were in fact no options at all for President Truman because both clashed sharply with what he perceived to be his ultimate goals in resolving the dispute. He had made his goals very clear in remarks before a meeting at the White House on May 3rd with representatives from the steel industry and labor.

First, it is absolutely necessary, for the safety of the country, that steel production must continue during the emergency . . . .
Second, it is essential to the economic health of our country and the welfare of our people that wage and price increases in the steel industry shall be held within the limits of sound stabilization policies.

A runaway inflation in this country could wreck our economy and impose terrific hardship on millions of families.[28]

In light of the above, it is not surprising that these two options were immediately discarded.

It is important to note two things in relation to Truman's stated goals during 1952. First, that Truman's domestic concerns vis-a-vis a steel settlement were every bit as great as his defense concerns vis-a-vis a steel strike. Second, Truman had already experienced firsthand the economic consequences of yielding to exorbitant steel company price demands during the steel dispute of 1946. It was then the stated policy of Truman's reconversion/ stabilization program to allow for price adjustments as a consequence of increased wage payments only *after* a six-month period during which time the increased wages were paid. This would give the administration time to assess accurately what level of price adjustment was made necessary by the wage increase. However, during the 1946 steel dispute, a situation very similar to that of 1952, the steel companies refused to agree to the wage demands of the unions until they were granted immediate price increases. Steel was essential to the reconversion effort both here and abroad, and a settlement was greatly desired. Truman, accepting the advice of Office of War Mobilization and Reconversion Director John Snyder, agreed to an immediate five dollars per ton price increase, thereby violating his own administration's policy of a six-month waiting period.

As a consequence of Truman's action the strike was immediately settled, but the economic repercussions were also swift in coming. "There was brave talk that this was only a 'bulge' in the price line that would eventually be smoothed out, but in reality it was the beginning of the end for price control."[29] During the year following the settlement wholesale prices rose at an annual rate of 20 percent and consumer prices at a rate of 12 percent, both unprecedented levels since the end of World War I. In light of this prior experience Truman may have made up his mind to stand more firmly by his stabilization policies in 1952, and not yield to steel industry pressure.

Options three through six were all statutory alternatives. Option three involved the use of the Emergency Provisions of the Taft–Hartley Act. Options 4, 5 and 6 will be discussed first, and then we will return to a consideration of Truman's actions regarding Taft–Hartley.

As a consequence of Truman's declaration of a national emergency at the beginning of the Korean War, Congress passed the Defense Production Act of 1950. The intent of the Act was to ensure continued production of materials essential to the defense effort. "Title II empowered the President to requisition property, or the use thereof, whenever he determined 'that the use of any equipment, supplies or materials or facilities necessary for the manufacture, servicing, or operation of such equipment, supplies or component parts, is needed for the national defense.' "[30] Commenting upon the effect of Title II, Senator John J. Williams stated during debate on the bill, "under this bill as it now stands, the President could authorize the nationalization of our great steel industry, along with the nationalization of such of our other large industries, as he saw fit."[31] Action pursuant to Title II was Truman's fourth alternative.

However, before a plant could be seized under Title II, the government had to file in court a declaration of taking for each and every plant to be seized and deposit in banks prior to seizure whatever amount the government thought to be just compensation. This was a very costly procedure, both in time and in money, and would require Congressional acquiescence for the appropriation of funds for just compensation. Given the fact that by April 8 Truman had less than twenty-four hours to prevent a work stoppage, the Title II option, which would take weeks if not months to effectuate, was not a viable option in light of Truman's previously stated goals for dispute settlement. Furthermore, Title II required Congressional approval. Since Congress was in favor of usage of the Taft–Hartley Act, it could not be expected that Congress would cooperate with the Title II process. In light of these facts it is not surprising that Truman rejected Title II of the Defense Production Act of 1950 as an adequate means of bringing about a settlement.

A second statutory option available to Truman was Section 18 of the Selective Service Act of 1948. "Section 18 authorized the President to place orders with any manufacturer that produced material needed by the armed forces . . . as long as procurement of that material had been approved by Congress. If the company failed to fill the order in the time specified by the President, he was empowered to take immediate possession of the property . . . ."[32]

Truman's advisors told him that seizure of the mills could be done via Section 18, but that to do so involved a number of obstacles, all similar to those presented by the Defense Production Act of 1950. Specific orders had to be placed with specific plants and this had to be done with Congressional approval. Furthermore, time had to be allowed for the companies to fill the orders before Truman could take possession of the mills. All these steps would take time, even assuming Congressional cooperation, time which was simply not available given the April 9 strike deadline. Hence, Truman discarded the Selective Service Act of 1948 as a viable option to avoid the impending steel strike.

Yet another statutory option open to Truman would have been to request that Congress pass special legislation specifically authorizing him to immediately seize the steel mills. If done as quickly as possible, perhaps only a one- or two-day work stoppage would occur before Congress could pass such a bill. However, the likelihood of a seizure authorization bill passing through either house, let alone both houses, was essentially zero. Ever since the industry had reacted strongly against the Wage Stabilization Board's recommendations of March 20, Congress had been calling for Truman to invoke Taft–Hartley should the union call a strike. Now, on the eve of the strike, Congress was vociferous in its demand that Truman use Taft–Hartley. Truman knew a special bill had no chance of passage in a hostile Congress. Wishing not to embarrass either the Office of the Presidency or himself in an effort sure to end in a lopsided defeat, he never seriously considered employing such an option prior to April 9.

Having discarded five options, Truman was left with only two of the original options. One of them, the use of the emergency provisions of the Taft–Hartley Act, was statutory. The other, seizure of the mills under his inherent powers as both Commander in Chief and Chief Executive, was constitutional in nature. Both options might serve equally well to avoid any work stoppage on April 9, one of Truman's primary goals.[33] Concerning Truman's second professed goal, a settlement of the price issue consistent with his stabilization policy, perhaps one option might be more effective than the other in Truman's mind. At least that is one point that will be argued in the following discussion as to why Truman rejected Taft–Hartley.

Truman's Rejection of Taft–Hartley: Active-Positive Combat in Action

The most commonly discussed reasons why Truman chose not to invoke the Taft–Hartley Act during the steel crisis of 1952 are 1) his long history of being pro-labor, and 2) his deep resentment toward the Taft–Hartley Act, which was passed over his strenuous veto. I will first argue that neither of these reasons are sufficient to explain why Truman acted as he did. Then I will show that it was Truman's presidential character, along with the power situation confronting Truman at the time, which best explains why Truman decided not to use Taft–Hartley but chose the seizure alternative.

As to the contention that Truman acted during the steel dispute of 1952 from a basic pro-labor stance that would have precluded him from ever taking a stand that might be perceived to be anti-labor, Truman's actions during the labor troubles of 1946 seem to belie the point. During the coal and railroad strikes of that year Truman showed that he could be very severe with labor, and no amount of arguing could have convinced labor leaders such as John L. Lewis, Alvanley Johnston, and A. F. Whitney that Mr. Truman was pro-labor.

Truman's attitude was generally pro-labor, but his support for labor was not unconditional. In discussing Truman's presidential character it was earlier maintained that he had a very highly developed sense of national responsibility. In Truman's mind all leaders, be they inside or outside government, had a duty to subordinate their own interests to the good of the nation when the times demanded it. The coal and railroad strikes of 1946 proved to labor that Truman could be a formidable adversary.

When workers in both the coal and railroad industries walked off the job in May of 1946 Truman seized both industries under the Smith–Connally Act of 1943. This Act gave President Truman the authority to seize "essential" strikebound industries. As both coal and rail transportation were critical to the reconversion effort Truman saw any nation-wide strike in these areas as irresponsible and intolerable. These seizures incensed labor in general and John L. Lewis, head of the United Mine Workers, A. F. Whitney, head of the Brotherhood of Railway Trainmen, and Alvanley Johnston, leader of the Brotherhood of Locomotive Engineers in particular.

As Truman saw it, union leaders had a dual responsibility: to protect the welfare of their membership and to do the same with respect to the welfare of the country. Truman would not let his generally positive attitude toward labor allow labor leaders to sacrifice the latter duty for the former when to do so would cause serious economic dislocations. Truman's revulsion at what he saw to be the irresponsible actions of the coal and railroad leaders during 1946 was expressed in a telegram he sent to another union official. "There should be, however, a sense of shame in all the hearts of the leaders of labor for the manner in which Mr. Lewis attempted to defy the Government. His action is in line with the action of Whitney and Johnston and does labor no credit."[34] Nor did Truman leave any doubt as to his willingness to take strong action against labor leaders should the need arise again in the future. "We used the weapons at hand to fight a rebellion against the government, and I am here to tell you that I expect to use whatever powers the President and the Government have, when the law and the Government are defied by an arbitrary dictator, such as Lewis."[35]

As a consequence of their 1946 encounters Lewis did not think

much of President Truman either, as he made plain in a speech
before the United Mine Workers Convention in October. "He is
a man totally unfitted for the position. His principles are elastic,
and he is careless with the truth. He has no special knowledge of
any subject, and he is a malignant, scheming sort of individual
who is dangerous not only to the United Mine Workers, but
dangerous to the United States of America."[36]

Such exchanges between Lewis and Truman hardly seem to
indicate an unswerving pro-labor stance on the part of Truman.
Rather, the 1946 incidents make evident the fact that when
anyone, labor included, violated Truman's sense of national
responsibility, the active and combative elements of Truman's
presidential character would manifest themselves. Therefore, to
attribute Truman's rejection of Taft–Hartley during the 1952
steel dispute to an unconditional pro-labor stance is to misinter-
pret the level of support Truman in fact held for labor. If
President Truman was influenced by his admittedly positive
attitude toward labor in 1952, it was because in his mind the
union had acted in a manner consistent with its dual responsibilities to its membership and the nation. Whether or not this
was the case will be examined in detail when the reasons why
Truman chose seizure are discussed later in this paper.

A second, often-mentioned reason for President Truman's
refusal to use Taft–Hartley in 1952 was his supposed resentment
toward both the Act itself and the Congress that had passed the
Act over his veto. It is certainly true that Truman did everything
in his power to prevent passage of the Act, attacking it viciously
both in public and in private. His veto message to Congress,
over 5,500 words long, and which called the Act "dangerous,"
"arbitrary," "discriminatory," and "drastic" was characterized by then Senator Wayne Morse as "one of the most powerful
vetoes in all our history."

However, in assessing Truman's positive outlook toward his
job as President, one important aspect mentioned was the fact
that such an attitude prevented him from building up resentment
from battles lost. He was a "good loser" in so far as he would
not dwell upon his defeats but would immediately move onto

new ground. Truman seemed to adopt this forgiving attitude regarding the Taft–Hartley Act when he said in his 1948 State of the Union Message that despite his prior opposition to the Act, now that it had become the law of the land, "I shall carry out my constitutional duty to administer it."[37]

However, the clearest evidence that Truman's refusal to use Taft–Hartley in 1952 was not due to any aversion to the Act per se is the fact that he had invoked its national emergency provisions on previous occasions. "He invoked these powers six times before the campaign of 1948: three times in maritime strikes, twice with coal mine disputes, and once before an impending strike at the Oak Ridge atomic plant."[38] If anything, Truman's antipathy toward the Taft–Hartley Act could be expected to have been greater in 1948 than it would be in 1952, and he had invoked the Act six times between its passage and the 1948 campaign. For this reason it seems hard to imagine that the primary reason why Truman chose seizure over a Taft–Hartley injunction in 1952 was his obstinate refusal to invoke an act which he found personally repugnant. His real reason then for rejecting Taft–Hartley was not a publicly expressed distaste for the Taft–Hartley procedure, rather it can be explained best in terms of Truman's presidential character.

The keys to understanding why Truman chose seizure over injunction are 1) an appreciation for the power situation facing Truman on April 8, 1952, and 2) a knowledge of which party, labor or management, Truman held responsible for precipitating a strike Truman strongly believed to be inimical to the national interest.

The Power Situation

There were two outstanding factors to be taken into account when considering the power situation in which Truman had to seek a resolution to the steel dispute. The first was that on March 29, 1952 Truman had announced that he would not seek re-election to a second term as President. This in effect made Truman a "lame duck" president during a most crucial time in the steel dispute. As it is generally believed that lame duck presidents lose much of their ability to influence Congressmen and others crucial to the formulation and implementation of government policy, his announcement almost certainly reduced in the minds of others the amount of influence they believed Truman could exert. Therefore, those opposed to Truman and his policies, such as the steel company executives and members of Congress, found it easier to organize effective resistance to Truman's price policy. This in turn might have forced Truman to take actions which otherwise might not be taken, such as to assume a more vigorous stance in order to prove that as a lame duck president he was not powerless to promote his policies.

The other major factor affecting Truman's power situation during the spring of 1952 was his very low public approval rating. Richard Neustadt, in his landmark book *Presidential Power*, established that the only real power a president possesses is the power to persuade others, and that a president's powers of persuasion are to a very large degree predicated upon his personal popularity. Generally speaking, the more popular a president is with the public, the more popular he will be with Congress and the more effective the president will be as a leader. The converse is also true. The less popular the president, the less ability he has to persuade others to follow his policy leads.

In a Gallup poll released on February 8, 1952, 25 percent of those responding approved of President Truman's handling of the office. Sixty-two percent disapproved, and 13 percent had no opinion.[39] A second polling, announced on March 26, only three weeks prior to Truman's April 8th decision vis-a-vis the steel dispute, produced identical results.[40] Both polls indicated that Truman's public support was very low and that this condition was stable over time.

Not only was Truman's personal popularity at nearly historically low levels, but the Korean conflict, an issue intimately related to the steel dispute, was also becoming increasingly unpopular by April of 1952. When asked to respond to the question, "Do you think the United States made a mistake in going into the war in Korea, or not?" 51 percent answered yes,

35 percent no, and 14 percent had no opinion.[41] So in effect what those who wanted to oppose President Truman in the steel dispute were faced with was a very unpopular president trying to conduct an unpopular war. This made Truman an easier target to oppose than most Presidents, at least in the minds of his detractors.

The consequence to Truman of his low approval ratings was that he could not "go to the people" in the hope of engendering popular and/or Congressional support for his policies, or to influence those in the steel industry. When, on April 10, 1962, U.S. Steel announced sharp increases in steel prices, then President Kennedy, a much more popular president at the time with both Congress and the public, went on an immediate public offensive against the price increases. During a press conference the following day Kennedy denounced the price rises as exorbitant and against the national interest. As a consequence of the resultant public and private pressure, steel industry executives announced a price rollback. Due to his low popularity such public "jawboning" by Truman against the steel industries would have had no effect, either on the public, Congress, or the steel executives.

These two elements of the power situation, Truman's lame duck Presidency and his very low popularity surely acted, both singly and in concert, to deprive Truman of influence and therefore reduce the options truly open to the President to settle the steel dispute in 1952. Due to the power situation, Truman could not rely upon persuasion via the exercise of subtle, informal political influence. Rather, if he was to have any effect at all upon the final outcome, he would have to rely heavily upon his formal executive powers, and preferably upon a formal power which required as little outside cooperation as possible.

Another repercussion of the power situation facing Truman was that it most likely triggered the "combative" aspect of Truman's character. Truman did not always use aggressive or abrasive rhetoric, and his personal style was often portrayed by those close to him as surprisingly mild and friendly. However, when he perceived himself to be in the midst of a fight, Truman would quickly resort to "fighting words." Truman was firmly resolved not to appear weak or to back down to the steel industry's price demands in 1952 as he had done in 1946, and, given his nature, his resolve was intensified when faced with a power situation that left him to fight very nearly alone for his policy positions.

The Issue of Responsibility

In addition to the power situation, the second key factor necessary to understanding why President Truman chose seizure over Taft-Hartley is a knowledge of which party, industry or labor, Truman held responsible for the perpetuation of a strike he strongly believed to be inimical to the national interest. It was noted earlier that Truman had developed a very strong sense of national responsibility throughout his political career. This sense was not only with regard to his own actions, but also applied to all national leaders, inside and outside of government. From his action during the 1946 labor troubles we saw how Truman, given his character, was most likely to react toward the parties he deemed to have been irresponsible toward the national interest. During the 1952 steel dispute labor attempted to blame management for the lack of a settlement, while management tried to place that responsibility on labor. Perhaps both sides were equally at fault in reality, but the question is what was President Truman's perception on this issue? Which party did he feel was responsible, and how would this feeling affect his choice among the options still open to him?

It is clearly evident from President Truman's address to the nation announcing the seizure decision, delivered on April 9, that at that time he held the steel companies responsible for failure to settle the dispute via collective bargaining. In talking about the Wage Stabilization Board's March 20 recommendation, which labor was willing to accept as a basis for settlement, Truman stated, "They were entirely consistent with what has been allowed in other industries over the past eighteen months. They are in accord with sound stabilization policies. The fact of the matter is that the settlement proposed by the Board is fair to both parties and to the public interest. And what's more, I think the steel companies know it. . . . They are raising all this hullabaloo in an attempt to force the Government to give them a big boost in prices.''[42] This was nearly identical to the situation during the 1946 steel dispute in which Truman had yielded to the companies' price demands. The economy and the country had paid dearly in terms of inflation for that action. This time around it seems President Truman was more determined to hold the line.

The companies had said that if they accepted the WSB guidelines they would need a $12 per ton price increase. To this demand President Truman responded angrily, ''that's about the most outrageous thing I ever heard of! They not only want to rise their prices to cover any wage increase; they want to double their money on the deal!''[43] President Truman was of the belief that the steel companies could and, therefore, should absorb the entire wage package recommended by the WSB without any need for a price rise. ''. . . If the steel companies absorbed every penny of the wage increase, they would still be making profits of $17 or $18 a ton on every ton of steel they made.''[44] Truman labeled such profit ''extremely high'' and noted it was far above pre-Korean war levels of steel industry profits.

Another thing that was clearly evident from his April 9 address was that Truman was as concerned, if not more concerned, about the steel dispute's effects upon the domestic economy than about its effect upon the country's defense efforts in Korea. Well over three-fourths of the text of his address dealt with the economic repercussions of the steel companies' demands. President Truman asserted that if the companies' demands were agreed to, ''that would be a terrific blow to the stability of the economy of the United States of America . . . if we broke our own price control rule for steel, I don't see how we could keep them for any other industry.''[45] Truman noted that other industries had asked for higher prices and were denied them, but they had kept on producing. Truman's sense of duty is expressed when he remarked, ''that's what any law-abiding person does when he is told what he would like to do is against the rules. But not the steel companies. Not the steel companies . . . the steel industry wants something special. . . ."[46]

President Truman summarizes and reiterates his position on the issue of responsibility for the strike call by saying, "It is perfectly clear from the facts I have cited, that the present danger to our stabilization program comes from the steel companies' insistence on a big jump in steel prices. . . . the steel companies are recklessly forcing a shutdown of the steel mills. . . . As President of the United States it is my plain duty to keep this from happening."[47]

From the above statements it is quite evident that on April 9 President Truman believed the steel companies had acted contrary to the national interest. Furthermore, he was intent upon taking actions to bring pressure upon the steel industry to conform to his conception of national responsibility. The question then becomes which of the two options still left on the table, a Taft–Hartley injunction or seizure of the mills pursuant to Executive Order, would exert the most pressure upon the *companies* to settle?

Regarding a Taft–Hartley injunction, Truman's feelings were made plain in a special message to Congress delivered on June 10, 1952. Noting that labor had voluntarily worked for ninety-nine days without a contract, he said "In these respects, the union and its members have cooperated freely with the government in the public interest. And yet the effect of a Taft–Hartley labor injunction would be to penalize the workers and give the advantage to the steel companies. I want to make it very plain to the Congress that the result of using the Taft–Hartley type injunction in this dispute would be to take sides with the companies and against the workers."[48] Therefore, in Truman's mind, in terms of punishing the "guilty" party in the dispute, Taft–Hartley would not fill the bill.

On the other hand, if the steel companies were seized and administered by the government, the government might alter the terms of employment, raising workers' wages, while the mills were in their possession. If this possibility were made known to the industry, it would almost certainly act as an impetus for settlement via collective bargaining rather than by governmental fiat where the companies would have no input. This was Truman's grand design behind the seizure option; to bring as much pressure as possible to bear upon the companies, not labor. "The White House had hoped, by threatening to increase the wages of the steelworkers while the government was in possession of the mills, to exert pressure on the steel companies to settle with the union on terms which would not harm stabilization policy. Since seizure ensured the continued production of steel, the industry would, it was thought, have no leverage to obtain the price adjustment it wanted."[49] Furthermore, the symbolic aspect of seizure was also consistent with President Truman's aims, for ". . . unlike the Taft–Hartley injunction, it was directed at the steel companies as well as the union. Indeed the President's speech clearly indicated that the steel seizure was being used as a weapon against the industry as the recalcitrant party."[50]

Given Truman's presidential character in general and his sense of outrage at the steel companies' evasion of their national responsibility in particular, combined with a power situation which made the choice of less drastic measures impossible, seizure appeared to be the only option which would satisfy all of President Truman's goals for dispute settlement. These goals had by now grown to four from the original two. President Truman wanted 1) no stoppage of steel production, 2) no price increases over and above those allowed by his stabilization policies ($3 to $4 per ton), 3) a method of settlement that would put the most pressure upon the steel companies due to the fact that Truman believed it was their intransigence and irresponsibility which precipitated the April 8 crisis, and 4) a method of settlement that, given the power situation, had the greatest likelihood of success with regard to the previous three goals.

Therefore, on April 8, with collective bargaining stalled and only a few hours until the strike was to begin, President Truman issued Executive Order 10340. This order instructed Secretary of Commerce Charles Sawyer to administer the steel mills in the name of the government until a settlement could be reached.

Thus, government seizure of the steel mills was effectuated solely by resort to the inherent powers of the President acting in his capacities as Commander in Chief and Chief Executive. Such a seizure did not require any cooperation from Congress to become effective, nor was there any time lag involved.

President Truman firmly believed he had sufficient constitutional powers to justify seizure of the mills. "In my opinion, the seizure was well within my constitutional powers, and I had acted accordingly. . . . I believe that the power of the President should be used in the interest of the people, and in order to do that the President must use whatever power the Constitution does not expressly deny him."[51]

By issuing Executive Order 10340 Truman specifically rejected the Taft–Hartley injunction option. In his address to the nation explaining his action of April 8 he cited two factors for the rejection. First, "the overriding factor is that the Taft–Hartley procedure could not prevent a steel shutdown of at least a week or two."[52] This was so because under Taft–Hartley a board of inquiry had to be appointed to investigate the issues before the Attorney General could go to court to request an injunction. Second, President Truman felt that even after the Attorney General requested an injunction there was no assurance that the courts would grant an eighty-day cooling off period due to the fact that the unions had already postponed their strike for ninety-nine days without result.

As a consequence of Executive Order 10340, the Government would have possession of the mills and steel production would continue until June 2, 1952. On that day the Supreme Court declared the seizure to be an unconstitutional exercise of executive power. The decision was 6–3 and was without a clearly enunciated majority opinion.[53] Upon hearing the Court's decision, a severely disappointed but nevertheless dutiful President Truman ordered the immediate return of the mills to their private owners. When this was accomplished a fifty-two-day strike ensued.

Conclusion

This paper identified all the options available to President Truman for settlement of the steel dispute of 1952, established Truman's presidential character, and then applied his character to the options available in order to explain Truman's choice of seizure over the others. From this look into Truman's presidential character and decision-making options, two things become evident. First, President Truman was at least as much concerned with the steel dispute's domestic economic repercussions as he was about the effect of a stoppage in steel production upon U.S. defense efforts in Korea. Second, that Truman's actions during the steel strike of 1952 were consistent with those you would expect of active-positive presidents in general, and of Truman's presidential character in particular.

When viewed in terms of President Truman's presidential character, his actions during the 1952 steel dispute become more clearly understandable. In 1946 it had been labor who had acted "irresponsibly" and had consequently felt Truman's wrath. In 1952 it was the steel companies who acted irresponsibly, and they were treated by Truman in an identical fashion. Hence, President Truman's actions during the steel dispute of 1952 were not those of a rash, vengeful decision-maker, but were rather consistent products of particular elements of his presidential character. The steel dispute became a matter of principle for Truman, and he acted as he had always acted in such matters. As Truman himself said, "it is much better to go down fighting for what is right than to compromise your principles."[54]

So was it spoken; so was it done.

References

[1] *Youngstown Sheet and Tube* vs. *Sawyer*, 343 U.S. 579 (1952).

[2] Veto Message to the House of Representatives, June 20, 1947, Truman papers, 1947, pp. 288–97.

[3] James Barber, *The Presidential Character* (Englewood Cliffs, N.J., 1977) Chapt. 8.

⁴ What follows is a very broad-brush discussion of Barber's analytical scheme and Truman's presidential character as developed by Barber. This brief sketch will allow us to examine Truman's actions during the steel crisis of 1952 in terms of his presidential character. For those wishing to read a fully-developed explanation of both Barber's paradigm in general and his analysis of Truman in particular, please see Chapters 1 and 8 in *The Presidential Character*.

⁵ Barber, *The Presidential Character*, pp. 3–4.

⁶ Ibid., p. 8.

⁷ Ibid., p. 7.

⁸ Ibid.

⁹ Ibid., pp. 7–8.

¹⁰ Ibid., p. 6.

¹¹ Ibid., p. 11.

¹² Ibid., p. 12.

¹³ Harry Truman, *Years of Trial and Hope: 1946–1952.* (New York, 1956), p. 13.

¹⁴ James Barber, *The Presidential Character*, p. 250.

¹⁵ Ibid., p. 263.

¹⁶ *New York Times*, March 30, 1952, p. 64.

¹⁷ James Barber, *The Presidential Character*, p. 273.

¹⁸ Steinberg writes that "Thomas Jefferson once observed that the American people expect Presidents to be aloof and unsmiling in public. Truman could never achieve such a pose and assume a false front of aloofness. It was his openness and his grin, his love of horseplay and wisecracks . . . and his absolute lack of snobishness that added mortar to the brickbats thrown at him by opponents." See Alfred Steinberg *The Man from Missouri: The Life and Times of Harry S. Truman* (New York, 1962), p. 264.

¹⁹ James Barber, *The Presidential Character*, p. 261.

²⁰ Ibid., p. 277.

²¹ Harry Truman, *Years of Trial and Hope*, p. 45.

²² Ibid., p. 49.

²³ Statement by the President on the Labor Dispute in the Steel Industry. December 22, 1951, Public Papers of the Presidents, 1951, pp. 651–52.

²⁴ For details of the W.S.B.'s recommendations see Arthur F. McClure, *The Truman Administration and the Problems of Postwar Labor* (Rutherford, N.J., 1969) pp. 65–68.

²⁵ *New York Times*, March 22, 1952, p. 3.

²⁶ The Capehart Amendment allowed defense contractors to pass on increased costs of production incurred during the Korean War, but did not allow for increased profits.

²⁷ Letter to Charles Wilson, March 30, 1952 Presidential Papers 1951–1952, p. 226.

²⁸ Presidential Papers 1952–53, p. 315.

[29] Bert Cochran, *Harry Truman and the Crisis Presidency*. (New York, 1973), p. 205.

[30] Maeva Marcus. *Truman and the Steel Seizure Case: The Limits of Presidential Power*. (New York, 1977), pp. 6–7.

[31] *Congressional Record*, 96:12412.

[32] Maeva Marcus. *Truman and the Steel Seizure Case*, p. 76.

[33] This is assuming a) that the Courts would agree to issue an injunction in spite of the fact that the strike had already been voluntarily postponed for ninety-nine days, or b) that the union would obey a Taft–Hartley injunction or a back-to-work order by the Government following a seizure.

[34] Harry S. Truman, *Years of Trial and Hope*.

[35] Ibid.

[36] *New York Times*, October 21, 1946.

[37] Fred L. Israel, ed., *The State of the Union Messages of the Presidents, 1790–1966*, vol. 3, p. 2956.

[38] R. Alton Lee, *Truman and Taft–Hartley: A Question of Mandate*. (Lexington, Ky., 1966), p. 107.

[39] George Gallup, *The Gallup Poll: Public Opinion 1935–1971* 2, 1040.

[40] Ibid., p. 1050.

[41] Ibid., p. 1052, poll released on April 2, 1952.

[42] Truman's Address to the Nation Concerning the Seizure of the Steel Mills. *New York Times*, April 9, 1952, p. 16.

[43] Ibid.

[44] Ibid.

[45] Ibid.

[46] Ibid.

[47] Ibid.

[48] Special Message to Congress Regarding the Steel Strike, June 10, 1952 Presidential Papers 1952–1953, p. 412.

[49] Maeva Marcus. *Truman and the Steel Seizure Case*, p. 83.

[50] Ibid., p. 47.

[51] Harry Truman, *Years of Trial and Hope*, p. 473.

[52] *New York Times*, April 9, p. 16.

[53] *Youngstown Sheet and Tube Co.* v. *Sawyer*, 33 U.S. 579 (1952). Truman may have been victimized by his power situation in the Supreme Court as well as in Congress. Noting that Supreme Court Justices had not lacked for ingenuity in upholding past exercises of presidential power when they *wanted* to, Bert Cochran wrote, "It is doubtful that the Court would have been this precipitate in taking the case (and finding against the President) but not for Truman's poor repute." See Cochran, *Harry Truman and the Crisis Presidency*, p. 335. The fact that Truman was also a lame-duck president may have made the Justice's ultimate decision easier to arrive at.

[54] Harry Truman, *Years of Trial and Hope*, p. 179.

13

On Presidential Character

Jeffrey Tulis

In 1972 Senator Thomas Eagleton of Missouri withdrew from the race for vice-president of the United States because of public reaction to the fact that he had been previously treated for mental illness. Presidential nominee George McGovern also fared poorly due, in part, to that incident; for while the public worried over Eagleton's medical history, they worried too about McGovern's political judgment and skill in selecting and firing Eagleton. The question of presidential character has loomed large in the public eye since 1972, because of political events like the Eagleton debacle and later the Watergate affair. The Eagleton-McGovern incident illustrates nicely the range of issues that have been conflated into the concept of "character." On the one hand are psychological considerations, and on the other are political or judgmental considerations. In everyday discourse, one often distinguishes between people who are in the grip of syndromes and those who are exercising "poor judgment." The line between the two is sometimes fuzzy, as lawyers will often point out in murder trials, but it is noteworthy that the law itself, like our common parlance, captures the distinction between psychological and judgmental causes.

Our common parlance and our everyday understanding of "character" may be changing, due in large measure to a book which first appeared the year of the Eagleton incident—James David Barber's *The Presidential Character*. After Barber, many Americans may no longer be concerned primarily with presidential judgment as such, but rather with personality "types" that lie behind the judgments. To be more precise, many commentators now see "judgment" as a reflection of a psychological variable rather than as an independent cause. Barber's study is not the first study of political personality, or even of presidential personality, but it is the most important because it may be shaping the way citizens evaluate their presidents and presidential candidates. One may consider the examination of the meaning of Barber's enterprise to be a matter of public policy, since Barber has employed his studies in efforts to support candidates in the last two elections.[1]

In addition to the practical concern, there is a scholarly impetus to seriously examine the Barber study. Barber appears to have avoided several of the significant flaws attributed to earlier studies of political personality. The model typological analysis before Barber was Harold Lasswell's *Psychopathology and Politics*.[2] Lasswell constructed a typology based upon data collected in interviews with men who had held political positions, but who, in most cases, subsequently became mental patients. Most of the political positions that these men had held were as low-level functionaries. Lasswell assumed that all were "political men," each embodying a mix of three types: the agitator, the administrator, and the theorist. He sought to discern these types by employing an avowedly Freudian analysis. Thus, Lasswell attempted to fathom the meaning of a political personality from a vantage point that appeared far removed from politics: the men he examined were not significant politicians; he did not focus upon politicians *within* particular political roles; he employed the psychological approach which probes most deeply into the private aspects of his subject's minds. This brief sketch of noteworthy characteristics certainly does not do justice to the Lasswell study. These characteristics are noteworthy, however, because none of them is present in *The Presidential Character*. To be sure, many of the often praised aspects of Lasswell's work have found their way into the Barber study, and these are noted by some of Barber's reviewers.[3] But one should also note that Barber, building upon his previous work examining state legislators, looks at important politicians in their political settings and he eschews strictly Freudian theory. Barber prefers an eclectic approach which, remaining closer to the surface, takes more seriously the actors' own perceptions.

> The psychological approach is simple; some will find it too simple. With a few quite minor exceptions, included for their wider interest, psycho- analytic interpretations at the symbolic level are avoided. . . . My approach to understanding Presidents is much closer to the psychology of adaptation, stressing the ways interpersonal experience shapes the person's self-image, his worldview, and his political style, and how, in turn these internalized lessons of experience are turned back to shape interpersonal experience.[4]

Barber's study also represents a departure from previous studies of presidential personality, because it is the first attempt to construct a generalized predictive theory of the presidency. A well-known earlier study, *Woodrow Wilson and Colonel House*, by Alexander and Julliette George, utilized a more sophisticated psychological approach, but its restriction to one case precluded the development of a political theory.[5]

Barber does not limit himself to prediction. As Alexander George noted in his very insightful review of *The Presidential Character*, "Barber's study emerges as the first systematic effort to apply personality theory to the task of *assessing* candidates for the Presidency."[6] Barber attempts to link specific kinds of character to specific kinds of policy making. In the final and most important step of the study Barber hierarchically orders the kinds of policy making in an effort to encourage selection of a particular kind of man.

The Presidential Character is significant not only because it culminates in conscious prescription, but also because the prescription is rhetorical rather than institutional. In other words, Barber suggests criteria to guide citizen deliberation about candidates, rather than laws to affect either the selection process or the conduct of the presidential office. Because the presidency is "so highly personalized" Barber suggests that the office has little to do with presidential behavior. "You can organize [the] office in many different ways, but the person who inhabits the office is going to use those instrumentalities for his own purposes.'' Barber's key to improving the presidency is not to change the office, but rather to help the citizenry select the right man. ''If you can't really control the President effectively by law, if you can't really control him effectively during his term of office by a skeptical attitude of public opinion, then basically what you're left with is the thought that you'd better control him at the time you're picking him.''[7]

Although contemporary studies of presidential character show little regard for the constitutional order in explaining presidential behavior, the architects of the constitutional order were very much concerned with presidential character. For the founders, the question of character was a central consideration in their design of a selection system and of the presidential office.

Early in the deliberations of the Federal Convention, Benjamin Franklin reminded his colleagues to concern themselves with the character of their future presidents. Franklin proposed that the president should serve without salary, so that presidential ambition would be unable to unite with avarice. Since Madison indicates that the institutional proposal was not taken seriously by the other delegates, some historians have ignored or minimized the importance of Franklin's suggestion.[8] Although the specific proposal was rejected, there is evidence which indicates that the point behind the suggestion was influential. Franklin reminded the delegates that an office of honor that is at the same time a place of profit will attract a certain kind of man.

> And what kind are the men that will strive for this profitable preeminence, through all the bustle of cabal, the heat of contention, the influential mutual abuse of parties, tearing to pieces the best of characters? It will not be the wise and moderate, the lovers of peace and good order, the men fittest for the trust. It will be the bold and the violent, the men of strong passions and indefatigable activity in their selfish pursuits. These will thrust themselves on your government and be your rulers. And these too will be mistaken in the expected happiness of their situation: For their vanquished competitors of the same spirit, and from the same motives will perpetually be endeavoring to distress their administration, thwart their meaning and render them odious to the people.[9]

Moreover, Franklin argued that avaricious presidents would divide the nation into tumultuous factions because there would always be men on both sides of a continuing proposition to increase the salary of the president, and avaricious chief executives would constantly seek to augment their salary. It is important to note that Franklin's discussion of presidential character occurred in the context of an institutional issue: the salary provision. This was the characteristic way in which presidential character was discussed throughout the formation and ratification of the Constitution.

On the matter of salary, the convention did decide to pay the president, but it stipulated that the salary could not be increased or diminished during the president's term in office. Franklin's reasoning apparently affected the deliberations. According to *The Federalist*, "Judicious attention has been paid to this subject in the proposed Constitution. . . . [The legislature] can neither weaken [the president's] fortitude by operating on his necessities, nor corrupt his integrity by appealing to his avarice. . . . He can, of course, have no pecuniary inducement to renounce or desert the independence intended for him by the Constitution."[10]

As *The Federalist* indicates, the interests and motives of the president were to be attached to the structure and duties of his office. With respect to salary, this meant that the president's baser motives would be contained. However, the founders also attempted to build upon low, or selfish qualities of the incumbent, either by making self-interest coincide with public good, or by elevating and transforming selfishness itself. Self-interest would be made to coincide with the public good, for example, by means of the impeachment provision, because "so far as the fear of punishment and disgrace can operate, that motive to good behavior is amply afforded by the article on the subject of impeachment." The founders' deliberation over the provision for indefinite reeligibility illustrates how they believed self-interest could sometimes be elevated. By holding up the possibility of a long tenure, a president's selfishness, or greed, might be converted into a quest for fame, since the prospect of a lengthy tenure carries with it the prospect of monumental projects.[11]

The founders were not solely concerned with the structure of the office; they considered, too, alternative modes of selection. As in contemporary commentary, the question of presidential selection loomed large at the founding, but it was viewed as an institutional rather than rhetorical problem. The electoral college and the minimum age requirement were structural responses to the founders' fear that unqualified and dangerous men (particularly demagogues) might ascend to the nation's highest office. Presidents must be at least thirty-five, not only because the founders wanted experienced men, but also because they wanted men old enough to have revealed their character and ability. Thus the people would "not be liable to be deceived by those brilliant appearances of genius and patriotism which, like transient meteors sometimes mislead as well as dazzle."[12]

From this very brief sketch of noteworthy founding views, it should be clear that the framers of the Constitution considered institutions to be of more perplexity than character. The "new science of politics" of that time was less interested in discovering a new conspectus of human types than in discovering ways to control or mold commonly known qualities of men. James Barber finds character more perplexing than institutions. His political science is directed to developing a new typology of character different from that known to the average citizen, albeit intended to instruct the citizenry. This approach rests on an implicit criticism of the faith the founders had in institutional arrangements. According to Barber, recent history indicates that men "preeminent for wisdom and virtue" are often not elected president, and those elected are not always prevented "from steering a course which ends in tragedy for the nation." And even if the men who become president are a discrete set of character types filtered and molded by the founders' design, there is enough diversity in presidential behavior to push scholars beyond the "office" in their search for explanations of why presidents behave the way they do.

Conceding that the principles and structure of the office do not provide sufficient material for comprehensive explanation of presidential decision making, we wish to know to what extent Barber's theory does. After briefly summarizing Barber's theory, we shall reexamine it by replicating it. The theory will be applied to Abraham Lincoln and Stephen Douglas (a president and presidential candidate not examined by Barber) in order to illuminate the limits of Barber's enterprise.

The Presidential Character in Brief

Barber's objective is fourfold. He attempts to describe the bearing of presidential character upon presidential performance in the twentieth century. He attempts to predict presidential behavior in two ways. On the basis of fundamental characteristics which constitute a particular type of personality, Barber attempts to predict associated characteristics of men of that type. On the basis of study of early life, Barber attempts to predict behavior in later life. Finally, he attempts to assess which kind of personalities become the best (and worst) presidents.

There are four basic types of presidential personality generated from the combination of two "baseline" variables. All men are more or less active in their lives' endeavors and all men more or less enjoy those activities. On the basis of data culled from biographies of presidents, Barber classifies each as predominantly active or passive, and predominantly positive or negative with respect to enjoyment. This produces four cells arrayed below and filled in with respective presidents.[1]

Barber reconfirms his initial categorization with the aid of five major concepts: style, world view, character, power relations, and climate of expectations. The latter two concepts, "power relations" and "climate of expectations," represent Barber's attempt to depict the historical scene that surrounds each president. Barber finds that the "resonance" (or lack thereof) between man and circumstance illuminates personality.

Given depiction of the constellations of power and climate of expectations, "the burden of this book is [to show] that the

	Active	Passive
Positive	Jefferson FDR Truman Kennedy Ford Carter	Madison Taft Harding
Negative	John Adams Wilson Hoover Johnson Nixon	Washington Coolidge Eisenhower

crucial differences can be anticipated by an understanding of a potential President's character, world view, and his style.'' These three major concepts are utilized to discern the "integrated pattern" that constitutes each president's personality.[13] The concepts are delineated as follows:

> Character is the way the President orients himself toward life. . . . Character is the person's stance as he confronts experience.

> World view consists of [a President's] primary, politically relevant beliefs, particularly his conceptions of social causality, human nature, and the central conflicts of the time.

> Style is the President's habitual way of performing his three political roles: rhetoric, personal relations, and homework.[14]

Style is the most salient indicator of presidential personality, and Barber spends most of his analysis describing the disposition of presidents in their three political roles. However, Barber concludes that character is the most important factor within personality.

For purposes of prediction, Barber notes that "in general character has its main development in childhood, world view in adolescence, style in early adulthood." The three themes coalesce, and are expressed by style. The appearance of style is somewhat peculiar. Barber maintains that presidential style is most clearly visible at the point at which a youngster moves from home into a wider public, similar to the period labeled by others as the time of "identity crisis." Barber labels this period, "the first independent political success," although it involves running for office in only a few of the cases. According to Barber, the style surrounding the first independent political success *reappears* (having been somewhat dormant) upon election to the presidency. Barber does not know why this happens. "Something in him remembers this earlier victory."[15]

Barber's attempt to predict adult character on the basis of adolescent personality rests on the adequacy of the concept "first independent political success." However, it is Barber's other sort of prediction, the attempt to assess the probable texture and direction of policy making in the White House on the basis of the president's adult personality, that is our main concern here. This kind of prediction rests crucially upon the accuracy of the general description of the several basic presidential personality types. The following summary indicates the prevailing tendencies that Barber discovered in each:

> The 'active-positive' character is 'adaptive." He displays a congruence between much of his activity and his enjoyment of it, thereby 'indicating relatively high self-esteem and relative success in relating to the environment.' He shows 'an orientation toward productiveness as a value and an ability to use styles flexibly, adaptively. . . . He sees himself as developing over time relatively well defined goals,' and emphasizes 'rational mastery.'

> The 'active-negative' character is 'compulsive.' He experiences a 'contradiction . . . between relatively intense effort and relatively low emotional reward for that effort.' His activity has a 'compulsive,' compensatory character; 'he seems ambitious, striving upward, power-seeking. . . . He has a persistent problem in managing his aggressive feelings. His self-image is vague and discontinuous.'

> The 'passive-positive' character is 'compliant.' He is 'receptive' and 'other-directed,' a personality 'whose life is a search for affection as a reward for being agreeable and cooperative rather than personally assertive.' He experiences a contradiction . . . between low self-esteem (on grounds of being unlovable, unattractive) and a superficial optimism.'

> The 'passive-negative' character is 'withdrawn.' He is oriented 'toward doing dutiful service; this compensates for low self-esteem

based on a sense of uselessness.' His tendency is 'to withdraw, to escape from the conflict and uncertainty of politics by emphasizing vague principles (especially prohibitions) and procedural arrangements.'[16]

Barber suggests that the best policy and leadership for the nation comes from an active-positive president. His personality leads him to be flexible, and to avoid irrational decisions, to be open to criticism and advice. "This may get him into trouble; he may fail to take account of the irrational in politics," but on the whole the country is safest if its president is an active-positive type.

The worst kind of president for Barber is the active-negative. The active-negative tends to pursue a tragic "rigidification" of policy which is impervious to criticism, public opinion, or the surrounding power situation. Johnson's escalation of the Vietnam War, Nixon's continuance of the war and his behavior in the Watergate affair, Wilson's self-defeating League of Nations campaign, and Hoover's economic policies are all cited as examples of such rigidification. These policies are all considered "disastrous" or near-disastrous.[17]

Passive-positive and passive-negative presidents may in certain times provide the country with reassurance, and respite from previous tumult. But there is a danger that with a passive president the country may "drift," or be lulled into a false sense of security "which diverts popular attention from the hard realities of politics." "What passive Presidents ignore active Presidents inherit."[18]

All of the analysis and predictions in the first edition of *The Presidential Character* were retrospective, except one: the Nixon "tragedy." In the second edition Barber predicted the presidential characters of Ford and Carter, but due to the short tenure of each, Barber's pre-Watergate predictions of Nixon's second term remain "so far this scheme's main test."[19] Nearly one quarter of Barber's book is devoted to analysis of active-negative Richard Nixon. Of course Barber's study did not, and was not intended to, predict historical events like Watergate. Rather, Barber claims to have been successful in predicting

Nixon's manner of dealing with Watergate, and more importantly, he predicted that Nixon would probably seize upon and
pursue *some* line of policy in the manner of Watergate.[20]
Barber's Nixon prediction has been contested by Alexander
George, who suggests that Nixon did not "rigidify" his behavior
as did other active-negative presidents, most notably Woodrow
Wilson. George calls upon Barber to give greater weight to the
differences between presidents within each of Barber's types,
and less attention to similar tendencies. He suggests that Barber
expand the number of cells, adding "mixed types" to the four
original categories.[21] It is important to recognize that this kind of
criticism is not fundamental. That is to say, whether correct or
not, it remains within an horizon of agreement with Barber
regarding the theoretical possibility of his enterprise. Thus, the
issue between Barber and his critics appears to be over the
adequacy of Barber's individual interpretations and over the
relative merits of a simple versus a complex typology, not over
the limits inherent to a typological understanding per se.

Replicating the Barber Study

What follows is another "test" of Barber's theory, one which
is intended to raise questions about the nature and consequences
of his endeavor as a whole. Barber's theory will be partially
replicated by applying it to two politicians not examined by
him—Abraham Lincoln and Stephen A. Douglas. Lincoln is a
crucial case because his administration and political qualities
have been well studied and are so well known. Lincoln is widely
regarded as America's greatest president, possessed of qualities
so admirable that it is common for scholars, citizens, and pundits
to yearn for his uncommon kind of leadership. It is reasonable to
expect that a prescriptive thesis like Barber's would square with
the considered judgment of Lincoln, or at least not run directly
counter to the widely accepted view without explanation. But as
will be indicated below, Lincoln does not fare well by Barber's
criteria. He appears to have been an active-negative, the worst
type of president for Barber, while his opponent Douglas seems

to have possessed the praiseworthy active-positive character. It is striking that Lincoln is not mentioned, let alone analyzed in detail, by Barber, not only because the restriction to twentieth-century presidents is "more or less arbitrary" in *The Presidential Character*, but also because Barber examined the style of nineteenth-century Andrew Johnson in an early article.[22]

It should be emphasized that these brief case studies are intended to be faithful replications of the Barber mode of analysis in all details including style of presentation. While interpretations of the sort Barber employs cannot be replicated with the automatic ease of other political studies such as those employing survey techniques, it should not be assumed that no standards or guidelines are available. Barber has been extraordinarily helpful to scholars by making accessible background instructions that he gave to his research assistants as well as by publishing a reflective article that reconstructs the logic and method of his inquiry. To be sure, in *The Presidential Character* itself Barber does not devote much space to his methodology, preferring instead to get right to the business of actual interpretation. The same procedure will be followed here, but the reader is invited to compare these cases with Barber's to test the "faithfulness" of the replication. The best cases for this purpose are Barber's comparison of Nixon and McGovern because there Barber pits an analysis of an actual president against an interpretation of a candidate.[23]

Abraham Lincoln

Throughout his political career Lincoln worked incessantly. He campaigned for many candidates, rarely missed legislative sessions, and undertook his own research and clerical work. Biographer Benjamin P. Thomas gives this account: "Lincoln was diligent in the routine work of the House. He rarely missed a roll call and performed his full share of labor on his two committees—that of the Post Office and Post Roads, and the Committee on Expenditures in the War Department. *Few first term members have been more active*, yet his colleagues generally appraised him as a droll westerner of average talents."[24]

When Lincoln ran against Douglas in the now-famous senatorial battle (which Lincoln lost), he arranged the debates, preparing seven long speeches. The rigorous and long debates, however, represented only a small part of the campaign activity of both men. Thomas reports that "between the debates each man spoke almost everyday for four months to large crowds in the open air, and travelled incessantly between engagements, by railroad, steamboat, or horse and buggy, putting up with the scanty comforts and poor food of country inns and never, so far as the record shows, missing a single engagement."[25]

In the White House, Lincoln pursued the same frenetic pace. He started work early; by breakfast at 8 A.M. he had been at work for an hour. In the early days of the presidency he refused to limit visiting hours. (Later he was convinced to do so by his aides.) In addition to the usual policy preparation, Lincoln personally signed every officer's commission and promotion. He wrote his own speeches, state papers, and wrote many letters, often making copies for his files. Eating little, he would read the newspapers at lunch, visit hospitals at about tea time every day, work through the evening until about midnight. Before he went to bed he would visit the War Department telegraph office for the latest cables from the battlefields. He usually read before sleeping (often *Macbeth* or the *Merry Wives of Windsor*), and would finally doze off, sleeping "light and fitful." Once per week the White House would hold an open house reception; Lincoln's hand was reportedly swollen several times from greeting thousands of visitors each week. (It is claimed by Lincoln himself that such handshaking was the cause of his wavering signature on the Emancipation Proclamation.) The volume of Lincoln's writings is also a measure of his overall activity. It has been tallied that his published words "numbered 1,078,365 in comparison with 1,025,000 for the complete works of Shakespeare, and 926,877 for the entire Bible."[26]

It is clear enough that Lincoln had an active, rather than passive, personality, but where would he fall on the "positive-negative" spectrum? This broad dimension is intended to encompass the president's attitude toward his myriad activities and toward himself. In depicting Lincoln's subjective state, it will be helpful to delineate three predominate themes: his rhetorical style and skills, his world view revealed by his objects of interest (his singleness of purpose), and his character exhibited through expressions of inadequacy and mental torment.

Consistent with the styles of several "negative" presidents, (Wilson and Coolidge) speechmaking served as a release, a burst of exuberance, a surge of good feeling, for Lincoln. He wrote his own speeches, injecting literary allusions and polishing his style. There was a marked contrast between the excitement of his speeches and the ordinary character of his normal discourse. J. C. Randall comments that "no one could call his speeches crude; on the contrary they sometimes rose to the height of literary mastery, though in familiar conversation and in informal utterance he lapsed into colloquialisms." Another scholar notes the difference between Lincoln's prepared and unprepared remarks. "His best ideas and finest phrases did not occur in impromptu speeches. In public he seldom was ready with words."[27]

Lincoln's voice would change as audiences responded to his rhetoric. Beginning in a high pitched "squeaking" voice, Lincoln would gain confidence and mellow a bit in the midst of many of his speeches. When his public speeches were carefully prepared, they served as one of his most effective tools of leadership. "Mastery of language may have been that ultimate factor without which he would have failed."[28]

In his personal relations Lincoln was often reserved; he liked to draw out information without revealing his own thoughts and feelings. He was protective of his self, while inquisitive of others. The blatant contrast between the "prepared" public and the private Lincoln reminds one of Calvin Coolidge's "impenetrable silences."

> [Lincoln's] friends were fascinated by his enigmatic silences. Herndon, after sharing a law office with him for more than sixteen years, concluded that he was, when he wanted to be, "the most shut mouthed man who ever lived." David Davis, for many seasons a judge on the circuit court with him and in 1860 his campaign manager wrote: "I known the man so

well, he was the most reticent, secretive man I ever saw or expected to see." Leonard Swett, for eleven years a fellow lawyer on the circuit declared, "He always told only enough of his plans and purposes to induce a belief that he had communicated all; yet he reserved enough to have communicated nothing." Ward Hill Lamon, an Illinois crony who served as Lincoln's volunteer bodyguard during the war, stated that Lincoln "made simplicity and candor a mask of deep feelings carefully concealed, and subtle plans studiously veiled."[29]

Lincoln's rhetorical style cannot be completely depicted without mention of the place of humor in his speech. Humor served Lincoln several functions. He used "stories" to avoid discussion of sensitive topics, he told jokes to cheer himself up in times of stress, and he veiled some of his bitterest criticism in cloaks of sarcasm. Sarcasm, carefully planned, replaced a good fight for Lincoln. One Lincoln scholar labeled his humor "merciless satire," but pointed out that Lincoln the president matured to the extent that he suppressed the bite of some of his attacks. (Examples of the early *ad hominem* attacks include Lincoln referring to Douglas as a great man, "a lion in fact, a caged and toothless lion." ("A living dog though is better than a dead lion," he said.) Earlier Lincoln wrote to a friend that his party's strategy would be to ignore Douglas. "Isn't that the best way to treat so small a matter?"[30]

The personal attacking function became more and more suppressed as Lincoln grew into the presidency, but the other functions became more pronounced. At times, Lincoln would engineer his speeches around a joke. For example, Lincoln declared that "the Dred Scott decision made popular sovereignty as thin as homeopathic soup made by boiling the shadow of a pigeon that had starved to death."[31]

Lincoln's ability to joke in times of stress can be cited as a "positive" strand in his personality. As will be apparent later, however, his laughter was not enough to compensate for his feelings of inadequacy, and often his laughter itself might have been a kind of not-so-frivolous self-criticism.

A second "negative" theme is revealed in Lincoln's rhetoric. Two modes of justification were characteristic of Lincoln. One was an emphasis upon duty; the other a constant recourse to the will of God. Both of these justificatory devices remind one of style traits of active-negative Woodrow Wilson. Taken together, these devices reveal a tendency to appeal inflexibly to "principle."

As Lincoln emerged from obscurity and retirement, when the Kansas-Nebraska bill was passed, he affirmed that he was embarking upon a "moral challenge." The Kansas-Nebraska bill repealed the Missouri Compromise, thus allowing determination of the legality of slavery in new states to be left to "popular will." "The news aroused him, 'as he had never been before.' Three months later we shall find him back in politics. But he will emerge as a different Lincoln from the ambitious politician whose hopes were seemingly blighted in 1849. His ambition, reawakened, will become as compelling as before, but it will be restrained by devotion to a cause."[32]

Lincoln often justified his actions by referring to his duty to perform them. Shortly before his second presidential election, for example, Lincoln stashed a note in his desk which promised his opponent cooperation to save the Union between election and inauguration should Lincoln lose the election. After victory, Lincoln read the promise to his cabinet, prompting question as to what he would have done if he had lost the election and if his opponent McClellan had refused to cooperate. Lincoln replied, "At least I should have done my duty and stood clear before my conscience."[33]

Consistent with this adherence to duty was a tendency of Lincoln to "stick to" his decisions. "Those closest to the President had learned that while he came to his decisions slowly, once made he seldom reversed them."[34] As his friend Herndon described, Lincoln's mind was his final standard.

> There was no refraction there, in this man's brain: he was not impulsive, fanciful, or imaginative, but cold, calm, precise and exact: he threw his whole mental light around the objects seen. . . . In his mental view he crushed the unreal . . . the hallow and the sham: he saw what no man could well dispute, but failed to see what might be seen . . . by other men. . . . His own mind was his exclusive standard.[35]

An often discussed set of incidents which reveals Lincoln's duty-bound inflexibility occurred between his first election and inauguration. At that time Lincoln remained silent on major issues, sticking by his previous statements. He was besieged by newspaper editors for his "latest" views. Lincoln refused to budge.

> I could say nothing which I have not already said, and which is in print and accessible to the public. . . . Please pardon me for suggesting that if the papers like yours which have heretofore persistently garbled, and misrepresented what I have said, will now fully and fairly place it before their readers, there can be no further misunderstanding. I beg you to believe me sincere, when . . . I urge it as the true cure for the uneasiness in the country. . . . The Republican newspapers now, and for some time past, are and have been republishing copious extracts from many published speeches, which would at once reach the whole public if your class of papers would also publish them. I am not at liberty to shift my ground. That is out of the question.[36]

The death of Lincoln's son Willie affected him tremendously. It bolstered his duty-bound notions with a recourse to God. "More and more his official utterances and state papers breathed dependence on a Higher Power, whose existence he may have doubted in his callow years."[37]

Lincoln used the notion of God to justify singleness of purpose in his own mind. If there is a clear difference of opinion, both opinions could not be right, because God would not will a contradiction.[38] Lincoln's notion of duty and increasing recourse to God bolstered his belief that his specific policies were the right ones. Consonant with other active-negatives, Lincoln was often "inflexible." Rhetoric, humor, and other justificatory resources (duty and God) are all ways in which Lincoln made sense of his deeper feelings. That is, he attempted to obliterate, manipulate, or camouflage his feelings with the devices I have discussed. These all are devices that other active-negative presidents have employed.

More fundamentally, Lincoln had negative feelings toward himself. He was self-critical, and often doubted his ability to be president. Lincoln did not harbor bitter feelings over political

defeat (as had Richard Nixon, for example). Losing his Senate
battle against Douglas, Lincoln recalled thinking at the time that
"it's a slip and not a fall." Nevertheless, Lincoln did not have
positive feelings toward becoming president. Early in 1860,
Lincoln remarked to a newspaper editor, "I must, in candor, say
I do not think I am fit for the Presidency." This may have been
a political tactic. However, subsequent statements seem to
reinforce the sincerity of the claim. When he was "in the
running" Lincoln sent an autobiographical sketch to John Fell
(to serve as the basis for a campaign biography) with the
following note appended. "There is not much of it, for the
reason, I suppose, that there is not much of me."[39]

Shortly after the nomination, two fellow Republicans, cele-
brating with Lincoln in Springfield, noted his reaction to the
event.

> Lincoln looked much moved, and rather sad . . . feeling the heavy
> responsibility thrown upon him.[40]

> Lincoln's response had been modest and brief, yet not colorless: he
> almost wished the 'high honor' had fallen to another.[41]

Just before his train departure from Springfield which would,
after many victory stops, carry Lincoln to Washington, he said
goodbye to his law partner Billy Herndon: "The two men parted
with a firm clasp of hands. 'I am sick of office holding already,'
Lincoln said, 'and I shudder to think of the tasks ahead.' "[42]
Along the train route to Washington, Lincoln delivered thirty-
seven "greetings" in five days. "Often Lincoln struck the note
of self-depreciation. He referred to himself as an old man; once
he had a passage read by 'younger eyes,' at times he confessed
he had not the 'voice' nor 'strength' for longer speaking. . . . He
declared that 'without a reason why . . . [he] should have a
name,' there had fallen upon him, 'a task such as did not rest
even upon the Father of our country.' "[43]

During the middle of his first term Lincoln was under a
constant barrage of abolitionist criticism for not emancipating
slaves. Lincoln, feeling that the time was not right for a

proclamation, also felt the tremendous pressure of his delay: "I know very well that many others might . . . do better than I can; and if I were satisfied that the public confidence was more fully possessed by any one of them than by me, and knew of any Constitutional way in which he could be put in my place, he should have it. I would gladly yield it to him."[44]

Three months later, Lincoln was subjected to yet another shelling of criticism, this time concerning his cabinet. One of the cabinet members recorded Lincoln's statements at the time in his diary: " 'They (a Senatorial Committee) wish to get rid of me, and I am sometimes half disposed to gratify them. . . . We are now on the brink of destruction . . . I can hardly see any ray of hope. . . . The Committee is to be up to see me at 7 o'clock. Since I heard last night of the proceedings of the caucus, I have been more distressed than by any event of my life.' "[45]

Lincoln looked forward to a second term (which was contrary to the current presidential practice) but he did not look forward with any semblance of joy: "A second term would be a great honor and a great labor, which together, perhaps I would not decline if tendered." Clearly it was a sense of duty (not of enjoyment) that propelled Lincoln. "The President showed no elation at his renomination."[46]

Lincoln sometimes felt severely betrayed by his "friends." On one occasion, Lincoln supporters sponsored a strong bill (the Wade-Davis bill) which "repudiated the rebels." For example, it denied Confederate officers the right to vote for delegates to state constitutional conventions. Lincoln pocket vetoed the bill, and incurred the wrath of congressional radicals. The radicals published a scathing attack on the president, entitled the Wade-Davis Manifesto. Refusing to read the manifesto, Lincoln claimed, "to be wounded in the house of one's friends is perhaps the most grievous affliction that can befall a man."[47]

Lincoln's self-criticism and self-doubt manifested itself in physical forms. Much evidence suggests that Lincoln was "worn," "tired," and suffered from periodic depression. Herndon observed that "melancholy dripped from him as he walked." Another friend, W. H. L. Wallace, observed in 1860 before Lincoln had been inaugurated (although after the election), "I have seen Mr. Lincoln two or three times since I have been here, but only for a moment and he is continuously surrounded by a crowd of people. He has a world of responsibility and seems to feel it and to be oppressed by it. He looks more care worn and haggard and stooped than I ever saw him."[48]

Lincoln's haggard look increased throughout the presidency as indicated by successive photographs. Although Mary Lincoln also suffered increasing depression throughout her later life, her basic demeanor contrasted with her husband's. "Her qualities were complementary to those of her husband. She was to be a stimulus to him, even if at times that stimulus was somewhat of an irritant. His friends unaminously testify to his sadness, his periods of absent thought when he saw nothing around him." Mary Lincoln's fits of depression led her into irascible states; Abraham's depression manifested itself in melancholic silence— perhaps a response to the pressure of his wife's behavior.[49]

A distinctive development—a note of maturity—in Lincoln's later life, was his increasing ability to control his outward emotions. "So long as I have been here [in the presidency], I have not willingly planted a thorn in any man's bosom," he wrote.[50] Yet his outward control could not obliterate his inner torment. It cannot be said that Lincoln enjoyed being president.

Few of the presidents in *The Presidential Character* fit unambiguously into one of the four cells. Most reveal characteristics of several types, although one emerges as the dominant one. Such is the character of Abraham Lincoln. While his ability to joke reveals an active-positive strain, and his melancholy silence reminds one of the passive-negatives, overall Lincoln was an active-negative president—ambitious, an incessant worker who didn't enjoy his work, but doggedly unwavering in pursuit of objectives he considered to be "right."

Stephen Douglas

In contrast to the despondent Abraham Lincoln, Stephen A. Douglas possessed an active-positive character. The qualities associated with the broad dimension are not in all cases those that we would expect. Several indicators typical of active-negatives can be found in Douglas' life. That Douglas was generally active and enjoyed nearly all facets of his exciting life is apparent even to readers of Lincoln biographies; some of these indicators appear in the Lincoln material analyzed previously. The view is confirmed and enlarged upon examination of the now authoritative biography of Douglas by Robert W. Johannsen.[51]

Douglas was born in 1813 on a farm in Vermont. He never knew his father, who died when Stephen was two years old. His surrogate father was his mother's brother, Edward Fisk, on whose farm Stephen lived until adolescence. "In this environment Douglas developed the physical and personal characteristics which would distinguish him in later years. Quick, alert, and proudly self-reliant, he made friends easily, combining a natural magnetism with a consuming energy." His teachers and classmates report him astute and studious. But Douglas found his situation in Brandon, Vermont, confining and he developed a resentment for his uncle, who, he thought, "held him back."[52]

At fifteen Douglas made the decision to leave home, family, and friends to see "what I could do for myself in the wide world among strangers." In Barber's terms, this was his "first independent political success," although his destination, Middlebury, was but fourteen miles from home.[53]

Douglas signed on as an apprentice cabinet maker. In that role characteristic active-positive style themes emerged: enjoyment of hard work, "an ambitious reading program," and an enthrallment with politics. Due to some disagreements with his employer, Douglas returned home after only three months, but throughout the rest of his adolescence the traits nascent at Middlebury fully emerged and developed. Douglas became active in school debate; he dug deeply into historical accounts of Alexander, Caesar, and Napoleon; he continued to follow contemporary politics avidly. By the time Douglas was twenty, he appeared to fit nicely into the type Barber designates "active-positive."

It is not implausible to argue that Douglas was at least as active as any president examined in *The Presidential Character* and as active as Lincoln. Biographer Johannsen noted that "Douglas was tireless in his congressional role of 1838, when he opposed and eventually lost to Whig John Stuart. Shortly after that campaign, Douglas secured a judgeship. Even Whigs noted the efficiency with which Douglas disposed of cases. Writing to his mother in 1841, Douglas boasted that his clearing of the court docket was the first time it had been done in seven years. "I have thus far led a life of extraordinary activity," he declared.[54]

In his first congressional term, in 1843, he "tackled the responsibilities of his position with characteristic energy." When periodically ill (often considered the result of his activity), Douglas chafed in his sedentary state. His activity is noted by most commentators at each stage of his career. Douglas' energy inspired one correspondent to dub him "a perfect steam engine in breaches." The following description of his activity during the famous 1858 Senate campaign provides a fitting summary example of Douglas' energy.

A *New York Times* correspondent who covered the campaign reported after the election that Douglas delivered 59 set speeches each of two to three hours duration, 17 shorter speeches in response to serenades, and 37 speeches in reply to addresses of welcome. All but two of these were delivered in the open air, and seven were made in downpours of rain. Douglas, in the course of almost four months of strenuous campaigning, traveled over 5,000 miles by railroad, steamboat and horse convey-ance. . . . What he lacked in size he made up in energy; square shouldered, broad-chested, tossing his large head "with an air of overbearing superiority," Douglas was, "the very embodiment of force, combativeness and staying power."[55]

Before examining Douglas' developed style, world view, and character, one should note the general bearing of his physical stature upon his disposition. The final sentences of the passage just quoted suggest the possibility that Douglas needed to compensate in some way for his distinctly small physical stature. More mention is made of Douglas' stature in his biographies than of any other element of his countenance or character. It is

noteworthy, however, that out of many references in the Johannsen tome, only once is Douglas' response to his physique
seen as a problem. At that point Johannsen tells us, "He
compensated for his lack of stature by developing a boisterous and
exuberant manner and a nervous energy that frequently put people
off."[56] While Douglas' energy was at times considered obsessive,
his stature was often described as concealing inner strength rather
than calling attention to his compensatory modes.

However, one may plausibly venture beyond the biographer's
assessment and suggest another possible reaction by "the Little
Giant" to his smallness. Douglas had a temper which erupted
over the course of his life into a number of now well-known
incidents. He went after a critical newspaper editor with a cane,
nearly involved himself in a duel, made several "unseemly"
outbursts in the Senate, and once lost his temper when taunted
by an unfriendly crowd. These outbursts, which were in all cases
short-lived, seemed to follow from Douglas' thorough enjoyment of the larger political fight. These nuisances which provoked Douglas did not preoccupy him; he didn't seem to hold
long-term grudges. Indeed, Douglas kept cool when the fight was
an important one. This demeanor was particularly noticeable
throughout his prolonged battle with the Buchanan Administration.[57]

With respect to "style," the important point is that Douglas
thoroughly enjoyed political speaking. His was not the case of an
active-negative, who, the more he indulged, the more miserable
he felt. With the aid of his second wife, Adele, Douglas began to
enjoy social life as well, and his home became a social center in
his later years. Earlier, he had not the time or inclination for
"frivolity," but as he aged there appeared to be no facet of his
life he did not enjoy.[58]

The truly complex themes of Douglas' character concern his
world view. In Barber's categories, this found expression in a
mix of devotion to the principle of popular sovereignty and
propensity to compromise. Both of these are consistent with
Barber's description of the active-positive world view as "a
liquid world in which realities and the opinions which reflect

them shift continually.''[59] As will be indicated in the concluding section below, a full analysis of the meaning of this "world view" (and of Lincoln's) would shake the framework constructed by Barber. Noteworthy here, from Barber's perspective, is the fact that certain character traits that Barber found in his "dutiful" presidents are not present in Douglas' case. For example, Douglas did not come to despise his enemies. It is well known that Douglas accepted defeat from Lincoln with grace; he did not respond, for example, the way Wilson responded to his several defeats. Also, Douglas' defeats cannot be reasonably construed as due to "dutifulness" or to a "principled" stance per se, however much the defeats may have been due to the particular principles that Douglas embraced. This is quite obvious in the presidential race, since both candidates were dedicated to carefully articulated principles.

From Barber's perspective, Douglas' demeanor is better characterized by the theme of compromise or accommodation than by "dutifulness." Douglas offers us a good depiction of that disposition. "He noted [that] if he wished to gain an object, it was sometimes better to yield to a little that one might desire, in order to get the support of a majority, rather than being impracticable, and insisting upon his own particular views to hazard the whole, and lose the object he had in view.''[60]

Douglas enjoyed politics. His career reflects characteristic active-positive themes of flexibility and an orientation toward productiveness. Threats to his self-esteem, expressed through his temper, were transcended; he was not plagued with feelings of inadequacy. He accepted defeat with grace, and did not seem to his contemporaries to conceal bitterness.

Lincoln and Douglas both revealed personality traits that persisted throughout their lives. As in the case of Woodrow Wilson, there was no large change in behavior between the "first independent political success," and later adult life. Thus, there is reason to suggest that Douglas would have continued to be active-positive, had he been elected president.

On Presidential Character

If the electorate in 1860 had been guided by Barber's theory, they would have rejected Abraham Lincoln, who as an "active-negative" had the worst type of personality, in favor of Stephen Douglas, whose "active-positive" personality is the type most highly recommended by Barber. Although it is impossible to know how successful a Douglas presidency might have been, the historical judgment of Lincoln's administration, both its sober praise and sometime adulation, contrasts markedly with the dire conclusion reached by applying Barber's theory.[61] Why is there such a disparity between the common assessment of Lincoln's presidency and the "active-negative" conclusion generated by Barber's theory? Perhaps the answer lies in the difference between the starting point of the political understanding of citizens and politicians from that of theoretical perspectives like Barber's. For Lincoln, Douglas, and their contemporary public, issue differences were at the heart of the political crisis. Barber, on the other hand, begins his study by assuming that the content of political issues is of little importance in assessing presidential behavior. Instead of looking through the eyes of the politician under study, Barber encourages his readers to look through the lens of a conceptual apparatus different from that common to political life itself.

By beginning with the assumption that political differences as understood by politicians are unimportant, Barber's theory rules out a myriad of hypotheses which might best explain the Lincoln presidency. Because Barber is attempting to construct a theory, and not simply a set of detailed descriptions of various administrations, he is forced by this theoretical objective to create categories which are formal enough to transcend the exigencies of this or that time, or the infinite variety of political opinions and issues. As a theory, Barber's project requires concepts like "rigidity" and "flexibility" because these are generally applicable, while issues and opinions are not.

Barber is quite aware of the nature of his, or any, typological theory. "What is de-emphasized in this scheme?" he asks. "Everything which does not lend itself to the production of potentially testable generalizations about presidential behavior. Thus we shall be less concerned with the substance or content of particular political issues." Barber is not unconcerned with the content of political issues, but his concern is different from that of the politician. For Barber, political debate covers or partially hides more fundamental aspects of the participants' personalities.

> By moving a step up the ladder of abstraction, from particular issue stands and standardized ideological expressions to the leader's world-view we begin to get at themes at once more persistent and more significant in shaping action. A close review of what he has said over the years may reveal a fairly consistent set of assumptions—about how history works, what people are like, what the main purposes of politics are (to use the three I have found most useful). The product is a cognitive operational code of sorts, a set of politically relevant perceptual habits, *hardly ever put together in a systematic way by the leader himself* but derivable from his many comments as he experiences practical problems.[62]

The locus of thought relevant to personality is "worldview." The advantage of this concept to the theory builder is that one can focus upon static or at least enduring attachments. Thus, thought is transposed for the purposes of this kind of research into "belief-systems" which are visible to the investigator but not to the investigated.

To be fair, Barber did not adopt this kind of analysis simply because that was what "theory" inherently required. Rather, he turned to constructing a theory because he found issue positions and "ideology" of little help in describing what presidents did.

> The straight-out analysis of the content of the reasons the actor offers for his actions is of limited utility. Variations in the actual responses of political leaders to roughly the same circumstances warn against relying too much on the leader's plain spoken explanations. . . . Nor are his expressed intentions much help. . . . Nor have Presidents' ideologies—left or right—helped much in explaining what they did.[63]

Barber's first study of presidential personality was devoted to the political styles of Calvin Coolidge and Herbert Hoover. Barber does not indicate why Hoover's or Coolidge's reasoning can't account for their behavior, but he goes on to make an even more startling claim—that if his theory works with these presidents, it can work with all presidents.

> The dull Presidents are a trial for the political analyst, particularly for the student of personality and political leadership. . . . They . . . provide "hard case" tests for the supposition that personality helps shape a President's politics. If a personality approach can work with Coolidge and Hoover, it can work with any chief executive.[64]

But why so? The need for parsimony concomitant with the development of theory *may* be compatible with the characteristics of most presidents. It may be necessary to simplify the "variables," including thought, that impinge upon a weak or common president in order to discern the determinants of presidential behavior. If this proves true, Barber's kind of approach might be the most fruitful way to study most presidents. However, Barber is wrong to suggest that his theory "can work with any chief executive." A theory that explains the behavior of mediocre presidents cannot be assumed prior to investigation to explain the actions of great presidents.

Like the view that political issues and political judgment matter, the notion that some presidents are great in terms of political skill and perspicacity is one common to the citizen perspective. Scholars frequently denigrate the appellation "great" because it often betrays unreflective hero-worship rather than sober analysis, but it is hard to deny that some of our political leaders have had uncommon abilities. Barber might respond that he does not mean to deny that some presidents are greater than others, but rather to identify a clearer and more adequate basis for evaluation. Yet Barber's theory precludes one of the important traditional qualities of greatness—uncommon perspicacity. If one takes seriously the possibility that a politician may be great in this sense, one must begin by assuming that the politician may have been able to see and understand things which, without his assistance, remain inaccessible to the inquiring scholar. In short, one must begin by assuming that one may learn something *from* a president before, or at least while, one attempts to learn *about* a president. This procedure by no means prevents one from reaching the conclusion that a particular president had nothing to teach, but proceeding as Barber does in assuming that he is capable of knowing Lincoln's most important thoughts better than Lincoln precludes the scholar from discovering that he is mistaken. The "great" presidents pose special difficulties because they are supposed to have had minds incapable of description according to criteria simple and formal enough to be applied to most men.

Among Barber's own case studies, one can find some evidence that this problem plagued Barber. Noteworthy is his admitted difficulty in describing Franklin Roosevelt. Barber considered FDR "the most remarkable of all modern Presidents." Not surprisingly, he also proved to be for Barber, "the least self-revealing President."[65] Although FDR held the longest presidential tenure in history, Barber devotes relatively few pages to discussion of FDR's White House years. In fact, he devotes twice as much space to the discussion of each of the Truman and Kennedy presidencies. Barber spends most of the brief FDR discussion explaining away two incidents that appear to reveal active-negative tendencies. While obviously "active" and obviously "positive," FDR (like Lincoln and the active-negatives) does not unambiguously resemble other presidents of his type, when one proceeds beyond the "baseline" variables.

Does the possibility that presidential understanding molds behavior mean that "thought" is a completely independent variable, attaching itself to the things presidents see? Is it not quite plausible, as a personality theorist might argue, that presidents don't see everything around them, but rather have selective perception, seeing and discussing some things and not others? Certainly this must be true, but the fact that presidents like everyone (even personality theorists) have selective perception should not propel one to the immediate conclusion that the spectacles through which presidents view the world are unknown to them. One of the most striking facts about pre-Civil War politics is the degree to which Lincoln and Douglas chose to view the issues of their day through a constitutional lense. Without going into the merits of their respective arguments— one beginning from the principle of equality, the other from popular sovereignty—it must be emphasized that the agenda of issues that constituted their dispute and framed their arguments was set by the Constitution. The character of the political dispute just prior to the Civil War derived from a widespread deference to "issues." And in this case constitutional issues were the crucial political consideration.[66]

What is the practical consequence of the theoretical deprecation of issues? In considering this question, we move from the adequacy of Barber's theory as explanation to reflection upon the worth of his theory as a pedagogy. Barber is quite explicit in offering his teaching as a guide to the citizenry's selection of future presidents. Implicitly, Barber's theory is also a pedagogy for presidents themselves, because presidents will try to appear to be what their electorate expects. V. O. Key noticed this same political consequence when he criticized the denial of issue voting in seminal studies of voting behavior.

> If leaders believe the route to victory is by projection of images and cultivation of styles rather than by advocacy of policies to cope with the problems of the country, they will project images and cultivate styles to the neglect of the substance of politics. They will abdicate their prime function in a democratic system, which amounts, in essence, to the assumption of the risk of trying to persuade us to lift ourselves by our bootstraps.[67]

To the extent that Barber's vocabulary enters the realm of politics itself, politicians may come to believe that success depends primarily upon appearing to have the right character. This poses difficulty for Barber's future empirical work, because statements which were formerly uttered naïvely by politicians unaware of the use to which they would be put (statements like "I enjoy my work") may now be uttered with the conscious purpose of projecting the right character. While the record is not complete on Carter's personality, for example, he is a president who admired Barber's book and seems to have been influenced by it. How do we know whether Carter's active-positive smiles and repeated claims that he enjoys his work represent his character, or rather his artfulness? (Despite Barber's efforts to "steer clear of obvious puff jobs put out in campaigns" one of the main sources for his data on Carter is *Why Not the Best.*)[68]

The main problem, however, is not the future adequacy of Barber's empirical studies, now that his theory is public, but rather the relative merits of a constitutional pedagogy versus the new personality teaching for the actual conduct of the presidency. Certainly no personality theory, even one wholeheartedly embraced by a president and his public, could obliterate the president's day-to-day concern with issues or with constitutional matters in times of crisis—that is not the danger. Presidents will continue to fashion policies and defend them before Congress and the public. But how sound will these policies be, and how capable will the public be to judge them? Isn't it probable that presidential policy will be better formulated and presidential rhetoric more intelligent if presidents function under the auspices of a public opinion informed by a theory emphasizing policy and reason than by a theory that places a premium on character and style?

References

[1] James David Barber, *The Presidential Character* (2nd ed.; Englewood, N.J.: Prentice Hall, 1977; orig. pub. 1972). See also Barber's other writings: "The President after Watergate," *World*, July 13, 1973; "Tone-Deaf in the Oval Office," *Saturday Review/World*, January 12, 1974; "Active-Positive Character," *Time*, January 3, 1977; "Comment: Qualls' Nonsensical Analysis of Nonexistent Works," *American Political Science Review*, LXXI (March, 1977); "The Question of Presidential Character," *Saturday Review*, October, 1972. See also Michael Mandelbaum, "Political Science: A Discipline Shaped Not by Accord But by Disagreement," *New York Times*, March 27, 1977.

[2] Harold Lasswell, *Psychopathology and Politics*, (Rev. ed.; New York: Viking Press, 1969). For a thorough assessment of Lasswell's work, see Robert Horwitz, "Scientific Propaganda: Harold D. Lasswell," in Herbert J. Storing (ed.), *Essays on the Scientific Study of Politics* (New York: Holt, Rhinehart

and Winston, 1962). Some of Barber's conceptual improvements are noted by Alexander George in "Assessing Presidential Character," *World Politics*, XXVII (January, 1974), 2. For a complete survey of previous work in this field, see Fred Greenstein, *Personality and Politics* (Rev. ed.; New York: W. W. Norton, 1975).

[3] George, "Assessing Presidential Character," 246; James H. Qualls, "Barber's Typological Analysis of Political Leaders," *American Political Science Review*, LXXI (March, 1977), 185; Erwin Hargrove, "Presidential Personality and Revisionist Views of the Presidency," *American Journal of Political Science*, XVII (November, 1973), 4.

[4] Barber, *Presidential Character*, vi.

[5] Alexander George and Juliette George, *Woodrow Wilson and Colonel House* (New York: Dover, 1964). There have been many other important single-actor studies (for example Erik Erikson's *Young Man Luther*), but except for George and George, the best of these do not examine American presidents. There has been one atheoretical, and very interesting, study of the personalities of six presidents: Erwin C. Hargrove, *Presidential Leadership, Personality and Political Style* (New York: Macmillan, 1966).

[6] George, "Assessing Presidential Character," 278 (my emphasis).

[7] "The State of the Presidency," (interview) Chicago *Sunday Sun-Times*, September 23, 1973, Sec. 1A, p. 2.

[8] See, for example, George Ticknor Curtis, *Constitutional History of the United States* (New York; Harper & Brothers, 1889), 292.

[9] Max Farrand (ed.), *Records of the Federal Convention of 1787* (4 vols.; New Haven: Yale University Press, 1966), I, 82–85.

[10] Alexander Hamilton, James Madison, and John Jay, *The Federalist Papers*, ed. Clinton Rossiter (New York: New American Library, 1961), No. 73, p. 441.

[11] *Federalist*, No. 64, p. 396. Without reeligibility, "an avaricious man who might happen to fill the office, looking forward to a time when he must at all events yield up the advantages he enjoyed, would feel a propensity not easy to be resisted to such a man to make the best use of his opportunities [and] might not scruple to have recourse to the most corrupt expedients," (*Federalist*, No. 72, p. 437.)

[12] *Federalist*, No. 64, p. 391.

[13] Barber, *Presidential Character*, 5.

[14] *Ibid.*, 7–8.

[15] *Ibid.*, 10.

[16] This summary of remarks by Barber was compiled by Alexander George. See George, "Assessing Presidential Character," 248–49, and Barber *Presidential Character*, 12–13.

[17] Barber, *Presidential Character*, 446–48, 458, 460.

[18] *Ibid.*, 145.

19 But see *ibid.*, 445.

20 *Ibid.*, 470.

21 George, "Assessing Presidential Character," 273–75.

22 James David Barber, "Strategies for Understanding Politicians," *American Journal of Political Science*, XVIII (May, 1974), 450; "Adult Identity and Presidential Style: The Rhetorical Emphasis," *Daedalus* (Summer, 1968).

23 Barber, "Strategies for Understanding Politicians"; Barber, "Coding Scheme for Presidential Biographies," mimeo (January, 1960), 39 pp.; Barber, "The Question of Presidential Character."

24 Benjamin P. Thomas, *Abraham Lincoln* (New York: Knopf, 1952), 121.

25 *Ibid.*, 184.

26 *Ibid.*, 456; J. G. Randall, *Lincoln the President* (2 vols.; New York: Dodd Mead & Co., 1945), II, 165; Richard N. Current, *Lincoln Nobody Knows* (New York: Farrar, Straus, 1958).

27 Randall, *Lincoln*, I, 49; Current, *Lincoln Nobody Knows*, 12.

28 Thomas, *Abraham Lincoln*, 500.

29 Barber, *Presidential Character*, 99; Current, *Lincoln Nobody Knows*, 12.

30 Thomas, *Abraham Lincoln*, 70; 181; 93.

31 *Ibid.*, 173.

32 *Ibid.*, 143.

33 *Ibid.*, 454.

34 *Ibid.*, 358.

35 Randall, *Lincoln*, I, 28.

36 Thomas, *Abraham Lincoln*, 226.

37 *Ibid.*, 303.

38 *Ibid.*, 339.

39 *Ibid.*, 195; 200.

40 Randall, *Lincoln*, I, 279.

41 *Ibid.*, II, 243.

42 Thomas, *Abraham Lincoln*, 239.

43 Randall, *Lincoln*, I, 279.

44 *Ibid.*, II, 160.

45 *Ibid.*, 243.

46 Thomas, *Abraham Lincoln*, 409; 425.

47 *Ibid.*, 440.

48 *Ibid.*, 135; 231.

49 *Ibid.*, 267; Randall, *Lincoln*, I, 63.

50 Thomas, *Abraham Lincoln*, 21.

51 Robert W. Johannsen, *Stephen A. Douglas* (New York: Oxford, 1973).

52 *Ibid.*, 8.

53 *Ibid.*

54 *Ibid.*, 67; 598.

55 *Ibid.*, 123*ff*, 658.

[56] "When sitting he appeared of medium height, but 'his legs were very short.' His massive and 'intellectual' head was crowned with thick black hair, his light blue or gray eyes sparkled and his mouth and chin were firm." *Ibid.*, 92; 204; 4; 92.

[57] *Ibid.*, 501, 342, 453; 551*ff.*

[58] *Ibid.*, see especially 256, 45, 236, 491, 79, 291.

[59] Barber, *Presidential Character*, 242.

[60] *Ibid.*, 177.

[61] See, for example, Arthur M. Schlesinger, "Our Presidents: A Rating by 75 Historians," *New York Times Magazine*, July 29, 1962, p. 12, and Erwin Hargrove, *The Power of the Modern Presidency*, (Philadelphia: Temple University Press, 1974), 4–6.

[62] Barber, "Coding Scheme," 3; and "Strategies for Understanding," 464 (my emphasis).

[63] *Ibid.*, 463.

[64] James David Barber, "Classifying and Predicting Presidential Styles: Two Weak Presidents," *Journal of Social Issues*, XXIV (1968).

[65] Barber, *Presidential Character*, 211.

[66] See Harry Jaffa, *Crisis of the House Divided* (2nd ed.; Seattle, Washington: University of Washington, 1971). For a discussion of Lincoln's character in light of his understanding of the political issues, see Lord Charnwood, *Abraham Lincoln* (New York: Henry Holt, 1916).

[67] V. O. Key, Jr., *The Responsible Electorate* (New York: Vintage Books, 1966), 6.

[68] Barber, *Presidential Character*, preface to the first edition.

14

"Presidential Senator" Ted Kennedy and a Character Test

William D. Pederson

Another bid for the presidency by Senator Ted Kennedy will most likely raise again the question of his character. Two sides of his personality have been noted by observers for a number of years: on the one hand, he has often been an immature risk-taker in private life, and, on the other hand, a mature political leader in public life. His college cheating episode, law school traffic incidents, Chappaquiddick affair, and failed marriage contrast sharply with a quarter-century as a hard working United States Senator, as well as the responsible behavior he has shown toward his children. Despite the former behavior, the latter has contributed to his third-place rank among the most admired men in America, according to a Gallup poll (*Facts on File*, 1970: 988).

The purpose of this chapter is to explore Senator Kennedy's behavior in terms of James David Barber's approach to legislative and presidential behavior, and to conduct an empirical check on Kennedy's character derived from these theories. For purposes of analysis, the remainder of the chapter is divided into five sections: (1) a review of the Kennedy literature and the theories of James David Barber; (2) a six-part empirical check of Senator Kennedy's behavior in terms of Barber's theories; (3) the findings of these empirical checks; (4) a discussion of the findings; and (5) a brief conclusion. This exploratory study may help to determine the usefulness of Barber's theories of political behavior as a guide to selecting presidential candidates.

A "Barberian" Approach to the Kennedy Literature

There are more biographies on Ted Kennedy than any other living member of congress (Burton, 1972; David, 1972; Honan, 1972; Burns, 1976; Lerner, 1980; Levin, 1980). There are monographs on his campaigns (Levin, 1966; Chellis, 1985), and his legislative career (Lippman, 1976), in addition to the host of works on Chappaquiddick (e.g., Olsen, 1970; Rust; 1971; Tedrow and Tedrow, 1976; Willis, 1980), as well as those which deal with him as part of the whole Kennedy family (e.g., Clinch, 1973; Collier and Horowitz, 1984; Davis, 1984; Goodwin, 1987). In sum, the history and politics of Ted Kennedy are much better known than those of most candidates for public office. On the other hand, no serious effort has been made to place the senator's personality within the context of social science theories of political behavior. After a quarter-century of Kennedy's legislating and assuming the role of a "presidential senator," it may be useful to explore the theoretical context of his behavior.

The work of James David Barber on the behavior of state legislators (Barber, 1965) and his more controversial theory of presidential behavior which claims that political behavior can be predicted on the basis of worldview, style, character, and climate of expectations (Barber, 1972) provides an avenue to explore Senator Kennedy's legislative behavior and his likely performance in the White House, if he should win the presidency. Recent empirical checks offer some support for Barber's theories (Pederson, 1977; Pederson and Williams, 1980; Tays, 1980; Green and Pederson, 1985).

"Lawmaker" legislators and "active-positive" presidents, as the psychologically healthiest leaders, exemplify high self-esteem. The healthiest politicians appear to be those who self-actualize via the political arena—they have active and flexible personalities. The other types of legislators and presidents that Barber considers in his four-fold typologies suffer from low self-esteem. The most unpleasant legislators ("advertisers") and the most dangerous presidents ("active-negatives") are aggressive and power-seekers. The more passive legislators ("spectators'' and ''reluctants'') and presidents (''passive-positives'' and ''passive-negatives'') are drawn to politics in a search for affection or an obligation to perform a duty.

In a poll of 50 experienced political observers in Washington, D.C. in 1975, a majority rated Senator Kennedy as an active-positive. Yet Hubert Humphrey and Nelson Rockefeller scored much higher in the poll as active-positives than Senator Kennedy (Burns, 1976: 371). On the other hand, a minority viewed Kennedy as an active-negative, and an even smaller number considered him a passive-positive.

It may be useful to attempt to construct objective ''indexes'' to measure Senator Kennedy's personality (or ''character'') on the basis of Barber's theories of legislative and presidential behavior. Is it possible to assess the public Kennedy and the private Kennedy who has attracted so much media attention? What ''manner of man'' is Edward M. Kennedy?

Some ''Barberian'' Tests of Character

Rather than rely exclusively on Barber's unique procedure for predicting the performance of political leaders on the basis of ''worldview, style, character, and climate of expectations,'' this paper uses empirical checks of Barber's theory to measure Senator Kennedy's political personality. The hypothesis to be tested is as follows: If the majority of informed observers are correct in classifying Edward M. Kennedy as an active-positive personality, then his behavior in the United States Senate should provide evidence for it. Six factors of ''lawmaker'' or ''active-positive'' behavior will be used to attempt to measure Senator Kennedy's character. Some of these factors are based directly on Barber's work while others are refinements made indirectly from it:

1. *Active-passive Index.* Does Senator Kennedy demonstrate the high level of activity and legislative accomplishment associated with ''lawmakers'' and ''active-positives'' (Barber, 1965; Barber, 1972)?

2. *Commitment-Enjoyment-Flexibility Index.* Does Senator

Kennedy show the commitment to office (Barber, 1965), the enjoyment in office (Barber, 1972), and the flexibility (Pederson, 1977) which are associated with "lawmakers" and active-positives"?

3. *Lawyer Index.* Does Senator Kennedy's legal training make him different from the vast majority of active-positives who have not been lawyers (Green and Pederson, 1985)? Is he a lawyer or a politician by nature?

4. *Clemency Index.* Does Senator Kennedy display the generosity of spirit that is reflected in the clemency record of active-positives (Pederson, 1977)?

5. *Personal Security Index.* Does Senator Kennedy have a preoccupation with secret service protection unlike the other active-positives (Tays, 1980)?

6. *Staffing Index.* Does Senator Kennedy use his staff in an open, non-hierarchical arrangement with an emphasis on equality and dialogue, as is the tendency of active-positives (Pederson and Williams, 1980; Buchanan, 1987: 153–169)?

The Findings

Regardless of how its substance might be evaluated, the empirical evidence on Senator Kennedy's legislative output is recognized as substantial. After a cautious start in the Senate, he has compiled an impressive legislative record. He has been rated as one of the most effective members in the United States Senate by polls of informed observers, as well as by academics (Levin and Repak, 1980: 42; Randolph, 1982). In terms of seniority, he ranks ahead of all but six senators. If he is re-elected in 1988, he will soon have served half of his life in the senate—only 32 of the total 1,768 senators in American history have served that long (Wills, 1987). At times during his Senate career, he has developed a role for himself as "the shadow President" with a legislative agenda to enact (Lippman, Jr., 1976). His Senate career has been consistent with the incredible energy he displayed in his first campaign in 1962 (Levin, 1966), as well as with his active participation in sports (David, 1972: 245). If the

Senator is elected to the White House, his foremost biographer views the likelihood of an activist presidency as the safest prediction one could make (Burns, 1976: 339).

Senator Kennedy's attitude toward his work is almost as self-evident as the activity itself. His four re-election campaigns suggest his commitment to office is that of a "lawmaker" legislator, particularly when his career of satisfaction with legislative life is compared to that of his brothers, who used their legislative careers only as stepping stones to executive office. In contrast to them, Ted Kennedy has won the respect of his colleagues and became the youngest majority whip in the history of the United States Senate. Although that position did not work out as successfully as his other legislative work, it suggests a degree of flexibility in his senatorial role. His unusually flexible personality allows him to get along with political opponents (Burns, 1976: 310; Levin and Repak, 1980: 158). Although he is often caricatured as a radical liberal, the predominant focus of his legislative career has been in the broad area of "human rights" abroad (especially the plight of refugees) and at home (especially in terms of health issues regarding the lower and middle classes). He seems to enjoy politics in the same sense that most "lawmakers" and active-positives derive satisfaction from political office.

The empirical record also suggests that Ted Kennedy consistently has had more interest in politics than in law as a career. He won his earliest elective offices in elementary and junior high school. His debate skills were developed in high school and were refined in law school as reflected in his winning of the moot court competition at the University of Virginia Law School with John V. Tunney, who would later join him in the United States Senate. Ted Kennedy put more time into the moot court competition than in studying for law courses (Hersh, 1972: 140). He was training more for a career in politics than in the law (Pederson, 1987: 239).

Politics overwhelmed his legal training just as it did his marriage (Chellis, 1985: 35). Ted managed Jack's re-election campaign for the Senate while he was in law school, and immediately took part in the presidential campaign as soon as he graduated. He wrote on his application to the Massachusetts bar that his "ambitions lie in the public service of this state" (David, 1972: 93). His short stint as an assistant county prosecutor was merely designed to serve as a basis for claiming a public service career before running for the Senate. One of the youngest senators in American history, Ted Kennedy is a lawyer by training unlike most active-positives. But his behavior is similar to them in that he quickly chose politics over law as a career (Green and Pederson, 1985).

The clemency record of Senator Kennedy also closely resembles that of active-positives who grant the largest number of amnesties and offer amnesties on the most generous terms (Pederson, 1977). During the Vietnam War he favored amnesty as early as 1968 (Lippman, 1980: 84), and he became the first person in Congress to hold amnesty hearings (Burns, 1976: 17). More recently, he became an advocate of a broader amnesty for illegal aliens (Thornton, 1985). His public positions on clemency matters seem to reflect a personality which is generally forgiving and rarely vindictive, except perhaps in his early days in sports (Burns, 1976: 337; David, 1984: 724; 696–697). Even after his first real political defeat when he lost re-election as Senate majority whip, he did not become vindictive (Burns, 1976: 337). He is known for his ability to bounce back as a survivor with a sense of humor—particularly and most recently in his 1980 victory-in-defeat campaign for the presidency (Pederson, 1987: 242).

Senator Kennedy seems to have an unusually secure personality. He is not obsessed with his personal safety, which is a pattern consistent with other active-positives (Tays, 1980). Although he seems more reluctant in meeting the public in large crowds after the loss of his two brothers in the recent upsurge of political assassinations (Hersh, 1972: 484) than in his early career, he generally does not like secret service protection. He is uncomfortable when there are too many uniforms around him (Burns, 1976: 242).

The staffing arrangements that Senator Kennedy uses as a

"presidential senator" also seem to reflect the patterns that active-positives tend to use. It is generally acknowledged that he has either the best, or one of the best, staffs on Capitol Hill (Burns, 1976: 244; Levin and Repak, 1980: 31). Active-positives tend to attract the most talented staff assistants (Pederson and Williams, 1980). He makes a special effort to draw on outside sources for advice. His decentralized staff encourages competition, dissent, and dialogue (Lippman, 1980: 261; Levin and Repak, 1980: 54–55). He tends to treat subordinates as equals, and has an ability to empathize with others (Burns, 1976: 244–248, 313, 340; Levin and Repak, 1980: 42).

Discussion

The findings of the six empirical checks on Senator Kennedy's character are at odds with the media's obsession with the Chappaquiddick incident. They also contradict the impression that there is an immature side of the Senator's personality, perhaps due to his spoiled "baby" position in the Joseph and Rose Kennedy family. In any case, these risk-taking episodes seem to have diminished over time. Kennedy may have been attempting to achieve a separate identity in a very competitive family. For the sake of perspective, such episodes need to be placed against a history of responsible public service. Apart from the foolish episodes he participated in while he was young, most of the later incidents seem to have been associated with a marriage that failed to grow after the first five years (Chellis, 1985: 36). Despite his marital problems, he remained responsible to his three children at the same time that he performed his demanding role in the Senate.

It would be unfortunate to disqualify a candidate for political office for the wrong reasons. Despite the media's effort to sensationalize the private episodes of Senator Kennedy's life, his whole record needs to be evaluated. The findings of this chapter suggest that this has not been done very well. The empirical "indexes" seem to strongly suggest that he possesses a healthy personality. His lack of experience when he first ran for the senate and the subsequent record of accomplishment, indicates the type of personality which grows in political office. Reporters who covered his 1980 presidential campaign came to admire this "hidden" aspect of his character during the final months (Devin, 1982).

There is at least one parallel during a recent state campaign in Oregon when the issue of character became an issue. In the final days of the campaign to re-elect the Democratic incumbent, the late Senator Wayne L. Morse brought up the issue of an early automobile accident involving the Republican challenger, Mark O. Hatfield. Morse found that raising this issue provoked a backlash vote of sympathy for the challenger who was viewed by the voters as having outgrown his past (Smith, 1962). The same might be the ultimate result in a presidential campaign where the public is more forgiving than the press, and in a campaign in which the public sees more clearly the dimensions of the character issue than the press.

Conclusion

A test of six empirical checks on Senator Kennedy's political personality sheds new light on the "character issue." His activity, commitment to office, training, clemency behavior, security, and staff utilization support the hypothesis that he is a "lawmaker" legislator and would likely be an active-positive president. These six empirical measures of his personality call into question attempts to sensationalize a long and responsible public career which ranks as one of the best in the United States Senate, according to informed observers. The empirical measures derived from James David Barber's theories of legislative and executive behavior offer another possible method to verify his predictions based on worldview, style, character, and climate of expectations.

References

Barber, James David. *The Lawmakers*. New Haven: Yale University Press, 1965.
———. *Presidential Character*. Englewood Cliffs, N.J.: Prentice-Hall, 1972.

Buchanan, Bruce. *The Citizen's Presidency. Standards of Choice and Judgment.* Washington, D.C.: Congressional Quarterly Press, 1987.

Burns, James M. *Edward Kennedy and the Camelot Legacy.* New York: Norton, 1976.

Burton, Hersh. *The Education of Edward Kennedy. A Family Biography.* New York: Morrow, 1972.

Chellis, Marcia. *Living with the Kennedys: The Joan Kennedy Story.* NY: Simon and Schuster, 1985.

Clinch, Nancy G. *The Kennedy Neurosis.* New York: Grosset and Dunlap, 1973.

Collier, Peter and Horowitz, David. *The Kennedys. An American Drama.* New York: Summit Books, 1984.

David, Lester. *Ted Kennedy: Triumphs and Tragedies.* New York: Grosset and Dunlap, 1972.

David, John H. *The Kennedys: Dynasty and Disaster. 1848–1984.* New York: McGraw-Hill, 1984.

Devin, L. Patrick. "An Analysis of Kennedy's Communication in the 1980 Campaign." *Quarterly Journal of Speech,* 69 (1982), 397–417.

Facts on File, Vol. 30, No. 1574 (December 24–31, 1970), p. 988.

Germond, Jack W. and Jules Witcover. "Kennedy Should Stay Home in '88." *Shreveport Times,* September 7, 1985.

Goodwin, Doris Kerns. *The Fitzgeralds and the Kennedys.* New York: Simon and Schuster, 1987.

Green, Thomas M. and Pederson, William D. "The Behavior of Lawyer-Presidents." *Presidential Studies Quarterly,* 15 (1985), 343–352.

Honan, William H. *Ted Kennedy: Profile of a Survivor.* New York: Quadrangle Books, 1972.

Lerner, Max. *Ted and the Kennedy Legend: A Study in Character and Destiny.* New York: St. Martin's Press, 1980.

Levin, Murray B. *Kennedy Campaigning: The System and the Style as Practiced by Senator Edward Kennedy.* Boston: Beacon Press, 1966.

Lippman, Theo, Jr. *Senator Ted Kennedy: The Career Behind the Image.* New York: Norton, 1976.

Olsen, Jack. *The Bridge at Chappaquiddick.* Boston: Little, Brown, 1970.

Pederson, William D. "Amnesty and Presidential Behavior." *Presidential Studies Quarterly,* Vol. 7, No. 4 (Fall, 1977), 175–183.

———— and Stephen N. Williams. "The President and the White House Staff," in Edward N. Kearny, ed., *Dimensions of the Modern Presidency* (St. Louis: Forum Press, 1980), 139–155.

————. "Edward Moore Kennedy," in Bernard K. Duffy and Halford R. Ryan, eds., *American Orators of the Twentieth Century.* (Westport CT: Greenwood Press, 1987), 239–244.

Randolph, Eleanor. "The Best and the Worst of the U.S. Senate." *Washington Monthly,* 13 (1982), 30–43.

Robinson, Michael S. and Burgess, Philip M. "The Edward M. Kennedy Speech: The Impact of a Prime Time Television Appeal." *Television Quarterly*, 9 (1970), 29–39.

Rowan, Carl T. "Yes, Kennedy Will Run." *Washington Post*, September 25, 1985.

Rust, Zad. *Teddy Bare, the Last of the Kennedy Klan*. Boston: Western Islands, 1971.

Smith, A. Robert. *Tiger in the Senate*. Garden City, NY: Doubleday, 1962.

Tays, Dwight L. "Presidential Reaction to Security." *Presidential Studies Quarterly*, Vol. 10, No. 4 (Fall, 1980), 600–609.

Tedrow, Thomas L. and Richard L. *Death at Chappaquiddick*. Gretna, LA: Pelican Publishing Co., 1980.

Thornton, Mary. "Kennedy Plan to Expand Aliens' Amnesty." *Washington Post*, September 14, 1985.

Will, George F. "A Liberal's Waiting Game." *Newsweek*, March 16, 1987, p. 82.

Willis, Larryanne. *Chappaquiddick Decision*. Vale, OR: Better Books, 1980.

An Annotated Bibliography

William D. Pederson

This elemental bibliography of twenty-six books and articles on the American presidency and the work of James David Barber is divided into five sections: theory, critiques, empirical tests, applications in other settings, and reference works. It is meant as a brief tool for further reading and research.

Theory

James David Barber. *The Lawmakers: Recruitment and Adaptation to Legislative Life*, New Haven, Connecticut: Yale University Press, 1965.
A quantitative study on state legislators with personality types similar to those in *The Presidential Character*.

James David Barber. *The Presidential Character. Predicting Performance in the White House*. 3rd. ed. Englewood Cliffs, N.J.: Prentice-Hall, 1985.
The first edition was published in 1972 to attempt to influence the presidential election.

James David Barber. *The Pulse of Politics. Electing Presidents in the Media Age*. New York: W. W. Norton & Co., 1980
A 12-year cycle theory of presidential elections in the twentieth century.

Critiques

Alexander L. George, "Assessing Presidential Character," *World Politics*, Vol. 26, No. 2 (January, 1974), 234–282.
The longest book review that the editor of this reader ever encountered.

James David Barber, "Quall's Nonsensical Analysis of Non-Existent Works," *American Political Science Review*, Vol. 71, No. 1 (September, 1977), 212–225.
One of the more lively articles in the profession of political science.

Bruce Buchanan, *The Citizen's Presidency. Standards of Choice and Judgement*. Washington, D.C.: Congressional Quarterly Press, 1987.

A normative study with a useful discussion of Barber's approach to the presidency.

James H. Qualls, "Barber's Typological Analysis of Political Leaders," *American Political Science Review*, Vol. 71, No. 1 (September, 1977), 182–211.
A sophisticated methodological test of Barber's work, or at least of Quall's view of it, which seems to want total consistency in everything Barber has written.

Comparative Tests and Case Studies

Ronald H. Carpenter and William J. Jordan, "Style Discourse as a Predictor of Political Personality for Mr. Carter and Other Twentieth Century Presidents: Testing the Barber Paradigm," *Presidential Studies Quarterly*, Vol. 8, No. 1 (Winter, 1978), 67–78.
A speech professor and English professor attempt a check on political style alone without much success in using a part of Barber's theory.

Jeffrey Cohen, "Presidential Personality and Political Behavior," *Presidential Studies Quarterly*, Vol. 10, No. 4 (Fall, 1980), 588–599.
An elaborate statistical test of Barber's theory which finds little support for Barber's theory, but the test is more ambiguous than Barber's theory.

Eric B. Herzik and Mary L. Dotson, "Public Expectations and the Presidency: Barber's Climate of Expectations Examined," *Presidential Studies Quarterly*, Vol. 12, No. 4 (Fall, 1982), 485–490.
A partial investigation into one of Barber's less predictive factors in his theory of presidential behavior results in ambiguous findings.

John S. Latham. "President McKinley's Active-Positive Character: A Comparative Revision with Barber's Typology," *Presidential Studies Quarterly*, Vol. 12, No. 4 (Fall, 1982), 491–521.
Although most historians find William McKinley a passive president, this study argues he was active. As in the case of Dwight Eisenhower, McKinley was probably more active than most passive presidents, but still not as active as the most active presidents.

Dean Keith Simonton. *Why Presidents Succeed: A Political Psychology of Leadership*. New Haven, Connecticut: Yale University Press, 1987.
The latest in quantitative analysis on presidential greatness which does not find support for Barber's approach.

Applications in Other Settings

James L. Payne, et al. *The Motivations of Politicians* Chicago: Nelson-Hall Publishers, 1984.
A cross-national study of legislators with many links to Barber's theory, although a much different methodological approach is used.

Alan Shank and Ralph W. Conant, "Community Leadership: Mayors and Managers," in *Urban Perspectives: Politics and Policies* (Boston: Holbrook Press, 1975), 143–172.
A useful application of Barber's theory to chief executives at the local level.

John G. Stoessinger. *Crusaders and Pragmatists: Movers of Modern American Foreign Policy*. New York: W. W. Norton, 1979.
Although much less insightful than Barber's theory, this study of presidents and secretaries of state suggests similarities.

Reference Works

ABC-Clio Information Services. *The American Presidency: A Historical Bibliography*. Santa Barbara, California: ABC-Clio, 1984.
Covers material from 1974 to 1982.
Bibliographies of the Presidents of the U.S. 1789–1989. 50 Vols. Westport, Connecticut: Meckler Publishing Corporation, 1987–1991.
Annotated bibliographies on each American president.
Kenneth E. Davidson. *The American Presidency: A Guide to Information Sources*. Detroit: Gale Research Company, 1983.
An extremely useful tool with sources from 1787 to 1982. Emphasis since 1945, particularly since 1960 with annotations.
William A. DeGregorio. *The Complete Book of U.S. Presidents*. New York: Dembner Books, 1984.
An almanac on the American presidency.
Carol Bondhus Fitzgerald. *Cumulated Index to Meckler Publishing's Bibliographies of the Presidents of the U.S. 1789–1989*. 2 Vols. Westport, Connecticut: Meckler Publishing Corporation, 1989.
Robert U. Goehlert and Fenton S. Martin, *The Presidency: A Research Guide*. Santa Barbara, California: ABC-Clio, 1985.
An excellent one-volume work on sources to the American presidency with useful appendixes.
Robert U. Goehlert and Fenton S. Martin. *The American Presidency. A Bibliography*. Washington, D.C.: Congressional Quarterly, 1987.
In 600 pages there are 8,000 citations.
Robert U. Goehlert and Fenton S. Martin. *American Presidents. A Bibliography*. Washington, D.C.: Congressional Quarterly, 1987.
In 1,000 pages there are 13,000 citations.
Henry F. Graff, ed. *The Presidents*. New York: Charles Scribner's, 1984.
A very useful collection of articles on each president.
Joseph N. Kane. *Facts About Presidents: A Complication of Biographical and Historical Information*. New York: H. W. Wilson Company, 1981.
An almanac on the American presidency.
William D. Pederson and Ann M. McLaurin, eds. *The Rating Game in American Politics*. New York: Irvington Publishers, 1987.
A collection of quantitative and qualitative "rating games" on American presidents and other politicians.

John L. Andriot, *Guide to U.S. Government ...* Abstracts of Media Programs for the Public. New York: ... Publishers, 1977.

Although out of date, a good introduction to this area of this study and sources of statistical information.

Reference Works

The *Congressional ...* Service, 1970 ... a review of ... Bibliography, Santa Barbara: Clio ... 1970 to date.

Correspondence ... in 1970 to date.

Bibliographies of the President, ... vol. 2 ... 1975, 1976. Compiled ...

... language publications ...

James E. Davison, *Vice American Press ...* York: ... Inc., Corporation. ...

An extensive ... and with ...

William A. DeGregorio, *The Complete Book of U.S. Presidents.* New York: Dembner Books, 1984.

An almanac on the ... Presidents.

... Media ... Publishing ... in ...

Robert U. Goehlert and Fenton S. Martin, *The Presidency: A Research Guide.* Santa Barbara: California: ABC-Clio, Inc. 1985.

A collection of ... volumes of resources on the American presidency, including ...

Robert U. Goehlert and ... Sabato ... Washington, D.C. ... 1977.

In two ... the ... Presidents.

Carol ... Washington, D.C. ... Publishers, ...

In 1,200 pages there are 13,000 entries.

Henry F. Graff, *The Presidents.* New York: Charles Scribner's, 1984.

A very useful collection of articles on each president.

Roger A. Kane, *Facts About ...* Reference Publications, ...

An almanac of the American presidency.

William D. Pederson and Ann M. McLaurin, eds. *The Rating Game in American Politics.* New York: Irvington Publishers, 1987.

Subjective, quantitative, and qualitative ... approaches to the ranking of presidents and prime ministers.